The Set-Up Men

THE SET-UP MEN

Race, Culture and Resistance in Black Baseball

Sarah L. Trembanis

McFarland & Company, Inc., Publishers

Jefferson, North Carolina

ISBN 978-0-7864-7796-8 (softcover : acid free paper) ∞
ISBN 978-1-4766-1657-5 (ebook)

LIBRARY OF CONGRESS CATALOGUING DATA ARE AVAILABLE

BRITISH LIBRARY CATALOGUING DATA ARE AVAILABLE

On the cover: Publicity photograph of the
Indianapolis Clowns

Printed in the United States of America

*McFarland & Company, Inc., Publishers
Box 611, Jefferson, North Carolina 28640
www.mcfarlandpub.com*

For my family:
Art, Ella, & Sam
Ron, Ellen, & Erik

Table of Contents

Acknowledgments

Acknowledgments have always been my favorite thing to read in any book. I love how they serve as a glimpse into the author's personality as well as a record of the creation of a piece of work. This work has had a gestation that has outlasted an elephant's. At times, I feared that the Cubs would finally win the World Series before I finished. Consequently, I owe a great deal of thanks to many people.

The faculty of the History Department of the College of William and Mary have assisted me immeasurably in the drafting of this manuscript. During its earliest stages as a dissertation, the project benefited from the oversight of Kimberley L. Phillips, advisor extraordinaire, as well as a number of wonderful faculty members: Fred Corney, Cindy Hahamovitch, Charlie McGovern, and Leisa Meyer. James Whittenburg, though not a reader for this project, provided summer income through teaching opportunities as well as a master course in Colonial history. An external committee member, Patrick Miller provided valuable commentary and suggestions. I am forever grateful for the ways in which these wonderful scholars encouraged, engaged, and enlivened my understanding of the past. Thank you.

Graduate school not only deepened my knowledge of history, it also introduced me to the best friends I could have ever hoped for. To Beth Kreydatus and Melissa Ooten, thank you for all your support, visits, long talks, and love as well as for a welcoming place to stay. I am also grateful for the extended family you have brought to my life: Matthew, Andy, and May Kreydatus and Jason Sawyer.

Every scholar owes an unpayable debt to the librarian and archivists wizards who make our work possible. The library staff (especially the interlibrary loan specialists) at William and Mary's Swem Library and Immaculata University's Gabriele Library were incredibly helpful throughout the research process. Similarly, the staff at the National Baseball Hall of Fame and Museum were extraordinarily welcoming and accommodating, alerting me to sources I might have otherwise missed.

Continuing my streak of great luck, I also have found fantastic colleagues at Immaculata in the History and Politics Department—Gene Halus, John Hill, and Bill Watson. I am grateful for their support, especially that of John Hill, who has served as an encouraging mentor to me. My other colleagues at IU have been kind, gracious, and immensely positive. I would be remiss not to thank my students at Immaculata University. They have challenged me and supported me. I feel so grateful to have taught such wonderfully enthusiastic students who teach me just as much as I teach them.

To the external reviewers and colleagues who have read my work, commented on drafts, and asked questions at conferences, I am indebted to you. My own scholarship has been greatly improved by the input of historians from NASSH, PCA/ACA, MAPACA, and other organizations. The anonymous external reviewers for this book pushed me to refine my arguments and prose. Any errors that remain are mine alone.

In moving to Delaware, I have been fortunate to find a community of supportive friends who have cheered me on during this process or just offered playdates, walks, or a girl's night out. Much thanks and love to Claire O'Neal, Amy Shay, Mara Gorman, Niki Tantalou, and Sharon Fullerton. To my extra family and Friday night dinner buddies, Dana, Fabrice, Camille, and Noah Veron, thank you for the laughter and love over these many years.

Finally, I need to thank my family. My grandmothers, each in her own way, instilled in me a great love of history. Though they are no longer with me, I feel their presence as I write. My paternal grandmother, Lucille Hughes Kramer, would mail me newspaper clippings about black baseball, and my maternal grandmother, Eula Stoll, never failed to ask about my project and even read up on Satchel Paige.

I also owe a special thanks to my late grandfather, Charles Stoll. As a child I spent many evenings watching baseball games on television while simultaneously listening to the radio broadcast of his beloved Cincinnati Reds. He taught me the truisms of the game—that hustle is important, that good pitching will always trump good hitting, that you always swing away on 3–0. He also instilled in me a real love for the game. After I started this project, I found out that he and my grandmother spent their honeymoon traveling to Cleveland to watch Satchel Paige pitch for the Indians. I can only hope that this book, completed almost 60 years later, in some small way is a continuation of that journey.

Likewise, my brother, Erik Hughes, has gone above and beyond the call of duty. On numerous occasions, Erik has served as a sounding board, listening and questioning, as I described the most recent issue in my research or writing. His input has improved the manuscript and his companionship is a true gift.

My parents, Ron and Ellen Hughes, deserve a tremendous amount of credit and gratitude. I would not have been able to complete this book without their generous and unfailing support. In the most direct sense, they enabled me to finish by making trips to Delaware to provide childcare and help with house-keeping while I worked on the initial drafting, and by welcoming my children and me into their home for weeks at a time, while I frantically revised and reworked drafts. Of course, this large sacrifice is just the tip of a much larger iceberg. I can never properly thank them for all they have done for me over the years.

On a daily basis, three people contributed to the completion of this book, my husband Art, my daughter Ella, and my son Sam. Art washed dishes and watched the kids so that I could squeeze in a few more minutes of work. He listened to rambling discussions of culture, agency, folklore, and nicknames and always seemed interested. Most of all, he has been my biggest fan. Art has trumpeted my work to friends, family, colleagues, and complete strangers. For all of his help, love, and confidence, I owe him mackadocious props.

Lastly, to my darlings, Ella Matina and Samuel Patrick, you two have been my greatest motivation and my greatest procrastination. I've abandoned work sessions to go play at the park with you and put off puzzles for just a few more minutes of work. At the end of long days of writing, your hugs and smiles have brightened my world. It fills me with great joy that you both love going to see our Blue Rocks play baseball and that you now collect baseball cards with the same eagerness that I once did. In this book, I hope you will find a record of hard work, of community, and of the importance of a sunny day at the ballpark.

Preface

The American mythology of sport as the ultimate meritocracy has continually been disproven by historians, sociologists, and others. It has been a convenient and much embraced myth as it integrated the ideals of the American Dream into the American pastimes, particularly *the* American pastime—baseball. From the 1880s until 1960, baseball's meritocracy was a mere smokescreen for racially based discrimination. Remarkable black athletes, whose names have now been reinstated into the public history of baseball through the work of scholars and fans starting in the 1970s, played America's game on all-black squads, forbidden to prove their own abilities through integrated competition. Despite the great work of researchers in compiling their statistics and records, many regard their achievements as "less than" or marked with the asterisks that now accompany the baseball players of the recent steroid era. Their white counterparts, who did not face Satchel Paige or Josh Gibson during regular season play, are regarded as American athletic heroes—men whose feats of strength and skill have rarely been rivaled.

Like so many other American children, I came of age as a baseball fan. Summer vacations were structured around stops at baseball fields, both minor and major. I eagerly collected baseball cards, carefully preserving my most treasured rookie cards. I was always aware of the legendary lost baseball cards of older generations, the Mickey Mantle cards thrown out by an overeager mother after her sons had left for college, and I wanted to avoid the same terrifying fate. Every grown-up baseball fan I knew (including my uncles) had these stories and years later still mourned the loss of their precious cards. Memorizing statistics—batting averages, ERA, home runs, and no-hitters—meant I could keep up with the boys and best any local expert in an impromptu trivia challenge (made all the more incongruous to my opponents considering I was an 11-year-old girl).

Baseball connected the generations in my family and made me aware of the immense weight of history. To really perform as a fan, one needed to understand historical context. What did a 30–30 season mean? Why was it rare? How was one to comprehend Nolan Ryan's 5,714 strikeouts and seven no-hitters?

1

What about Joe DiMaggio's 56-game hitting streak? How did you rank the best hitters or pitchers of all time? Should you rely on individual statistics? Value added to their team? Buried in the footnotes of the books on baseball statistics I scoured at bed time, there would occasionally be hints of another history—one lurking at the edges—Josh Gibson's 800-plus home runs, Cool Papa Bell's speed.

In graduate school, searching for a dissertation topic, that slightly hidden history seemed to emerge in unexpected places and ways. Reading about black film or the Harlem Renaissance made me question how black baseball players (clearly celebrities in many African American cities and towns) participated in those pivotal cultural moments. Monographs about the Great Migration and the transformation of American demographics and public spaces reminded me that many black baseball players who toured with the Negro Leagues likely made that same migration. These players were the young men who left family, church, culture, and climate in the South to seek better economic opportunities in Northern industrial cities. Theoretical work on black cultural practice and the employment/development of the black vernacular seemed to describe the humor and folktales so prominent in the oral histories of black baseball players. The more I read of the African American experience generally, the more I was surprised by the lack of mention of black baseball players.

Diving into the literature that did exist regarding black baseball, mostly in the field of sport history and sport studies, I found rich and rewarding scholarship that explored the practicalities and lived experiences of those black baseball players, team owners, and league officials. Yet, questions remained. How did these players perform their racial identity in a politically charged moment? How did the ephemera—the visual "stuff" of black sport—reveal and reflect messages of racial resistance? Within the constraints of a segregated country, how did these players, their fans, and their owners construct their own sense of identity, purpose, citizenship, and meaning? I was struck by the sheer radicalness of the images, humor, and stories that littered black baseball throughout the Jim Crow period. As many historians have argued, notably Jules Tygiel, Jackie Robinson's breaking of the color line was the first and perhaps most significant early victory for civil rights in the United States. What was that victory built on? Was it merely the Double V Victory campaign and a grateful nation's debt to black soldiers who gave their lives in World War II? Or was it a more long-term story—one with small challenges and victories that cracked the foundation of white supremacy and segregation in a way that made it impossible to withstand the major blow of meritorious black wartime service? In this book, I delve into these questions and find that the cultural resistance African Americans employed in and around the "national pastime" of baseball during a time of great national separation, segregation, and suppression set the stage for the civil rights successes of the 1950s and 1960s. Jackie Robinson's debut as the first African American baseball player in the formerly all-white major leagues was not the starting point for later civil rights achievements but a reflection of the toil and struggle of the black athletes, fans, writers, and owners who preceded him.

Modern baseball's expanded rosters have brought about increased specialization. In the days of black baseball, teams struggled to maintain a reasonable roster size because of financial constraints. Negro League's clubs carried just enough players, so the idea of having specialized relief pitchers would have been completely unfeasible. Negro Leagues' teams worked just to maintain enough of a rotation that their star pitchers could grab a day or two of rest (a prospect made all the more difficult by punishing holiday and Sunday double and triple-headers). White major league teams had typically drawn relief pitching from the ranks of aging veteran pitchers when necessary, but black teams generally still needed to promote their veteran stars as starters to encourage attendance. It was not until after World War II that being a relief pitcher became a viable career position for professional baseball players.[1] By the 1980s, relief pitching itself had been specialized. Relief pitchers could be middle relievers, closers, or set-up men.

Set-up men are those relief pitchers who take the mound before the closer. They usually enter the game in the seventh or eighth inning with the job of holding the score so that the closer can come in and finish the game. Set-up men have a high-pressure job—they need to have masterful control—and hand off the pitching duties to a closer who brings it all home (hopefully with a win). The set-up men also face a number of disadvantages in their job. There is no recognizable statistic that truly measures their performance. Closers earn saves, not set-up men. An unofficial statistic, the hold, exists to provide some reward to effective set-up men. According to Major League Baseball's rules and regulations:

> The hold is not an official statistic, but it was created as a way to credit middle relief pitchers for a job well done. Starting pitchers get wins, and closers—the relief pitchers who come in at the end of the game—get saves, but the guys who pitch in between the two rarely get either statistic. So what's the most important thing one of these middle relievers can do? "Hold" a lead. If a reliever comes into a game to protect a lead, gets at least one out and leaves without giving up that lead, he gets a hold. But you can't get a save and a hold at the same time.[2]

Set-up men can earn a hold, but as the major league regulations note, it is not an official statistic, merely a bone thrown to those who toil in the relative obscurity of middle relief.

Rare is the set-up man who rises to glory and fame. Because of the regulations, set-up men compete in a high risk/low reward environment. They cannot win or save, they can only hold or lose. They pour their effort into pitching for the good of the team rather than personal gain, becoming visible in terms of statistics only when they record a loss.

All-Star selections are reserved for outstanding starters and closers, not the set-up men who manage the gap in between their work. Because their worth to the team is often less tangible, as it less visible in the measured stats so prized by fans, owners, and managers, set-up men are often the also-rans. Hardcore baseball fanatics know their names and abilities, but the casual fan little notes their presence. Set-up men also are relatively low earners in the world of professional baseball. They are not the players showered with tens of millions of dollars in salary and bonuses. They tend to have salaries on the low end compared to their peers.

In many ways, the black baseball community in the first half of the 20th century functioned as set-up men, setting the stage for the closers, like Jackie Robinson, who would get the glory, but also have hard ninth innings in which they had to battle. This book attempts to tell the story of these set-up men (and sometimes women) who fought and resisted on the field and, just as importantly, off the field. Just like their modern successors, Negro Leagues baseball players played in relative obscurity within larger American society. Their fans and press knew of their accomplishments and successes, but their audience was much smaller than that of the white major leagues. Despite grueling schedules and amazing feats of strength and skill, the statistics of black players like Satchel Paige, Buck Leonard, and Josh Gibson are not part of official major league baseball records. Their records and statistics are unofficial, and because of insufficient media coverage and inconsistent opposition, murky and unreliable. Even with diligent work by baseball historians and statisticians to gather all extant box scores, the legacy of these players is somewhat tarnished or diminished by their absence from "official" record books. Like set-up men, they generally were paid far less than their more famous (and in this case, white) counterparts.

Just like set-up men, they also had a huge impact on the game. These were the men who fought to reform and challenge the very white supremacist ideals that classified them as "less than," "inferior," and "unqualified." They used all the tools at their disposal, be they remarkable athletic displays, transgressive humor and nicknames, or critiques of white baseball's hypocrisy, to set up the ultimate opportunity for their closers, Jackie Robinson and Larry Doby. James "Cool Papa" Bell, a Negro Leagues star known for his speed, once was asked if he regretted the timing of his career, timing that meant he was not able to be part of the group who integrated the major leagues. He, like Buck O'Neil, who famously said he was "right on time," claimed no regrets. Instead he argued it was major league baseball that had missed out, having "opened the door too late." The set-up men, black baseball's promoters, players, fans, and press, worked diligently behind the closed door, knocking, pushing, and eventually forcing open the door. This book is an attempt to tell that story—the story of the set-up men.

Introduction

"A jim-crow affair": Negro League Baseball

During the first half of the twentieth century, African Americans grappled with how to define and negotiate black baseball within the confines of a Jim Crow society. This book explores the intersections among African American life, sport (in this instance, baseball), culture, and racial identity politics during those decades. In particular, I examine various arenas through which baseball provided a forum for African Americans to negotiate the meaning of race under Jim Crow. African Americans used baseball to construct and challenge early twentieth-century access to public and semi-public spaces, definitions of black manhood, visual depictions of black athletes, black vernacular folklore and humor, team and individual naming practices, and baseball clowning. Within these literal and figurative spaces, African Americans resisted the strictures of segregation, highlighted the ambiguity of racial classification and identity, refuted white supremacist stereotypes and theories, and debated black political ideologies.

To fully understand the implications of black baseball for African Americans, one first needs a brief history of black baseball in the United States. The story of black baseball is not a static history of one established professional league. Instead, the history of black baseball leagues is dynamic and ever changing. Between 1885 and 1960, black baseball ebbed and flowed as new leagues and teams formed and disbanded in response to various economic and social conditions, and in response to the maneuvers of high-powered team owners. Almost every scholar and historian writing about the Negro Leagues has employed a slightly different time frame, reflecting their individual perspectives. Consequently, the field lacks a standard time frame. I mark the beginning of black organized baseball with the founding of the professional and all-black Cuban Giants in 1885 and mark the end of professional black baseball with the dissolution of the Negro American League in 1960.

The vagaries of Jim Crow society greatly influenced the history of professional black baseball. As organized black baseball began in earnest at the same time that segregation was codified in the South and ended a few years after the *Brown vs. Board of Education* decision in 1954, the major events that formed, maintained, and challenged racially-based segregation similarly marked black baseball. World War I, the Great Migration, the New Negro and Harlem Renaissance of the 1920s and 1930s, the Great Depression, and World War II each had a significant impact on the fortunes (and bankruptcies) of black baseball squads.

African Americans have played baseball since the inception and growth of the sport concurrent with the Civil War and postbellum urbanization and technological advances.[1] A few African American men managed to compete in professional baseball prior to the exclusion of blacks from the major leagues in 1889. Bud Fowler played for a number of small-semiprofessional traveling teams in the 1870s and 1880s.[2] Moses Fleetwood Walker became the first African American major league baseball player when he suited up as catcher for Toledo, an American Association team, in 1884. A few other players, including Walker's brother Welday, followed in his footsteps.[3] Integrated baseball, however, was short-lived.

In 1887, Adrian "Cap" Anson, an influential player-manager and future Hall of Famer, refused to play against a racially integrated team. His refusal to compete against an integrated team was not new; he had made similar, unfulfilled threats in 1884. This time, however, Anson found a more favorable reception for his segregationist stance. The ten-member International League met in July of 1887 and voted to prohibit member teams from signing future contracts with black players. The vote was 6–4, with the six all-white teams voting in the majority.[4] Shortly after this decision, a number of other professional leagues, most of which already practiced informal segregation, upheld or instituted bans against black baseball players.[5] Historian Jules Tygiel has attributed these increasingly formalized color bans in professional baseball to a larger, late-century focus on "professionalism." In this "culture of professionalism," baseball players and owners tried to use "racial and ethnic exclusion" that "often constituted a means to define the distinctiveness of a given profession."[6] In other words, the justification for true professional status for baseball players could only come through the racially based exclusivity of the game.

For Walker and the other International League black ball players, this new rule signaled the end of their careers in major league baseball. Although the new regulation did not terminate current contracts with black players, the atmosphere on the integrated league teams was not welcoming in 1888. One player, George Stovey, was released from his contract prior to the start of the 1888 season. Two others, Bud Fowler and Bob Higgins, resigned midseason in the face of vitriolic abuse from teammates and spectators. A fourth player, Frank Grant, requested a raise after completing a strong season and was consequently denied a salary increase and let go. As the 1889 season approached, only one black player, Fleetwood Walker, remained in the professional leagues. Walker played a portion of the 1889 season and then resigned, officially beginning an almost 60-year period during which the professional leagues would employ only white players.

African Americans, however, were not willing merely to step aside and stay out of organized baseball altogether. All-black teams and leagues had been established in the 1860s, primarily on the Eastern Seaboard. The Pythians of Philadelphia, led by Octavius Catto, were the most notable of these early black baseball teams. They were, however, victims of the racial politics of the time. The National Association of Base Ball Players (NABBP) denied the Pythians membership and recognition. Although the Pythians persevered without NABBP recognition, they folded after the murder of Catto in 1871.[7] Other early black teams, often composed of hotel or restaurant employees, competed against each other in resort areas such as Long Island and Atlantic City, drawing crowds of baseball fans.[8] Meanwhile, a fledgling league was established in the South. Consisting of ten teams, the Southern League competed in 1886 and established clubs in major Southern cities, including Memphis, Atlanta, and New Orleans. Despite some positive notice in the press, the Southern League folded at the end of the year, with its member teams unable to support themselves financially.[9] In general, these early teams and leagues lacked an overarching power structure and firm financial footing. Consequently, teams encountered significant scheduling difficulties and were unable to sponsor a legitimate championship.[10]

During the first two decades of the twentieth century, black baseball increasingly made its mark in Northern urban centers. A small but growing number of teams regularly competed in cities such as Philadelphia and Chicago, facing other professional and semiprofessional clubs. The owners, both black and white, of these clubs formed casual alliances and arranged games under the supervision of promoters and booking agents. It was during this early stage of black baseball that a true star emerged. Rube Foster, a pitcher with the Leland Giants, compiled an overwhelming win-loss record and brought a number of new fans to the game. Still, owners were unwilling or unable to establish themselves as a league and frequently raided other black baseball teams for their stars.[11] Thus, even as black baseball became more popular, institutional instability threatened its survival.

Meanwhile, the advent of World War I had implications for African American communities and black baseball. As national immigration policies slowed the influx of European workers into the industrial cities of the North, increasing numbers of African Americans migrated from the South in search of greater opportunities and a more welcoming racial climate. The majority of these migrants were young men seeking jobs in the steel mills and factories of cities like Chicago, Cleveland, and Pittsburgh. In many cases, these early male migrants sought to establish themselves before sending for their family members to join them in the North. As young black men, these migrants often played on community baseball teams sponsored by local churches and business. Those who did not play most likely attended local baseball contests as spectators.

This increase in black urban populations in the North, ushered in with the first waves of the Great Migration, created a favorable environment for the creation of an organized black baseball league. Moreover, the push for greater racial equality domestically that accompanied black U.S. soldiers returning from World War I fostered a sense of solidarity for black businesses that benefited a fledgling black leisure enterprise.[12]

In 1920, Rube Foster capitalized on both the increasing popularity of black baseball and the growing urban black populations, by establishing the Negro National League.[13] Foster was motivated to begin a league to ensure that his Chicago American Giants had good, regular competition and to institute contractual obligations that would prevent other teams from raiding players or venues for their own personal gain.[14] Foster believed that black baseball could grow and prosper as a collective enterprise, bringing in greater numbers of fans and employing the best black talent.[15] Foster also resented the power of white booking agents like Nat Strong and sought to assert a leadership role for African Americans in black baseball.[16] Ultimately, Foster would be unsuccessful in eliminating the influence of Strong and others. Strong maintained his importance as a booking agent for the Negro Leagues and white semipro teams despite Foster's disdain. Although other baseball owners and black sportswriters shared Foster's dislike of Strong, Strong's connections made him invaluable to the survival of Negro Leagues teams, especially during the difficult Depression years.[17] Instead it would be the other elements of Foster's professional league that would have the greatest positive impact on black baseball.

One of the other founding members of the Negro National League, C.I. Taylor, felt the same pressures as Foster. In a 1920 article he noted that "[w]e will never have playing grounds until we can get an organization of such strength as to enable us to procure them, and to guarantee the public a standard schedule of games on those grounds after we get them." Taylor also detailed the difficulties owners encountered in dealing with players who lacked meaningful contracts.[18]

Strategically, Foster also hoped to take advantage of local movements that encouraged African Americans to patronize black enterprises whenever possible. Publicly, Foster promoted the Negro National League and particularly his

Chicago American Giants as black businesses to attract positive publicity and loyal fans. This strategy had its benefits, particularly in Chicago, where black leaders, including Beauregard Moseley, a Foster associate, had established the Leland Giants Baseball and Amusement Association to build and maintain black-owned recreational facilities, including a proposed ballpark. Moseley had also tried and failed to establish the National Negro Baseball League in 1910.[19]

Foster's 1920 timing was fortuitous. Black enterprise building, which had first become popular in Chicago at the turn of the century, had even more appeal during the 1920s.[20] Nationally, Marcus Garvey was gaining popularity and extolling the virtues of black enterprise and black racial purity. Foster's stated desire to build a racially pure black institution complemented Garvey's rhetoric. Even Foster's motto, "We are the Ship, All Else the Sea," echoed Garvey's Black Star Line and his Back to Africa campaign.[21] Yet privately, Foster focused primarily on establishing black baseball as a profitable business with little concern for the racial background of those he needed to ensure financial success for the fledgling league. Foster's difficulties in balancing his business relationships with his public call for black baseball to be a race enterprise will be discussed in greater detail in Chapter One.

Throughout the Negro Leagues era (1920–1960), leagues formed and disbanded frequently. Foster's own Negro National League fell on hard times after Foster's 1926 illness and subsequent death. Without Foster's strong, controlling presence, the league lacked the necessary leadership to continue, and folded in 1931.[22] In the 1920s and 1930s, black baseball fell into a set pattern. Team owners would collaborate as a league only to break apart as they began to bicker over player contracts and scheduling. The details differed based on the circumstances and personalities involved but the outcome was always the same—a folded league or a severely damaged league that was a shadow of its former self.

The Great Depression provided yet another obstacle for black baseball as a professional sport. According to historian Neil Lanctot, the Depression allowed white booking agents and "black underworld figures" (i.e., number runners) to gain a foothold into black baseball. With expendable incomes scarce, attendance dropping, and personal financial resources strained, team owners began to cut salaries and travel costs, scrimping everywhere they could.[23] Forced to adapt to a new economic environment, teams welcomed the deep pockets of number runners like Gus Greenlee, who established a Negro Leagues team in Pittsburgh. To maximize their ability to reach fans, the Kansas City Monarchs and the Pittsburgh Crawfords began playing night games. Perhaps the most significant innovation, however, was the establishment of the East-West All-Star Game in 1933. The East-West game quickly became one of the highlights of the year for black sport fans. Held in Chicago, the game brought together the best Negro Leagues stars and, most crucially, reignited the interest of black baseball's fan base. Mark Ribowsky has argued that because of the constant ebb and flow of players from team to team, "the strength of the black game consisted of its transcendent stars."[24]

The success of the East-West All-Star Game, slow improvement of general economic conditions, and support from the black press along with the financial influx from new owners allowed black baseball to survive the Great Depression. By 1939, fans started to return to the ballparks, bringing a more steady revenue stream to the financially strained clubs. Still, Negro Leagues baseball could not be described as particularly stable or economically secure. The long, difficult Depression years had left their toll on most black baseball teams and owners. As historian Lanctot has noted, despite the lessening of the Depression in the late 1930s, most African Americans still lacked the expendable income necessary to attend games on a regular basis.[25] World War II, however, would bring with it a change in circumstances for black baseball specifically and for African Americans in general.

Unlike white major league baseball, which was decimated by the loss of key players to the war effort, Negro Leagues baseball thrived during the war years, as did women's professional baseball.[26] Increased employment among African Americans translated into higher attendance numbers for black baseball teams, as did the still growing African American population in northern urban centers. On the field, black clubs were able to field competitive teams with star players due to the fact that the Negro Leagues, which marketed themselves on the basis of their celebrity players, needed players to compete long past the age when most white ballplayers had retired. Negro Leagues stars could expect to remain employed as an active part of the black baseball world for as long as they attracted fans to the ballparks.

The success of black baseball during World War II was a double-edged sword. Coffers were no longer empty, players were regularly compensated, and fans were enthusiastic. At the same time, however, increasing numbers of African Americans, as part of the Double V Victory campaign, advocated for an end to segregated institutions. Clearly, black baseball, with its call for race patronage, did not easily fit into this agenda.[27] Although fans did not immediately abandon black baseball, the black press and community leaders devoted their time and resources to the campaign to integrate the major leagues.

As the growing popularity of black baseball, a change in the major league commissioner, and a slightly more tolerant post-war racial climate coincided with calls for integration from both the black and white press, major league officials finally and publicly denounced the unwritten color line. This change in policy opened the door for Branch Rickey to sign Jackie Robinson to the Brooklyn Dodgers in 1946. In 1947, after one minor league season, Robinson entered

Ebbets Field as the first African American major leaguer since Fleetwood Walker in 1889.[28]

Larry Doby, Monte Irvin, and other Negro Leagues stars soon followed in Robinson's footsteps, and black fans were not far behind. Black fans were eager to see their baseball idols compete in a formerly forbidden arena and threw their support wholeheartedly behind these integrating pioneers. Patronizing black enterprises was no longer viewed as a contribution to racial success or uplift, but as a relic of an older style of racial politics. Instead African Americans fought for integrated schools, transportation, and leisure spaces. This change in ideology was actually a return to the more integrationist philosophy of late nineteenth-century African American leaders.[29] Black baseball quickly lost its importance for many African Americans. Plagued by waning interest on the part of fans, the last all-black baseball league folded in 1960, although the Kansas City Monarchs and Indianapolis Clowns held on as barnstorming teams until 1963 and 1965, respectively.[30]

A number of historians and sportswriters have examined the black baseball experience. The earliest works covering the Negro Leagues attempted to make visible the seemingly forgotten story of black baseball and its stars. In *Only the Ball Was White* and *Invisible Men,* Robert Peterson and Donn Rogosin recounted the terrific athletic accomplishments of Negro Leagues players while bringing to light the atrocious conditions under which they toiled.[31] These works, along with a number of biographies and autobiographies, successfully introduced the names of players like Josh Gibson to general readers of sport history.[32] At the same time, documentary efforts by John Holway, James Riley, and Brent Kelley preserved the oral histories of black baseball stars, preserving their memories for future readers and researchers.[33]

Groups like SABR (Society for American Baseball Research) have been particularly active in finding and collating statistics from the Negro Leagues. Although black newspapers covered Negro Leagues action, they did not have sufficient staff or resources to send writers on the road with the teams. As a result, box scores were often missing or provided limited information. Critics have alleged that even the extant statistics are flawed because black teams regularly competed against semi-professional teams that were not playing at a level comparable to major league baseball at the time. In 2006, an expert committee, commissioned by Major League Baseball, studied the records and accomplishments of black players, managers, and owners from the Jim Crow Era. The committee recommended that 17 Negro Leaguers be inducted into the National Baseball Hall of Fame in Cooperstown, New York. This group of 17 included the first female member of the Baseball Hall of Fame, Effa Manley. They were inducted on July 30, 2006. With their induction, the Hall of Fame now includes

35 members who played on, managed, or owned teams primarily before the modern integration of baseball.[34]

Most of the more recent full-length works either take a strict regional approach or examine the institutional history of the Negro Leagues. The regional manuscripts have provided a much-needed local context for the day-to-day operations of clubs such as the Homestead Grays, Kansas City Monarchs, and Hilldale Daisies.[35] Other larger works have taken the approach of exploring the Negro Leagues as a black business and enterprise. Thus, these works focus on the owners and agents who held much of the power in black baseball.[36] These newer works do place black baseball into the context of the larger history of African Americans in the first half of the twentieth century, yet they are centered on the experiences and accomplishments of the Negro Leagues' power brokers. As a result, they devote most of their analysis to the formation and dissolution of Negro Leagues teams and the personal relationships among club owners. This focus on owners and league politics ignores or gives only fleeting attention to a number of important features of black baseball. In particular, these authors neglect to examine the cultural products of black baseball and to explore the racial contestation and resistance that were integral to the sport.

Appropriately, considering his larger-than-life personality and out-sized emphasis on black baseball, another significant thread of recent scholarship has focused on Negro Leagues and major league pitcher Satchel Paige. Paige, known for his attention-getting antics on and off the field, has been a juicy and fruitful subject for interested scholars, historians, and biographers. Expanding on earlier works, Larry Tye has written a thorough and engaging biography of Paige that reconstructs his life and sheds light on the various apocryphal stories that star the great pitcher.[37] In 2012, Donald Spivey published a detailed and analytical biography of Paige, in which he delved into all the gray areas, discerning what could be documented as historical fact and what was better left to the storytellers of black baseball.[38] Likewise, Leslie Heaphy has contributed to and edited a collection of analytical papers that examine Paige's life and influence on baseball (in addition to covering other adjacent topics regarding black baseball more generally).[39] These new works on Paige highlight and interrogate the mythologies that surrounded his life story (often because of his own penchant for story telling and mythmaking), but only rarely delve into the larger cultural meaning of the folklore that was such a large part of his public persona.

Scholars of early twentieth-century African American history have also largely neglected black baseball.[40] These scholars have provided an invaluable examination of the ways in which African Americans worked, lived, organized, and played during Jim Crow. As most of these authors have constructed local studies, their concentrated focus on particular urban centers has resulted in multi-faceted portraits of specific black communities. Historians studying the interwar period have highlighted the important roles of social and cultural life (including leisure) in the formation of African American communities, yet they have rarely considered the implications of black baseball, specifically for black community formation, political strategies, racial identification, or public morality. Instead, these authors have been content to merely note, often without further comment or contextualization, the existence of a baseball park or Negro Leagues franchise within specific black communities.

By moving black baseball to the forefront of the black experience during the Jim Crow era, historians can answer a number of important questions. For instance, although we know a good deal about the significance of black religious institutions as property owners and community centers during this time period, by studying black baseball we can examine the implications of black ownership of secular, leisure spaces in African American communities. Furthermore, black baseball spawned a significant oral and visual culture that was a consistent presence in African American communities during this time period. Historians have explored the cultural meanings and significance of the visual and literary culture of the Harlem Renaissance while neglecting the illustrations, folklore, and cartoons of black baseball that were present almost daily in the pages of the black press, in the barbershops, and in the stores, churches, and community centers. By critically evaluating these cultural productions, one can better understand African American conceptions of racial identity and classification during Jim Crow.

In this book, I build upon the work undertaken by scholars of African American history and culture. Scholars such as Robin D.G. Kelley have produced important recent works of African American cultural studies that explore and document the cultural and social resistance of racially oppressed people. These monographs have served as a model for this work and have contributed to the analytical framework through which I have evaluated the visual and oral culture of black baseball. They are particularly useful for their interrogation of cultural expressions to determine both everyday resistance and larger racial and political meanings.[41]

Based on an understanding of the institutional functions of the Negro Leagues and the trials and triumphs of black baseball players, I examine the cultural meanings of black baseball for African Americans living under Jim Crow. In particular, I explore the ways in which black baseball, as space, as a model for manhood, as a visual image, and as the setting for trickster tales, provided an avenue through which African Americans were able to define and reshape their identity on their own terms. Baseball's accessibility and centrality in black life during the early twentieth century made it a uniquely important venue for discussion of race and gender norms, as well a crucial site on which to challenge segregation and claims of racial inferiority.

The first five chapters fit within the timeframe of 1900–1947. Prior to 1900, black baseball, though a presence in American life, lacked the attention and fan base it would gain after the turn of the century. In the first decade of the twentieth century, black baseball would begin to attract the notice of both African American and white audiences. In particular, a young, talented pitcher named Rube Foster would "inspire the national imagination and pump up a national agenda."[42] Foster's accomplishments and star power coincided with a large expansion of semi-professional black baseball in the population centers of the East coast, especially in the Philadelphia area. According to historian Mark Ribowsky, "[i]n the space of two years, at least nine new teams, all bearing the name 'Giants,' were born within a hundred miles of the city—as were two *genuine* Cuban teams based there, the Cuban Stars and the Havana Stars."[43] This expansion would immediately precede and inspire the formation of Foster's Negro National League in 1920. Thus, the vast majority of the time period coincides with the Negro Leagues era and so-called Golden Age of black baseball (1920–1947).

The sixth chapter spans the time period from the 1920s with the emergence of early clowning teams to the continued touring of the clowning teams into the 1980s. Most of the focus remains on the Negro Leagues period, but the clowning teams themselves acted as a bridge and extension of the black baseball tradition. Clowning teams struggled to find their place within the organized black leagues but rarely struggled to find fans. Their story complements and complicates the story of black baseball.

The epilogue explores the 13 years after Jackie Robinson's integration of major league baseball, during which time professional black baseball teams still took the field on a regular basis. Black baseball did not immediately end with the cessation of the color line, but the entrance of African American baseball players into the majors drew attention and fans away from the Negro Leagues and began a long period of disenchantment among black baseball fans. Although African Americans had great pride in the black baseball leagues, most black fans and sportswriters wholeheartedly supported the integration of the majors. For the majority of African Americans, integration was the only acceptable end result for black baseball. Consequently, black fans quickly turned their attention to black major leaguers, determined to support Robinson and his fellow color-line breakers as they forged ahead in a previously all-white world. As such, the last chapter will explore the ways in which these black players in the formerly white leagues negotiated identity and culture during a liminal time marked by racial quotas and continued discrimination. As of 1947, the Negro Leagues did not represent the only possible professional baseball environment for African American players. The stories of the men who chose the major leagues and their navigation of recently opened space are significant and illuminate many of the themes discussed in previous chapters. This small cadre of black men worked within an often still racially hostile environment. Even as the initial protests and death threats faded, the black major leaguers developed strategies to combat and survive the continued racial oppression in professional baseball.

To uncover the role of baseball in the lives of African Americans, this book relies heavily on contemporary black periodicals. Although these periodicals were produced by members of the black elite and therefore represent a particular viewpoint, they also provide the most extensive and consistent treatment of black baseball in the time period.

Through the use of black newspapers, I examine the public discourse and visual imagery surrounding black baseball during the time period. These sources reflected the agenda of the sportswriters and black press, as well as the expectations of the readership. In particular, I have utilized the major black periodicals of the time: the *Chicago Defender,* the *Pittsburgh Courier,* the *Crisis,* and *Opportunity.* Many scholars have also relied upon these sources in writing about the Negro Leagues, for good reason. They retain their value due to their large readership, one that crossed geographic boundaries, and their extensive coverage of black sport. Based on their wide national circulation, one can make inferences about the national impact of black baseball that would be impossible to make merely by reading local publications. The newspapers of smaller locales provide an important look at the various regional and local differences of black baseball coverage. At the same time, cities and towns that lacked an established professional black team primarily covered black baseball during stops by barnstorming clubs, as these smaller papers did not have sufficient staff or resources for more national coverage. Because of this book's broad scope, I have focused on the larger papers to identify and analyze the most commonly disseminated images and information.

To gain a better understanding of the meaning of black baseball for African Americans, I have examined portions of these periodicals that scholars of black baseball have largely ignored. The illustrations, photographs, and editorial art of the black press comprise a significant portion of the primary evidence for this book. These incredibly important and frequently provocative images reflected and challenged contemporary conceptions of race and gender. Through a close reading of these images, I have recovered the meanings and messages of these images and highlight their significance for African Americans during the Jim Crow era.

Similarly, I analyze the oral histories and memoirs of black baseball players. These accounts provide a great deal of source material. The players recount their recollections of life in the Negro Leagues, discussing fan response and attendance, difficulties in traveling under Jim Crow, and the numerous trickster tales that highlighted the exploits of black ball players. Former player accounts, while valuable and often voluminous, have their problems. Memories are frequently faulty and unreliable, particularly as the years pass between these men's careers and their memoirs. Dates and names may be conflated, achievements exaggerated, and disappointments de-emphasized. Moreover, as products of a particular historical time and place (Jim Crow America), these men often minimize the difficulties that they faced as black ball players, perhaps as a means of self-protection. Having survived an era of lynchings and violence against black men, these players learned to be reticent when speaking publicly about racial injustice and may have maintained that custom years later when speaking to interviewers and ghostwriters.

Yet one should not discount these sources entirely on the basis of these potential inaccuracies. These men reveal a great deal about black baseball and its role in African American life and provide some of the only first-hand accounts of black baseball outside of press coverage. These memoirs reveal more direct information about the importance of baseball for working-class African Americans and recent black migrants, as most black ballplayers were from Southern working-class backgrounds. By emphasizing the commonalities among the accounts, one can find meaningful pieces of evidence regarding black baseball.

In this work, I have also focused on trickster tales about black baseball. The analysis and interpretations of these tales was informed by theories of resistance and signifying proposed by James Scott and Henry Louis Gates, Jr.[44] Scott's theory of the hidden transcript posits that public statements have two levels of meanings, particularly when performed by members of an oppressed group. In the public transcript, oppressed people express sentiments that can be clearly understood by the dominant societal group, yet in the hidden transcript there is a secondary meaning, visible only to other members of a the subordinate group. By playing between the public and hidden transcript, subordinate people can communicate potentially subversive messages without attracting the ire of their oppressors. Within the realm of the hidden transcript, signifying becomes a crucial discursive practice. Gates has explained that signifying practice allows for a discourse that operates and hinges double meanings. By discursively signifying, as black ball players did with nicknames and trickster tales, one can apply layers of reference to a single word or story, thus bestowing layered meanings to one's audiences.

During the era of segregated baseball, African Americans struggled to balance their desire for integration and their patronage of a race enterprise. Many African Americans expressed ideological support for the integration of the white major leagues. Yet at the same time, they valued baseball's role in the black economy. It is within this paradox that one can uncover the delicate negotiation of segregation, as black baseball advocates undermined the foundations of Jim Crow and advanced the cause of a race institution.

ONE

Sport and the Contest Over Space

July 5, 1930. On a warm and breezy Saturday afternoon in New York City, 20,000 baseball fans packed Yankee Stadium.[1] The patrons in attendance witnessed two closely-fought games between rival squads, the Baltimore Black Sox and the local Lincoln Giants. This doubleheader was the culmination of a four-game series played over two days in New York.[2] Staged as a benefit for the Brotherhood of the Sleeping Car Porters, the game attracted a well-dressed crowd composed of "thousands of attractive women in softly-tinted flimsy summer garments and nattily-clad men topped off by vari-colored berets."[3] The majority of the fans were African Americans (Chester Washington noted that the fans represented a "mighty mess of Harlem's sport lovers"), with a small but significant number of white Lincoln Giants fans also in attendance according to a promotional article in the *Pittsburgh Courier.*[4] Also taking in the game was the owner of the New York Yankees and Yankee Stadium, Jacob Ruppert, accompanied by a number of local city and baseball officials. The presence of a celebrity, Bill "Bojangles" Robinson, inspired a great deal of excitement among many in the crowd. Robinson delighted the fans "by winning a 100-yard handicap race running backwards pitted against a flock of youngsters."[5]

Despite the bonhomie and festival-like atmosphere, the financial devastation of the Great Depression lurked just outside the stadium gate. For many in the crowd, attending the game was both a monetary hardship and a necessary reprieve from the economic demands of the Great Depression. In the midst of this first summer of the Depression, record numbers of urban Americans were unemployed and struggling to make ends meet. In northern urban cities, the economic crisis was particularly acute, and the situation for African Americans was disproportionately difficult.[6] Indeed, the Depression had exacerbated the already strained financial circumstances faced by African Americans in Harlem.[7] According to economic historian William Sundstrom, "[w]ithin the North, unemployment rates were 80 percent higher for blacks than whites."[8] The large influx of Southern black migrants and West Indian immigrants that had swelled Harlem's population in the first three decades of the twentieth century found that the economic opportunities that had inspired their move to New York were rapidly diminishing.[9]

Amid the darkening economic times, black and white New Yorkers donned their Sunday finest and packed Yankee Stadium to cheer on the Lincoln Giants and to be part of the vibrant mass celebrating Independence Day. Above all, the patrons sought entertainment. Even those uninterested in the outcome of the game enjoyed the social aspects of the event and the extra entertainment. This particular game featured Robinson's comedic race, a large marching band, and a number of exhibition races. For fans, one constant yet unpredictable pleasure was the prime people-watching. Sportswriters covering the festivities remarked on the unusual attire of at least one patron. In addition to the scheduled entertainment, one fan "drew the spotlight away from the game upon his entrance." The man in question was "attempting to set a new fad" by wearing "a flawless tuxedo coat and the correct aviation collar and bat wing times, supported by a cane and a pair of white flannel trousers and sport shoes."[10] The assembled crowd undoubtedly thrilled at the sight of such a figure. For African American baseball fans suffering through the twin tragedies of Jim Crow and the Great Depression, games provided much more than an outlet for their interest in sport. Negro Leagues games also provided an opportunity to see and to be seen: to catch up with acquaintances and meet new associates, to flirt and date, to listen to bands and laugh at comedic routines, to gamble and hopefully to win much-needed cash.[11]

Accounts of this doubleheader provide not only important information about the ways in which Americans in the Depression sought out leisure activities for momentary pleasure and escape, but also a great deal about black baseball and African American spectators in the first half of the twentieth century. After an initial doubleheader at Dexter Park, the Giants' traditional home grounds, the action moved to Yankee Stadium.[12] Yankee Stadium was a much larger venue and had the added benefit of being a major league facility. Competing there, the Giants and Black Sox would have had access to finely maintained grounds and more comfortable clubhouse amenities. The trip was both a geographical and symbolic relocation. In undertaking this approximately 16-mile trip from Queens to the Bronx, the players and their fans traversed the much greater gulf of baseball's biracial color line.

For the African American fans in attendance, having Yankee Stadium as the venue would have added both difficulties and advantages. Yankee Stadium was not their home field, and while more fans could attend, the intimacy of Dexter Park would be missing. In addition, the "concrete-bowl" construction of Yankee Stadium undoubtedly trapped a great deal more heat and provided significantly less shade than the smaller venue, an important consideration in mid-summer.[13] Yet despite these inconveniences, witnessing a game in Yankee Stadium had a particular value for African American fans and was a closer destination for those living in Harlem. During a period of segregation and professional color lines, Yankee Stadium represented the pinnacle of major league success. "The House That Ruth Built" was the most important physical venue in the American baseball world in 1930.[14] Advertisements for the series capitalized on Yankee Stadium's significance, calling the series "the biggest event of the year" and encouraging "Harlem" to "fill the Yankee Stadium."[15] If that was not enticing enough for patrons, the ad continued by noting that these games would represent the "first time in history" that "the famous Yankee Stadium" was "donated to the colored people of Harlem." Despite the clear patronizing tone of white charity in the ads, access to Yankee Stadium on a holiday weekend was an opportunity that black baseball fans, players, and owners could not pass up.

For African American fans, players, and sportswriters, this doubleheader in Yankee Stadium provided a glimpse of what could be if black baseball stars could regularly compete in comparable facilities. Without contradiction, black baseball advocates dared to hope for two possible solutions: that the Negro Leagues would obtain the capital necessary to build their own "green cathedrals," subsequently flourishing as a successful black enterprise, and that the white major leagues would finally open the door to the many deserving blackball stars.[16]

This chapter discusses the ways in which players, fans, owners, and writers conceptualized and negotiated space for black baseball under Jim Crow. To establish the centrality of baseball within black life, I first trace the popularity and significance of baseball in black communities. Then I interrogate the role of black baseball in two aspects of the larger debate over segregated leisure: property access/ownership and transportation/travel. As contemporary concerns over segregated space and travel reflected national political debates over civil rights and racial equality, this chapter will also explore the ways in which shifting attitudes toward black enterprise and segregation complicated black baseball.

In the first half of the twentieth century, vast demographic shifts marked African American life. In search of greater opportunities, large numbers of African Americans moved first to urban centers in the South.[17] Temporarily settling in cities such as Houston, Nashville, Memphis, and Birmingham, previously rural-based African Americans sought to make a living in industrial mills and factories or at least enough money to finance a permanent move north.[18] Shut out of many unions, denied the opportunity for anything other than entry-level manual labor, and confronted with government-sanctioned segregation, a number of these migrants continued north when they were able.[19] Hoping for a less restrictive society and better job prospects, African Americans left the urban South for the industrial centers of the North and Midwest.[20]

Inspired by newspaper ads in black papers like the *Chicago Defender* and the *Pittsburgh Courier* and word-of-mouth, these migrants, most of whom were young males, boarded trains for cities like Pittsburgh, Cleveland, and Chicago. A 1918 study of African American migrants to Pittsburgh concluded that approximately 30 percent of migrants were accompanied by their families. Thus, 70 percent were single men or women, with the vast majority of that group consisting of young men. According to the study, 75 percent of all Southern migrants were "between the ages of eighteen and forty."[21] Within this context, then, it is unsurprising that a significant number of Negro Leagues players (young, black males) were either recent migrants or relocated from the South to the North to establish themselves as professional baseball players. To demonstrate the extent of this phenomenon, of the 17 former blackball players interviewed by John Holway in the 1970s, 13 were born in the South. Of those 13, four migrated either with their families or alone as young men to northern cities in search of employment (other than baseball). Two of the remaining 13 lived in a large urban southern city, Atlanta.[22] Upon their arrival in the northern industrial cities, these new citizens entered the local black enclaves, searching for lodging, employment, and, when possible, extended family members or other potential contacts.

As the Great Migration and the economic lures of World War I domestic employment brought a significant number of African Americans to northern urban centers, the new migrants negotiated a physical, cultural, and social space within their new communities. Leisure spaces, particularly baseball fields, were problematic sites of conflict as native-born whites, recently arrived immigrants, and African Americans clashed over access to recreational sites.[23] Depression-era scholars and authors of the landmark study of Chicago, *Black Metropolis,* St. Clair Drake and Horace R. Cayton observed that the Chicago color line was particularly unwavering for "recreational situations that emphasize active participation rather than merely looking on, and in which men and women participate together."[24] Race-based street-level clashes highlighted the ways in which different ethnic and racial groups claimed public spaces as exclusive sites of play, and the potential for violence and danger that surrounded those spaces.[25]

Within this increasingly tense and segregated environment, ensuring the success of black businesses became a central political issue for a number of African Americans. Community support for local black enterprise had a long history in the United States. African American leaders of all stripes, be they Washingtonian, Du Boisian, or Garveyites, championed black economic success and encouraged followers to patronize "race" merchants.[26] Although support for race enterprises came from widely divergent ideological camps, the message was clear. When possible, African Americans should patronize African American businesses.

This message became even more critical during the Great Depression but presented a challenge to the national leadership and expressed goals of the NAACP. Despite the favorable public sentiment toward cultivating black institutions and W.E.B. Du Bois's publicly-declared support of race institutions when appropriate, Walter White, as secretary of the NAACP, continued uncompromisingly to pursue integration and condemn attempts to build black-only institutions. White attempted to compromise slightly by supporting the building of community centers in black neighborhoods as long as the center encouraged interracial cooperation and participation whenever possible.[27] However, he was not willing to alter official NAACP policy regardless of public opinion or opposition from powerful black advocates like DuBois.

White's position did not dissuade other black reformers from encouraging black enterprise whenever and wherever possible. During the Depression, local black political and community leaders came to support "Don't Buy Where You Can't Work" campaigns as well as the concept of the "Double Duty Dollar."[28] With jobs scarce and African Americans disproportionately unemployed, black reformers encouraged people to spend their money in ways that would benefit the race and their local communities. One notable boycott took place in Harlem in 1934 and reveals the ways in which black reformers tried to navigate complex political and commercial relationships for the betterment of local black residents. Harlem elite—"ministers, newspaper editors and writers, politicians, radicals and others"—at first generally opposed an initial Harlem boycott movement as organized by Sufi Abdul Hamid. Hamid had previously led a successful boycott movement in Chicago. In Harlem, however, he found that citizens ... were hopelessly divided over the dilemma of Harlem." In particular, some ministers "supported the idea of giving Negro youth a chance at decent jobs in the community ... but ... wanted the thing accomplished in a spirit of Christian kindliness." In an attempt to win concessions from white business owners in a less confrontational manner, members of the Harlem elite, "led by Reverend John H. Johnson ... and Miss Effa Manley," established the Harlem Citizens League for Fair Play. Effa Manley would come to prominence in the late 1930s as the first lady of the Negro Leagues. Manley's husband owned the Newark (Brooklyn) Eagles. Effa Manley served as the business manager and ran the team in terms of daily decisions. The Citizens League failed to persuade a prominent local businessman to employ African Americans in greater number and "better positions." The League then adopted Hamid's boycott method to great success. Tensions remained high between Hamid and the League, much to the benefit of white merchants. In an attempt to prevent Hamid from overseeing the newly employed black workers, the League withdrew much of its support, entered into a détente with white merchants and "denounced the activities of irresponsible trouble-makers in Harlem."[29] Within this environment of boycotts and community-supported race enterprises, the Negro Leagues sought to define itself as a business both for and by African Americans.

The consistent and ever-increasing support for "race enterprise" within African American communities did not necessarily reflect the acceptance of seg-regation. Historian Herbert Aptheker observed that W.E.B. "Du Bois consis-tently fought against forced segregation and discrimination. At the same time, and without any contradiction in his own mind, he insisted that where separate Black institutions or organizations existed, it was necessary and proper to bring those to as high a point of efficiency and service as possible."[30] Similarly, African American fans, players, and writers promoted the Negro Leagues as a black enterprise at the same time that they lobbied for the eventual integration of the white major leagues. Under this reasoning, black baseball advocates argued that integration could only be achieved if the Negro Leagues functioned as a healthy and thriving example of black enterprise.

These two interrelated desires came to a head during the Great Depression. The economic motivations for supporting black baseball combined with what black sportswriters saw as a small opening through which they could sway white baseball officials. Throughout the 1930s, the black press publicized the com-parative success of Negro Leagues teams in attracting fans and suggested that white baseball would solve its attendance woes by abandoning the color line.[31]

Thus, black baseball's success as black enterprise ultimately led to its demise. Particularly with the advent of World War II and the racial inequities black wartime service exposed, African Americans became more willing to publicly combat and question segregation. Returning black soldiers refused to relinquish seats in the front of the bus and proudly wore their military uniforms at home. As a result, they faced court martials and assault. Quite notably, one of these black servicemen was Jackie Robinson. Robinson was arrested by military police for objecting to segregated bus seating on his Army post, segregation that was in contradiction to military policy after a number of high profile conflicts earlier in the war. The panel overseeing Robinson's court martial trial acquitted him after hearing the evidence, but for Robinson the situation was yet another case in which he played a public role in challenging a system that denied him his cit-izenship rights.

Other African Americans fought for full inclusion into professional sports and public education. For example, author and basketball advocate E.B. Henderson argued against segregated recreation in 1940. According to Henderson, "segregation connotes discrimination and becomes more costly as attempts to equalize opportunity increase."[32] At the conclusion of World War II, supporters of black baseball successfully lobbied for major league baseball to lift its color line. With Happy Chandler's 1945 statement to black sportswriter Ric Roberts that "[i]f a black boy can make it on Okinawa and Guadalcanal, hell, he can make it in baseball" and Branch Rickey's successful recruitment of Jackie Robinson, the integration of major league baseball became a reality.[33] Energized by their victory, African American baseball fans threw the weight of their support and their attendance to Jackie Robinson and the former Negro Leaguers who entered the majors. As Robinson left the world of professional black baseball for the formerly white major leagues, so did many black fans.[34]

*   *   *

Baseball has had a long history in African American cultural life. Nineteenth-century community festivals often included a baseball game, and the first all-black professional baseball team formed in the 1860s.[35] From the 1880s on, African Americans staged annual Emancipation Days—celebrations that intertwined politics, religion, and sports. Emancipation Day organizers frequently scheduled political speeches and intercommunity baseball games back-to-back, ensuring that both activities were well attended.[36] In cities and towns alike, African American commencement ceremonies frequently included a baseball game, as did Juneteenth and Fourth of July commemorations.[37]

As Negro Leagues baseball established itself as an important institution within black culture and society in the twentieth century, African Americans spent their limited leisure time at the ballpark. On Sundays, in particular, African Americans would crowd local ballparks, eager to participate in what was one of the more important weekly social events. Sunday games were the most profitable and well attended. In 1920, *The Competitor* noted that teams thrived in cities that permitted "Sunday baseball, a feature which almost insures success."[38] Team executives were well aware of the financial benefit of staging Sunday games. Dick Powell, general manager of the Baltimore Elite Giants, recalled that for Negro Leagues teams, "[t]he big day was Sunday at home. That's when we made our payroll."[39] Negro Leaguer Leon Day fondly recalled such days. "Sunday in Newark in the 1930s and '40s was church, a doubleheader, and then either out to dinner or to a friend's home for dinner."[40]

For other minority communities in the United States, baseball functioned in the same way. Japanese Americans who struggled to deal with racism and the consequences of the Great Depression also centered their weeks and their Sundays around baseball games. In his study of Washington State–based Japanese

American baseball, scholar Michael L. Mullan noted that "[b]y the mid–1930s, Sunday afternoon baseball in Wapato was the cultural event of the week attracting most of the Japanese American farming community in the valley. People came for baseball, but they also came to visit friends and to be counted among the ethnic gathering in the festival atmosphere of Sunday baseball."[41] In ways very similar to African Americans, Japanese Americans in these rural farming communities structured their weeks around Sunday baseball, a brief reprieve of leisure in the midst of difficult labor.

African Americans continued to celebrate holidays with a trip to the ballpark. The Fourth of July was particularly profitable for the Negro Leagues; clubs frequently staged daily doubleheaders during Independence Day weekends to take advantage of the holiday crowds.[42] Decoration Day (Memorial Day) baseball contests attracted fans by the thousands, eager to see their favorite teams compete.[43] In some cases, the demand was so strong that clubs would schedule tripleheaders for the holiday. These tripleheaders usually followed a doubleheader on the day immediately preceding the holiday. In 1932, the Pittsburgh Crawfords and the Homestead Grays played five games in two days over the Sunday and Monday of Decoration Day weekend.[44] Likewise, Emancipation Day organizers continued to include baseball as an important part of the day's events. In his memoir, *I Was Right on Time,* former Negro Leaguer Buck O'Neil remarked that it was an "Emancipation Day" for players as well. Because of the large crowds that attended those games, the players received a great deal of money and thus had more "freedom."[45]

Baseball was not merely a holiday amusement. The sport also had a symbolic value for African Americans. In the first half of the twentieth century, baseball was the unquestioned national pastime for whites but also, increasingly, for African Americans.[46] C.I. Taylor, owner and manager of the Indianapolis A.B.C.s, described baseball as a pervasive force in American society. "Baseball is their [African Americans'] national game as much as it is the national game of the whites, because it is above all things an AMERICAN game. It abides deep in the sport loving natures of all Americans regardless of their creed or color."[47] Ira F. Lewis went further and argued that in Chicago, baseball was "the fourth meal of the day" for black residents. African Americans could claim a part of a larger national institution by performing and supporting baseball.[48]

Football, on the other hand, functioned as a popular collegiate sport prior to World War II. Football matches among historically black colleges and universities were popular, particularly with the African American elite, and well covered in the black sporting press. Adding to African American interest, some white colleges in the north included African Americans on their football nines.[49] During this time period, professional football was unstable and unremarkable save for the few African Americans who competed for brief periods in the NFL. The NFL would establish a color line in 1934 and prevent African Americans from entering until 1946. Despite the lifting of the color line, integration in professional football was slow and restrictive. Most teams practiced a policy of excluding black players from all but a few positions and would recruit and drop black players on a regular basis. In this latter practice, team owners would claim to be actively pursuing black talent and point to their recruiting record as evidence. Yet by subsequently dropping those players from their rosters before the beginning of the season, they did not have to play or pay them.[50]

Throughout the Jim Crow era, African Americans embraced baseball as both a spectator sport and an amateur athletic pursuit. Particularly for young African American male migrants, participation in baseball games and leagues provided an outlet through which they could use their bodies for something other than physically taxing wage labor. Indeed, African American reformers promoted these leagues and other organized recreation as a favorable alternative to other expressions of leisure and physicality.[51] Robin D.G. Kelley has posited that "dance halls and blues clubs" provided arenas through which working-class African Americans could "take back their bodies ... recuperate ... be together."[52] Likewise the baseball park, both the stands and the field, functioned as a similar space. As with all public and semi-public spaces in the first half of the twentieth century, African Americans had to negotiate the local rules of segregation in accessing these physical spaces.

As African Americans fled rural southern farms in search of industrial jobs in southern cities, they found a strict enforcement of segregation in public recreation facilities. Local authorities maintained segregated parks and rarely funded parks for the African American population. Enforcement of these all-white leisure spaces was often strict and limited the ability of African Americans to participate in athletic competitions. Baltimore recreation officials denied high school athletes from a black city school access to field house facilities during a track and field meet, resulting in the school's withdrawal from competition.[53] In many locations, the only access many African Americans had to such facilities was through their role as caregivers for white children. *The Crisis* and progressive playground activists campaigned for the establishment of "separate and equal" black parks, but rarely found success. *The Crisis* took the notion of an all-black park to a satirical extreme, requesting that the city of Memphis establish a park for blacks with only black animals and "plenty of jim crows ... flying overhead."[54] In Atlanta, city officials designated recreational facilities by race, allocating the vast majority of public leisure spaces for white residents.[55] Unsatisfied with mere segregation and insufficient facilities for black residents, Atlanta officials prohibited black and white amateur baseball clubs from competing separately within a two-block radius of each other. Atlanta thus barred not only interracial competition, but also prevented black and white teams from competing in relative proximity.[56] Other southern cities enforced segregation by overcharging African American groups for the rental of local parks and other public recreational facilities.[57]

Cities like Cincinnati, on the border of the south, but growing in black residents during the early phase of the Great Migration, also struggled with the intersection of race and sport. In the early 1910s, the Cincinnati YMCA excluded African Americans entirely and then "rose in wrath" when black residents "started a branch ... and [in reaction, this YMCA] caused the colored organization to change its name to the YBCA" (The Young Boys' Christian Association). This name change also allowed white residents to diminish the manhood and masculinity of African Americans by linguistically rendering them as the "boys" of the YBCA while their white counterparts remained the "men" of the YMCA.[58]

In the North, African Americans had more opportunities for sports and other recreational activities. Mobilized as part of the growing recreation movement popularized by Progressive Era social welfare advocates in the first 30 years of the twentieth century, community groups constructed and maintained recreational facilities in various city neighborhoods.[59] In Chicago, the YMCA established recreational facilities and sponsored a number of baseball leagues and workplace-based baseball teams in black neighborhoods to provide for the leisure needs of the growing migrant population in the city.[60] The *Chicago Defender*'s sports page revealed the degree to which these teams were prevalent in the city. The *Defender* often listed as many as 50 games for any given spring or summer weekend. A perusal of the *Chicago Defender* and *Pittsburgh Courier* during the 1910s and 1920s reveals the pervasiveness of these leagues and teams. In the 1930s, the black press coverage of local teams diminished as editors filled their sports pages with articles about nationally known professional and semi-professional teams.[61] Likewise, other northern cities established recreational facilities in black neighborhoods. These facilities, however, were rarely large enough to fulfill the leisure needs of the adjacent black neighborhoods.[62]

These new recreational sites often became an arena of racial and ethnic conflict. While many of these facilities were not explicitly segregated, local custom (and sometimes, local law enforcement) often ensured that a color line was maintained.[63] In other instances in the urban North, the ambiguity of these unwritten segregation policies resulted in disagreements over access rights to recreational facilities.[64] In Chicago, playgrounds located near racially-based neighborhood boundaries witnessed the greatest conflicts over usage. Ethnic or racial groups would unofficially claim exclusive use of these contested spaces, and when outsiders would test that exclusivity, unrest frequently ensued. Whites who laid claim to disputed playground areas enlisted the assistance of police to maintain their unofficial color line, while African Americans relied on using mass attendance to dissuade whites from using their facilities. The Parks Bureau in Chicago assisted in this de facto segregation of city parks, hiring racially homogenous staffs in their parks and discouraging the patronage of African Americans at white-staffed facilities. According to historian Allan Spear, "[d]uring the summer of 1919, the Colts [a notorious Irish gang] and other young white hoodlums regularly attacked Negro boys who attempted to use the baseball diamonds in Washington Park." Moreover, "Negro groups that ventured into Fuller Park or Armour Square were assaulted even when accompanied by adult leaders."[65] In other cities, white officials denied African Americans access to recreation facilities or portions thereof. Bathing facilities, pools, and beaches were frequently hotspots in these local battles for access to public sites.[66] In 1919, conflict over a Chicago beach, coupled with already strained race relations, set off a race riot.[67] When African American groups were able to utilize these public spaces, they were overcharged for concession items and forced to use the less desirable areas of the space.[68]

Violence over recreational spaces also found expression in the practice of the "African dodger," a popular pursuit among white amusement park patrons. An attraction at numerous fairs and festivals, this practice involved an African American man placing his head in an opening, while white fairgoers threw baseballs at his head. The black man would try to duck "or dodge" to avoid being hit by the onslaught of baseballs. Although this practice was outlawed in some areas, notably New York, the African dodger placed African Americans in a position of vulnerability and highlighted the inherent dangers in seemingly innocuous leisure pursuits. The *Defender*, reporting on the new prohibition of the African dodger in New York, challenged other localities to take similar action. "Chicago and other cities that complain of the same trouble should get busy." Despite the ban, *New York Times* articles from the 1920s mention the African dodger as a still-popular sideshow attraction.[69] In 1926, the practice was still well known enough to be utilized in political commentary. A 1926 *Life* article compared the United States to an African dodger. According to E.S. Martin, the United States was "in the position of the Negro who puts his head through the hole in the canvas at the fair for persons who pay to throw baseballs at him."[70] In the analogy, "Europe" was the patron aiming the baseballs at the United States. This abhorrent practice was immortalized in a short 1931 film entitled *The African Dodger* and later featured in a Spencer Tracy movie, *Dante's Inferno* (1935).

Similarly, the 1933 World's Fair in Chicago featured a sideshow game called

"African Dips." This game echoed that of the African dodger. For the African Dips, a contestant was given a ball to throw at a target. If the contestant successfully managed to hit the target with the ball, a "'colored man' in a little cage was dropped into a tank of water."[71] An article in the *New York Times* disclosed that the "African Dips" had generated approximately $23,000 in revenue. It is listed as the fifth-most profitable game in the 1933 World's Fair.[72] In the late 1940s, the first African Americans to play integrated baseball matches faced a similar threat to the African dodger. Under the auspices of competition, hostile white pitchers would at times intentionally throw at the head of an opposing black batter.[73]

During the interwar period, race leaders advocated the establishment of black enterprises within urban centers as a means to combat Jim Crow. African American political leaders believed that these black business ventures would allow black consumers to avoid the discriminatory practices that they encountered during transactions with white merchants.[74] These businesses would also benefit the black economy by creating jobs for other African Americans.

Black baseball was one such enterprise. Founded by Rube Foster in 1920, the Negro National League grappled with the competing demands of benefiting the race and turning a profit.[75] For many African Americans, especially members of the black press, race ownership of league teams and facilities was a crucial aspect of its success and value. Ira Lewis, writing for *The Competitor* in 1920, noted that the fate of the nascent Negro National League would have implications for other black businesses. According to Lewis, "[t]he workings of this league will be watched with more than passing interest by everyone, if it is successful, as we all hope, look for a further merging of colored business interests on a national scale."[76] Reflecting on the success of the League and the beginning of a new baseball season one year later, Lewis suggested that the black baseball was becoming a true race business. "Western colored baseball has shaken off the yoke of the white man's control, almost completely, and the colored man of the East will do the same thing within a few years."[77] Lewis and the other writers and editors at *The Competitor* were committed to promoting black business as a solution to the race problems of the early twentieth century. The same 1920 issue that promoted the idea of a black baseball league also featured an article extolling the work of the Virginia Negro Business League and urging African Americans to use their collective power as consumers and business people for "their own racial benefit."[78]

Lewis's pronouncement would prove to be overly optimistic. For Negro Leagues team owners, fulfilling the obligations of a true "black enterprise" was difficult or impossible. As was the case with other black enterprises, African American business owners lacked sufficient capital to operate independently.[79]

In 1930s Chicago, black business owners interviewed by Drake and Cayton reported that they suffered because of a lack of buying power, inadequate credit with wholesalers, and insufficient capital.[80] From the very beginning, most Negro Leagues owners simply could not afford to purchase and maintain their own baseball stadium. Consequently, team owners had to enter into rental agreements with white park owners to stage games. These rental agreements were often facilitated through the use of a small number of powerful white booking agents. Black sportswriters frequently named one of these agents, Nat Strong, as a symbol of the unnecessary interference of white sporting figures in black baseball.[81] Without Strong's assistance, Negro Leagues teams were unable to secure necessary bookings or park rentals. Team owners depended on Strong for their financial survival. According to one former player, Strong was not above exacting revenge on teams that did not cede to his demands. Judy Johnson, in a 1970s interview, claimed that Strong doctored the baseballs when one of the teams he was promoting faced a club that he did not have a vested interest in.[82] Even within the league organization, there was white influence. In some notable cases, team owners themselves were white.

The most prominent of these white owners was J.L. Wilkinson, owner of the Kansas City Monarchs. Although players generally regarded Wilkinson as fair and even-handed, they did note that he did not relinquish his room when his players were forbidden from staying at a segregated hotel. The players camped in tents, while Wilkinson lodged indoors.[83]

From the inception of the Negro National League in 1920, black professional teams entered into contracts with white major league and semi-professional clubs to use their facilities.[84] Under these agreements, Negro Leagues teams would have use of the stadiums while the white team was away in exchange for either a fee or a cut of the gate, concession, and parking receipts. Numerous Negro Leagues teams engaged in such arrangements: the Black Yankees and New York All-Stars competed in Yankee Stadium; the Homestead Grays in Griffith Stadium in Washington, D.C.; the Brooklyn Eagles at Ebbets Field; and the Chicago American Giants in Comiskey Park.[85] These arrangements were often beneficial for all involved. The white major league stadiums had big capacities, and therefore could entertain larger crowds. Moreover, each party profited from the large gate receipts.

In at least one instance, the white park management raised the ire of assembled black fans. In 1926, an employee at Griffith Stadium halted a game moments before it was due to start. Fans had already gathered to see the white Community League All-Stars and the black LeDroit Tigers, when park manager William Smith "came upon the field and forbade the contest on the ground that colored and white teams were not allowed to play together."[86] In an open letter to Washington Senators owner Clark Griffith, *Pittsburgh Courier* reader Neval Thomas called on Griffith to "announce to your staff that such discrimination is not your policy" to appease the "thousands of daily colored patrons" who contributed to Griffith's coffers through their attendance at games featuring the Grays and other black professional and semi-professional teams.[87] Thomas and other fans stung by discriminatory practices found they had recourse through the threat of withholding patronage.[88]

During the Great Depression, these business relationships became even more important for both Negro Leagues teams and major league park owners. With the exception of Pittsburgh Crawfords owner Gus Greenlee, most Negro Leagues team owners continued to experience limited cash flow and remained dependent on these rental arrangements. Wary of worsening economic conditions, major league park owners began to depend on the extra revenue raised through rentals to the Negro Leagues and greatly desired to maintain those working relationships. White teams had great financial incentives to rent out their stadiums while away. Baseball historian Charles Alexander points out that during the Depression, white teams, in particular, needed to find funds in any manner possible. Even with the improved financial situation of World War II, white major league baseball continued to battle for profitability. With a number of white team rosters decimated by the draft and voluntary enlistments, major league clubs struggled to attract a sufficient number of paying fans. Consequently, the rental income from Negro Leagues clubs was even more valuable to white team owners. In 1942, the New York Yankees made $100,000 by renting out Yankee Stadium for Negro Leagues games.[89]

Satchel Paige provides a different interpretation in his memoir, arguing that Negro Leagues teams pushed the white teams to open their stadiums. According to Paige, the crowds that came to witness his exploits were too large for the usual Negro Leagues stadiums, so black baseball managers had to look elsewhere to accommodate Paige's legion of fans. Paige's explanation was consistent with his public persona as a trickster figure in black baseball. Paige's claim of his own popularity among baseball fans reflected a boasting tradition inherent in black vernacular expressive culture and signifying practice.[90]

These arrangements often put African American fans at a disadvantage. Black sports were popular with white fans. White fans attended all-black baseball games and "battle royals," boxing matches featuring two African American fighters. The fighters in these bouts often were amateurs and engaged in clowning to entertain the crowds. Battle royals drew a great number of spectators, both black and white.[91] Similarly, black baseball owners and officials welcomed white patrons and their money to league games.

Despite their promotion of black baseball as a race enterprise, league owners signed rental contracts that required segregated seating to secure the use of large ballparks. Many stadium owners and officials, particularly those in more southern cities like St. Louis and Baltimore, maintained preferential seating for white fans.[92] In these instances, much like at the Harlem music and nightclubs, white fans enjoyed prime seating at a black performance.[93] Langston Hughes lamented the degree of white ownership and control of leisure and entertainment spaces in Harlem during the 1920s and 1930s. According to Hughes, "The famous nightclubs were owned by whites, as were the theatres.... White downtown [was] pulling all the strings in Harlem.... Black Harlem really was in white face, economically speaking."[94]

In a number of baseball parks, black fans witnessed games in the bleachers under the elements while white fans enjoyed the grandstand seats under covers and awnings. According to Negro Leaguer Bill Drake, when his squad played at St. Louis's Sportsman's Park, "Negroes had to sit in the pavilion in right field and in the bleachers. Negroes didn't go in the grandstand."[95] Another Negro Leaguer, James "Cool Papa" Bell, recalled a physical barrier enforcing segregation. Bell described baseball fields where the officials "would have a rope to put across the stands" to separate fans by race.[96] As late as 1948, Negro Leagues players remembered black fans being confined to segregated sections in baseball parks, in one instance with chicken wire.[97]

Historian David Nasaw has expanded further on the ways in which ball park seating provided a map of race, ethnicity, and class. Nasaw has documented a class-based ethnic segregation at white major league games. According to Nasaw, "[t]he division of the park into separately priced sections resulted in de facto ethnic segregation, with the Irish and German Americans in the bleachers, and the rest of the crowd in the more expensive grandstand, pavilion, and box seats." Consequently, the "cheap section" of various ballparks (including Chicago's Comiskey Park, St. Louis's Sportsman's Park, and New York's Polo Grounds) were named for the predominantly Irish fans who occupied those seats. In this, as in other instances in Jim Crow America, race trumped class. Black fans occupied segregated seating regardless of their ability to afford preferred seating.[98] Much like in transportation, where one could not ascend to the status of gentleman or lady unless white, the financial ability to buy a good ticket was of no consideration.

Boxing, the other great sport for African Americans, was also beset with issues of segregated seating. Notably, at the Joe Louis–Primo Carnera fight in 1935, the majority of African American spectators were confined to the bleacher section, although "there were many *scattered* throughout the stands and a *few* occupied ringside seats." In addition to this partial segregation, the *New York Times* observed that there were policemen stationed every ten feet within the bleacher sections. Tellingly, the grandstands only had "scattered" policemen. One assumes they were "scattered" in a similar manner as the African American patrons.[99]

African Americans faced different degrees of segregation and accommodation within black baseball stadiums. In at least one instance, team owners promoted the fact that black fans would have access to seating usually reserved with white patrons. In 1909, a *Defender* article on a Cuban Stars vs. Leland Giants game at the White Sox's park at the 39th Street Grounds repeatedly emphasized that the honored guest, Mrs. Booker T. Washington, received priority seating. For this one game, officials had arranged "special reserved seats for Mrs. Booker T. Washington ... giving everyone a chance to see a real all-round race woman."[100] Mrs. Washington's status as the symbol of an accommodationist racial philosophy that did not directly challenge white supremacy and as the exemplar of black womanhood made her an ideal (and less threatening) choice for breaking segregated practice. Her evasion of Jim Crow seating through her respectability was consistent with her husband's political strategy and served as an aspirational model for African American women.

In contrast, other black baseball team owners highlighted segregated seating in an attempt to bring in white spectators and to placate local officials who were antagonistic to the idea of integrated public leisure spaces. The owners of the Baltimore Black Sox required that Maryland Park (where the Black Sox competed) had a "section of box seats *for whites only.*"[101] Smaller regional semi-pro black baseball contests also advertised similar accommodations. One advertisement promoting the Rocky Hill Tigers and East Point Red Sox highlighted a "reserve stand for white people."[102] Similarly, ads in the 1932 *Norfolk Journal and Guide* included a warning that "part of grandstand [is] reserved for white patrons."[103]

Conversely, the Kansas City Monarchs' Muehlebach Field had an open seating policy during Negro Leagues games.[104] Kansas City baseball fans held a special regard for the Monarchs and strongly supported them. Consequently, the Monarchs' success on the field and in fostering a large, loyal mixed-race fan base made them an integral part of the city. Opening Day for the Monarchs was a citywide celebration, complete with a parade that shut down the main traffic arteries, a band performance at the ball park, a flag raising that employed 500 boy scouts, and an opening pitch from the mayor of Kansas City, Missouri, to the mayor of Kansas City, Kansas. City officials even went so far as to allow all city employees a half-day holiday so that they could attend the opener.[105] The Monarchs and Muehlebach Field were an exception within Kansas City. Most other public amusements remained segregated, and Muehlebach Field itself almost always employed segregated seating when the all-white Kansas City Blues took the field. During a short period of time in the mid 1930s, the Blues allowed integrated seating. Once owner Johnny Kling sold the club in 1938, segregated seating returned.[106]

In many instances, black fans attending Negro Leagues games held in white stadiums required a significant amount of travel. Because most major league parks were located in the white sections of town, transportation was an issue for African Americans who traveled to the games. At times, public transportation would shut down the routes to the black neighborhoods before the end of the game, essentially stranding some fans. Even if they could successfully arrange transportation to the game, the work schedules of many fans made the time commitment untenable. In addition, black fans had to deal with spending their limited leisure time in what could be "hostile" space, neighborhoods that discouraged their patronage. Under Jim Crow, such travels could incite violence and therefore were dangerous.[107]

In the years following World War I, the politics of black baseball became more significant for its fans. As African American servicemen returned from duty and Northern cities continued to swell with newly arrived Southern migrants, African Americans began to place a greater degree of importance on their ability to establish and maintain black businesses and institutions. Scholar Robert L. Boyd has demonstrated that black businesses increased in number as local black populations increased within racially segregated sections of northern cities.[108] In particular, the black leadership, in the press, in the church, and in politics, called for African Americans to purchase property and claim a physical space in the city as their own.

African Americans also placed a great deal of value on the ownership of church property. In the late 1910s, white churches in Chicago began to relocate in response to the growing black population. Churches located in or near what would become the black belt sold their facilities to black congregations. Gaining ownership of church buildings held a great deal of importance for the parishioners. The procurement and establishment of black churches as black-owned entities reinforced the commitment to buy black and support black enterprise. Consequently, the purchase of a church building was cause for celebration. In the late 1910s, the Olivet Baptist Church bought a former white Baptist church resulting in the "members ... staging a parade of thousands that stretched from Dearborn Street to South Park Way."[109] Even earlier, in 1905, the editor of *Alexander's Magazine* advocated church ownership, bemoaning the fact that "not a single Negro church [in Boston] is owned by its congregation."[110] Similarly, the author of a 1921 article in *The Competitor* lauded the benefit of church ownership for African Americans, noting that black church holdings were valued at 76 million dollars.[111]

In the March 1925 issues of *Survey Graphic,* the noted black poet, novelist, and activist James Weldon Johnson lauded the exponential growth in black property ownership in Harlem as a symbol of African American success. "Twenty years ago Negroes were begging for the privilege of renting a flat in Harlem.... Today Negro Harlem is practically owned by Negroes."[112] Johnson also mentioned that black Harlemites were involved in fostering black enterprise. "Harlem is gradually becoming more and more a self-supporting community, Negroes there are steadily branching out into new businesses and enterprises in which Negroes are employed."[113] Despite Johnson's optimism, other African American intellectuals noted that black business in Harlem was constrained by a lack of sufficient capital. In the same issue, black sociologist and author Kelly Miller noted that

> [b]usiness is the last place in which prejudice shows itself, and it is in this field that its harvest is least manifest.... In Harlem, as in every other large city, the Negro proprietor conducts mainly sumptuary establishments such as eating-houses, barber-shops, beauty parlors, pool rooms, and such places as cater immediately to the appetite or to the taste. The more substantial stores which require a larger exercise of the imagination, such as those dealing in dry goods, shoes, furniture, hardware and groceries, are usually in the hands of whites. Race prejudice will sooner or later lead to race patronage in business.[114]

For black baseball devotees, these politics and concerns played out over the issue of property ownership. Rube Foster, universally acknowledged as the father of black baseball, was embroiled in a controversy over the ownership of the field where his Chicago American Giants competed in the late 1910s. Foster had an agreement with John Schorling, a white Chicago businessman, and Charles Comiskey, owner of the Chicago White Sox, to allow him to claim "ownership" of Schorling Field (formerly the 39th Street Grounds and home to the White Sox prior to the building of Comiskey Park), despite the fact that Comiskey truly owned the park.[115] Under the terms of their agreement, Comiskey's involvement was shielded from public knowledge. Schorling served as "operator of record," while Foster was granted ownership title to the grandstand section of the park.[116] Under this arrangement, Foster claimed to own Schorling Park and neglected to mention the involvement of Schorling or Comiskey.

For Foster, who had promoted his new Negro National League as a venture for racial uplift and progress, it was crucial to function successfully without financial contributions from white business interests. Consistent with the politics of the time, Foster was intent on framing black baseball as a truly black enterprise, one that only African Americans would truly profit from and be invested in. The black press and blackball fans embraced Foster's venture partially because of the importance they placed upon the financial success of black business.[117] At the time, black churches and the black press in Chicago championed the idea of a "Double Duty Dollar," money that was spent to both acquire an item and contribute to the success of "the race."[118] In addition, periodicals like *Half-Century Magazine* highlighted profitable black enterprise and property ownership as the solution for "the mire of prejudice and scorn."[119] Consequently, to continue to benefit from the integration of politics and baseball, Foster endeavored to keep his silent partners very silent.

Foster's reticence proved to be well-founded. In 1919, an article lauding Foster and his achievements, highlighting the construction of Schorling Park as one of Foster's finest moments, appeared in *Half-Century Magazine*.[120] In the feature, Howard Phelps avoided any discussion of who built the park or the origin of the financing for such a venture. Phelps argued that Foster's "next big achievement consisted in the building of the American Giants present home, the finest semi-professional ball park in the world. It was constructed for Foster's team and he prides himself in that it was expressly built and used only by him."[121] Shortly after the article's publication, an angry writer accused Foster of covering up the fact that Schorling Park was under "Jewish" ownership. In a letter to the editor, Gale Williams expressed concern that "Colored men overlook money-making propositions such as the American Giants baseball team."[122] In essence, Williams argued, African American business men were losing an opportunity to profit off of the emergent professional black baseball league.

By choosing to highlight that Foster's associate was Jewish, the writer capitalized on the strained relationship between African Americans and Jewish businessmen in Chicago and therefore leveled what he believed to be a truly damning claim that could have alienated Foster's black fan base. Many business owners in the "Bronzeville" district of Chicago were Jewish, and black residents resented their presence in the neighborhoods. In 1938, these tensions would reach a climax when a small black periodical made derogatory comments about Jewish business owners and promoted the expulsion of Jewish residents and business owners from "Bronzeville."[123]

Half-Century quickly came to Foster's defense, arguing that the owner of Schorling Park was in fact not Jewish and downplaying the involvement of local white interests in the park. According to the rebuttal by Frank Young, longtime sports editor of the *Chicago Defender* and Foster ally, the park was "not owned by a Jew" but "by a retired doctor, now a millionaire living in Europe." In Young's version, Comiskey had leased the park from the millionaire physician prior to establishing White Sox Park. With little need for the facility, Comiskey in turn leased the grounds to Schorling, who constructed the park in collaboration with Foster.[124] Although Young's evasive article helped to diminish the controversy over Foster's connection with powerful white businessmen, Foster's reprieve was brief. Two years later, Foster would come under fire when a fellow Negro Leagues owner, Tenny Blount, revealed the name of Foster's silent partner, John Schorling, in a newspaper interview. This time, Foster had no choice but to address the charges, telling reporters that Schorling was his landlord at the baseball field and thus received rent from the Chicago American Giants.[125] While this admission of white involvement did not permanently damage Foster's reputation or his league, it did make black baseball less useful as a political tool for African Americans. Personally and professionally, Foster bore a great cost for his pioneering work in establishing the Negro National League. In 1926, Foster was struck by a sudden and incapacitating illness, which resulted in his commitment to a psychiatric hospital. At that point, public concern regarding Foster's personal tragedy shielded him from any criticism in the black press. Thus, a 1931 article by black sportswriter Frank A. Young glossed over Foster's management of the Chicago American Giants and attributed the downfall of black baseball in Chicago to Schorling and his white successors.[126] In addition, because of baseball's significance to the black community in Chicago, the loss of Foster's field as a success story damaged the political and economic value of black baseball within the city as well as black baseball as a whole. Chicago black baseball struggled after Foster's death in 1930. The team was sold to a group of white investors who hoped to bankrupt the team and open a "dog race track." After two years of ownership and failure to obtain permission to establish a track, the Chicago club did not play in 1931, leaving Chicago, the symbolic center of organized black baseball under Rube Foster, without a competitive Negro Leagues team.[127]

Foster was not the only black ball owner, however, to cover up financial partnerships and arrangements with white business interests. Another Negro National League team, the St. Louis Giants, also was involved in racially complicated business deals. Negro Leagues pitcher Bill Drake recalled that when he was with the St. Louis Giants, owner Charles Mills had an agreement with Ed Brock, a local white businessman, who helped him gain access to Finley Park. "Charles Mills owned the Giants then. He was a saloon keeper, but he had a white fellow in the background named Ed Brock.... He's the one got us into that park."[128]

The fight to secure black ownership of black leisure spaces only increased through the 1920s and 1930s. The black press played a crucial role in the escalation of demands for black ownership and the eventual integration of baseball. As part of the campaign to encourage black ownership of baseball facilities and to speed the slow pace of integration, black sportswriters conducted campaigns to persuade black fans to boycott major league baseball games. *Courier* sportswriter W. Rollo Wilson sounded the alarm in the 1920s, encouraging his readers to shun the Philadelphia Athletics due to a history of discriminatory policies and racist behavior by club officials and team members like Ty Cobb, who played for the Athletics during the 1927 and 1928 seasons. Wilson asked *Courier* readers to consider such actions when they were deciding which team to patronize. If they insisted on attending major league games, Wilson suggested that they consider the Phillies, who had a better record in regards to the treatment of the black press.[129]

In the late 1930s, the campaign to protest the restrictive racial policies of the white major leagues gained steam. Led by Wendell Smith, *Pittsburgh Courier* sports editor and major player in Jackie Robinson's signing with the Brooklyn Dodgers, black sportswriters utilized their columns to point out the inequities of the baseball color line. Again echoing popular boycotting campaigns in cities, these writers urged African Americans to stay home from white games, thus not contributing to an industry that refused to grant them entrance.[130] Smith chastised African Americans for their patronage of the major leagues:

> The fact that major league baseball refuses to admit Negro players within its folds makes the question just that much more perplexing. Surely, it's sufficient reason for us to quit spending our money and time in their ball parks. Major league baseball does not want us. It never has. Still, we continue to help support his institution that places a bold "Not Welcome" sign over its thriving portal and refuse to patronize the very place that has shown that it is more than welcome to have us. We black folks are a strange tribe![131]

Similarly, the *Crisis* editorialized two years later, "Baseball is a million dollar business. As are most big businesses, it is a jim-crow affair. And as most businesses do, it takes in hundreds of thousands of dollars from Black men and gives nothing in return."[132] In the 1940s, these calls for an economic boycott of the major leagues were tied to the larger cause of domestic civil rights. In a 1942 *Defender* article, the author intimated that African American consumers could potentially hasten baseball integration, but acknowledged the many obstacles inherent in combating the color line.

> More, too, we continue to pour our money into the box offices without any return. The owners believe we are satisfied. Hurt their pocketbook by staying away as long as the Negro ball player is kept out of the game and maybe we'll get somewhere. I said maybe. This is America and despite the fact we are engaged in a war of freedom of all peoples (?), the color line or racial lines when it affects a Negro, has never been erased.[133]

During the Depression, the "Don't Buy Where You Can't Work" campaigns migrating to the leisure arena became even more critically important for African American activists, fans, and players. Although in some regions of the country the Negro Leagues games attracted numerous white fans, black fans were and remained the foundation of black baseball. As sporting fans of all races had increasingly limited amounts of time and money to spend on leisure activities, black fans could place financial pressure on team owners and officials to establish themselves as enterprises that benefited local black communities.

From a standpoint of fostering racial pride and identity, black baseball was also crucial. Numerous black baseball players and writers recall their earliest baseball memories centering on white players like Babe Ruth rather than black baseball icons such as Rube Foster.[134] By supporting black baseball, African Americans could help construct an alternative to the widespread popular image of baseball as a white's man game. Moreover, Smith and his fellow sportswriters rightly acknowledged that black fans could place financial pressure on white major league baseball. The major leagues opened their doors to African American players in part to expand their share of the black urban market.

In the 1930s, many Negro Leagues teams sought to find more amenable and less costly locations for their games. The New York Cubans established a home field, Dyckman Oval, located near Harlem. Unfortunately for Harlem baseball fans, this proximity was short-lived. Local black baseball teams would soon have to travel because there was no "suitable field in Harlem."[135] Similarly, the Cleveland Buckeyes competed at Luna Park during the 1932 season. The black press applauded the location of Luna Park and the corresponding benefits to local fans: "Within comfortable walking distance for better than 15,000 colored residents, and accessible via three of the city's main street car routes, no park in Cleveland is more conveniently located."[136] Despite the favorable location of the park, the Cleveland club failed to attract much interest among city residents. At least one observer felt that the Cleveland ownership did not go far enough in terms of their commitment to the black community. Despite the fact that they did choose a favorably located park, the ownership failed to hire significant portions of the populace to work for the organization. This failure to employ local residents was particularly galling due to the economic distress and widespread unemployment brought on by the Great Depression. African American fans in Cleveland wanted not only entertainment from black enterprise but also jobs.[137]

Gus Greenlee, owner of the Pittsburgh Crawfords, was not content to rent a park in a black neighborhood. Instead, he found another method of ensuring the comfort of his fans. In 1932, Greenlee financed the construction of his own field in Pittsburgh.[138] Named Greenlee Field after its less than humble patron, Greenlee Field was a rarity in Negro Leagues baseball, a team-owned and, in this instance, a black-owned field. Not only was the field free of segregation, it was also located in the Hill District, a historically black segment of the city.[139] The location of Greenlee Field eliminated one of the other major problems facing African American fans, transportation to and from the white section of town. Pittsburgh fans were spared the difficulties and vulnerabilities inherent in traveling to hostile sections of the city to watch the Crawfords compete. The club letterhead as well as the club bus highlighted the Crawfords' "own $100,000 Greenlee Field."[140] The letterhead also featured a picture of their team bus and individual headshots of the Crawfords players, a tactic that helped sell the team through its star players. Because Greenlee was notorious for raiding talent from other clubs, this ostentatious reminder of his wealth of resources and talent must have further alienated him from the rest of the Negro National League. Greenlee was able to use official league correspondence to remind his colleagues and competitors of his past deals, particularly those that resulted in the improvement of his squad at the expense of other Negro Leagues teams.[141]

Greenlee, an astute if not often legal businessman, took advantage of the prestige that came with owning his own field.[142] Greenlee was a well-known numbers man in Pittsburgh and became involved with Negro Leagues baseball to provide a cover for his gambling operations. The numbers game was a popular and profitable business for numerous African Americans in the first half of the twentieth century.[143]

Many black men and women spent a portion of their salaries playing the numbers each week, hoping to strike it rich or at least improve their financial situations. The numbers racket was an illegal version of a lottery and was incredibly popular in major American cities in the first half of the twentieth century. To play the numbers, a person would choose a three-digit number and buy a chance, much like buying a basic lottery ticket today. They would write the number on a piece of paper and pay the numbers fee to a runner. Runners would collect payment and record the numbers from their clients and return that to the banker. The winning number would be determined by a certain number or combination of numbers in the following day's newspaper. Anything from racing results to stock or banking numbers could be used depending on local custom or the preference of the numbers banker. As with any gambling system, the odds heavily favored the "house" or the numbers banker, who raked in high profits.

These numbers bankers were both condemned and celebrated within African American communities. Some members of the black clergy and devout parishioners shunned the numbers racket, arguing that gambling in all forms was immoral and antithetical to the goals of racial progress.[144] Yet many black leaders, both in and outside of the church, supported numbers men because of their willingness to employ African Americans both in their illegal policy games and in the legitimate businesses they established as fronts. To the delight of many in urban neighborhoods, black numbers kings frequently invested in community endeavors, such as baseball teams, and generously contributed to charitable causes within their communities. As baseball historian Adrian Burgos, Jr. has noted in his biography of Negro Leagues owner and numbers baron Alex

Pompez, African Americans only objected to numbers bankers who were incompetent and not truly interested in committing to running a baseball team correctly. As long as the owners were committed to the community and their team, many local African Americans were unconcerned with the origins of the team's bankroll.[145]

Black baseball was intertwined with the numbers business in the 1930s. The Negro Leagues counted among its owners a number of numbers bankers, including Abe Manley, owner of the Newark Eagles, and Pompez of the Cuban Stars. Pompez was a central figure in New York's prosecution of the Harlem numbers game. In 1937, Pompez "fled to Mexico" to avoid prosecution, but he returned in 1938 to face charges.[146]

These high-profile numbers bankers challenged the moral code of race reformers and respectable race men. *Chicago Defender* journalist J. Winston Harrington described the dilemma for Chicago ministers, and by extension other civic and political leaders, in relation to policy. Arguing for the legalization (and regulation) of the policy game, Harrington noted that "[a]s it is now a minister who gets a liberal donation to build or redecorate his church from a man who got it through extra-legal means, puts himself on the spot. His followers begin to question his sincerity, for it seems that he condones the donor, that he's a hypocrite." If policy was legal, it would allow "the numbers nobility to aid worthwhile charities."[147] In Harrington's calculation (and certainly in many others'), the tangible benefits of the policy men's largess outweighed the immorality and illegality of their profitmaking ventures. At a time when black business was highlighted as crucial to the ultimate success of the race as a whole, black political and church leaders were often unwilling to denigrate an industry that fueled some of the largest and most successful business ventures in black neighborhoods. These leaders also wished to avoid calling unnecessary attention to the gambling enterprises that were inconsistent with the ideal of racial uplift and respectability that they strove to instill in their communities. This reticence angered reformers and anti-policy crusaders, who longed for the support of the powerful black ministers in this campaign against the numbers racket. One such activist, Chicagoan George Lambert, had briefly secured support from an A.M.E. bishop in his campaign against policy, but his 1939 attempt to re-energize the black clergy for his cause was unsuccessful.[148]

Adding to the power and prestige of the numbers men, the economic downturn of the Great Depression did not significantly decrease the profitability of the policy racket. Numbers runners retained their power and wealth at a time when financial strains plagued many other African American merchants and businesspeople. Indeed, their unique ability to maintain their status and expand their wealth opened doors that previously had been closed to numbers men.

The numbers game was also a source of employment for black men during the Great Depression. Few would reach the highest and most profitable heights of the numbers racket, but many would function as low-level runners, collecting money for their bosses. *Defender* reporter Harrington estimated that 10,000 black Chicago residents were employed in the policy game in 1939.[149] In the 1930s, policy men entered into a higher level of African American society on the basis of their new-found wealth and status. The *Norfolk Journal and Guide* noted in 1931, "suave and debonair racketeers [were] crashing exclusive D.C. society."[150] As symbols of a successful race enterprise and as investors in their communities, numbers men were exalted as race leaders. Yet race reformers continued to denounce policy men as purveyors of vice.[151]

In cities and neighborhoods that lacked black policy men, African American critics found other areas of concern. Namely, they were displeased with the ways in which white men engineered and profited from the numbers game, pocketing money from poor and working-class African Americans. Calling back to the "Don't Buy Where You Can't Work" campaigns, writers like Langston Hughes decried a system in which poor African Americans were courted as customers but forbidden from employment within the industry. In some black districts, notably Harlem, whites actually ran most of the vice operations patronized by black residents. According to historian Marcy S. Sacks, white proprietors owned almost all Harlem saloons and prostitution houses. Likewise, Langston Hughes noted that many of the Harlem policy rackets were also run by whites. The *Chicago Defender*'s coverage of a 1938 trial of Harlem numbers kings supported Hughes's assessment of the situation. In an article, the reporter stressed that "[a]lthough the numbers game is considered a Harlem 'business' it is understood that the powers behind the throne live outside the district."[152]

Similarly, in 1938, the *Chicago Defender* reported that D.C. policy men believed that the federal government was targeting their businesses with the hopes of putting them in jail. The article also noted that "[o]f the known big-time operators of the game here, only one is a member of the Race. Many Race members, however, are chief aides and lesser cogs in the $2,000,000 annual racket." Those men "fear for their bosses, their jobs and the racket." According to these contemporary reports, black numbers bankers were relatively rare in Harlem and Washington, D.C. despite the large African American consumer base for the game.[153] This lack of black oversight represented the ways in which even underground and illegal black enterprise (in this instance in what would be considered vice) was endangered by more powerful white competition. As Hughes stated, "Negroes could not even play their own numbers with their own people. And almost all the policemen in Harlem were white. Negroes couldn't even get graft from themselves for themselves by themselves."[154]

Back at the ballpark, Greenlee Field's existence, regardless of its owner's involvement in illegal activities, held important symbolic meaning for African American fans and the Negro Leagues players themselves. With the field, an African American owned an impressive facility that visibly represented black success in a game that was supposed to be for whites only.[155] This is not to argue that Greenlee's motivation in building the field was to inspire his black clientele or to strike a blow against Jim Crow. Although by all accounts Greenlee was concerned with making black baseball a truly black enterprise, he also desired to bring more fans (black and white) to the ballpark to boost his bottom line and to triumph symbolically over his cross-town Pittsburgh rival, Cum Posey (owner of the Homestead Grays).[156] In the early 1930s, prior to the construction of Greenlee Field, the Crawfords struggled to stay afloat financially. The Crawfords primarily relied on donations through passing the hat during the 1930 and 1931 seasons. Unfortunately for the Crawfords, even when they drew large numbers of fans, they did not generate a proportionate financial returns. The *Pittsburgh Courier* reported that a crowd of 6,000 on Decoration Day (Memorial Day) in 1931 yielded only about $80, leaving the team without any cash after paying the umpires and the visiting team.[157] In essence, the team had only managed to collect about a penny per person as admission, not nearly enough to ensure the long term existence of the Crawfords.

The implications of the construction of Greenlee Field for African Americans during the Jim Crow era, however, were clear. Greenlee Field was a symbol of black self-sufficiency and successful enterprise. The large amount of money Greenlee invested in the field also contradicted stereotypes of the time. Greenlee had enough finances to bankroll a large construction project and continued to pour money into the field even after the opening. Greenlee's financial wherewithal was even more impressive within the context of the Depression. Hoping to distinguish his field among other Negro Leagues parks, Greenlee also invested in a permanent lighting system.

By choosing to allocate a portion of his money into lights for the park, Greenlee may have been influenced by the acclaim that Kansas City Monarchs white owner J.L. Wilkinson received for his portable lighting system. In 1930, only two years before the construction of Greenlee Field and at a time when Greenlee's Crawfords struggled to break even financially and longed for the name recognition of the Homestead Grays, the Monarchs brought their lights to Pittsburgh for a series with the Grays.[158] Fans and press alike marveled at the size and novelty of a lighting system. The *Pittsburgh Courier* noted "[t]he night games have caused the fans to talk more of baseball lately than ever before ... and it is believed that the crowds at all of the games will be the largest the Grays have ever performed before."[159] The fact that Greenlee's system was linked only to Greenlee Field enhanced the ballpark's uniqueness. [160] It also gave Greenlee and his Crawfords a small bit of leverage over their intra-city rivals. Cum Posey used a portable lighting system to stage night games for the Grays. During at least one series, Posey utilized "floodlights" at Forbes Field for games against the House of David.[161] These alterations allowed Posey to play night games but lacked permanence, professionalism, and safety.

For Negro Leagues teams, the ability to stage games at night, especially in industrial cities, was critical. The typical African American baseball fan worked long hours and could not attend early afternoon games. Through night baseball, the Negro Leagues, under Wilkinson and Greenlee, found a unique way to cater to their particular clientele and make their games accessible for larger portions of the black population. This move not only allowed Greenlee to attract a greater number of fans to the park, but also highlighted the technological advances of black baseball in contrast with the white major leagues.[162] The downside of night baseball was that the lighting systems often made it difficult for the players to see the ball, resulting in a more dangerous game for the players.[163]

In at least one instance, the desire of Negro Leagues teams to run night games and their habit of renting white major league parks coincided. In 1935, Abe Manley, owner of the black Brooklyn Eagles, persuaded Ebbets Field officials to install a temporary lighting system to facilitate additional Negro Leagues games. Although *Brooklyn Times-Union* sportswriter Irvin N. Rosee suggested that the Dodgers should adopt a permanent lighting system for their own games after the successful run of the Brooklyn Eagles during the 1935 season, the Dodgers did not install lights at Ebbets Field until 1938. Manley moved his Eagles from Brooklyn to Newark in 1936, driven by the promise of less professional competition (it had been difficult to compete for fans with the presence of three white major league teams in New York City) and a better lighting system at Newark's Ruppert Stadium.[164]

In Pittsburgh, Greenlee brought more than just black baseball to the field. To attract additional fans and revenue, he booked boxing matches at Greenlee Field to fill the open dates when the Crawfords were on the road.[165] For boxing enthusiasts in Pittsburgh, and particularly in the predominately black Hill district, Greenlee's willingness to host prizefighting bouts was a significant advantage of the new construction. Moreover, the black press and black boxing fans saw the potential for Greenlee to promote and encourage up-and-coming black boxers, by giving them "more consideration in the new arena than at any other place in the district."[166] Local African Americans hoped Greenlee Field would succeed as a race enterprise that benefited both black athletes specifically and black Pittsburgh as a whole.

The opening of Greenlee Field underscored the importance of the field to

Negro Leagues baseball. A number of local politicians and sportswriters attended the opening ceremony.[167] Greenlee himself took advantage of the occasion to make a spectacular entrance "in a red convertible.... Surrounded by a marching band, he received a standing ovation from the capacity crowd of six thousand. Clad in a white silk suit and tie, Gus walked to the pitching mound and threw out the first pitch."[168] The theatrics surrounding the opening of Greenlee Field provided great entertainment for baseball fans as well as a chance to celebrate the achievements of black baseball in the face of tremendous obstacles, most notably the Great Depression.

The *Pittsburgh Courier* glowingly reported about the new ballpark, lauding its many advantages.

> Pittsburgh has a new ball park, erected by a Negro, for Negroes, and with Negroes as participating factors. It is one of the finest independent ball parks in the country. With a left field longer than that at Forbes Field, with a right field which has yet to succumb to a home run wallop and with a seating capacity of close to 7,000 people, it stands as a monument of progress.[169]

For the *Courier* writer and Pittsburgh baseball fans, Greenlee's dedication to building a local black business was as significant as his ability to put together a competitive team. For this accomplishment, Greenlee was to be applauded and admired. To black Pittsburgh, Greenlee's field was not merely a better place to watch a baseball game, it was "a monument to progress," a symbol of black success in an often hostile Jim Crow America. In 1933, the *Courier* championed Greenlee as president of the Negro National League, noting that "no man in the country is more interested in the progress of Negro baseball, and certainly none will spend as much money as the Pittsburgh sportsman to put it across."[170] Despite the ample praise, Greenlee's motives were not entirely selfless. While undoubtedly interested in the success of the Negro National League as a race enterprise, Greenlee sought profit and championships from his baseball club above all else.

The symbolic importance of Greenlee Field was equally apparent in its grand opening as it was in its premature closing. In 1938, after a series of disastrous on- and off-the-field events, in which the intra-city rivalry between Posey and Greenlee came to a head, Greenlee closed his beloved field. His decision to do so was brought about by numerous financial struggles. Greenlee and Posey's fight for power over Pittsburgh baseball had reached a crescendo in 1937, when Posey aligned himself with white booking agents in an attempt to make it difficult for Greenlee to travel profitably with his team. Satchel Paige's defection to play for the Trujillo All Stars in 1937 only exacerbated Greenlee's troubles. Having lost his biggest star (and box office draw) and unable to make sufficient money traveling with his team, Greenlee was in dire straits.[171]

After the announcement that he would close Greenlee Field, Greenlee's supporters in his venture to build a black-owned Negro League park quickly became loud opponents of both his plan to shutter the park and his tenure as the Crawfords' owner. Members of the black press argued that Greenlee's failure to thrive merely reinforced the worst stereotypes about black baseball and black business in general. *Pittsburgh Courier* sportswriter John Clark implicitly accused Greenlee of failing the African American race by not assuming a "purer racial interest" in his baseball operations, thus linking the fate of black baseball with the larger issues of racial progress. Clark attributed the failure of Greenlee Field not to the internal power dynamics of Negro Leagues baseball or Satchel Paige's defection from the team, but instead to Greenlee's decision to employ whites at the park in greater numbers than blacks.[172] Clark argued that the economic demands and high unemployment of the Great Depression made Greenlee's hiring practice all the more distasteful to his black clientele and therefore, fans had responded by staying home and spending their money elsewhere. In the final analysis, Clark concluded that the closing of Greenlee Park sent the message to the rest of the country that "Pittsburgh is no place to attempt big things for Negroes."[173] If Greenlee had considered racial pride in his employment practices and staffed his park with African American workers, Clark implied, black fans would have become enthusiastic patrons to support such a race-based initiative. According to this contemporary interpretation, successful black baseball magnates had to consider baseball as part of a larger crusade for racial success and civil rights. Failure to do so would result not only in the failure of the club but also in a setback for the race.

The sensitive issue of the ownership of leisure spaces plagued black ball players throughout the Negro Leagues' existence. The symbolic importance of this issue became intertwined with one of the derogatory terms opponents of integration used to describe professional black ball players: "sandlotters." "Sandlot" baseball was not an insulting term in and of itself; members of the black press used "sandlot" team as shorthand for semiprofessional or amateur baseball clubs, thus contrasting sandlot teams with the professional Negro Leagues teams. Negro Leagues players also used the term "sandlot baseball" to refer to semiprofessional leagues, both black and white. For these players, there was an important distinction to be made between semipro baseball and the professional and organized Negro Leagues. Their talents and skills (and the fact that they were fully employed as athletes) placed them in a different category than the part-time players they often faced on tours.[174]

White reporters and major league baseball officials, however, often employed the term sandlotter in a more pejorative manner. By dubbing the black leagues "sandlots," these observers negatively compared the white and Negro Leagues by highlighting the widespread lack of physical home fields in black professional baseball. Consequently, the term implied that the black leagues operated at a significantly lower level than the major leagues. As "sandlotters," Negro Leagues players presumably lacked both the athletic ability and professionalism necessary to participate in the white major leagues. Indeed, the derogatory term reinforced the common perception that black baseball players were sideshow performers rather than athletes. This diminution of black athletic performance and professionalism helped to reinforce the necessity of maintaining a color line in major league baseball in the minds of white baseball officials, players, and fans.

William "Sug" Cornelius noted in an oral interview that major league commissioner Kenesaw Mountain Landis used the term when he prohibited white players from competing against black teams in barnstorming tours. According to Cornelius, after a white all-star team lost to Satchel Paige's black team, Landis "said they [the white all-stars] were a disgrace to organized baseball to let a bunch of sandlotters beat them."[175] Cornelius noted, however, "we were a bunch of *good* sandlotters."[176] Negro Leagues players resented the term "sandlotters" and the implication that they participated in second-rate baseball because of the arbitrary color line drawn by white baseball officials. Cool Papa Bell attributed the use of the term "sandlotters" to a greater plan on the part of white Americans to keep "the black hidden, not only in baseball, in any form of life that we had outstanding black people."[177]

Similarly, late twentieth century basketball players battled with similar implicit slights. In an article on Michael Jordan, writer and scholar John Edgar Wideman described the phenomenon. Wideman and Jordan reflected on the ways in which basketball coaches (presumably white coaches, considering the dearth of African American coaches in college and professional basketball, particularly prior to 1990 when Wideman first published his piece) criticized black players for "playground moves." As Wideman notes, that designation "meant there was something wrong with it, which also meant in a funny way there was something wrong with the playground, and since the playground was a black world, there was something wrong with you, a black player out there doing something your way rather than their way."[178] By rejecting the term sandlotter (just as years later, Jordan and others would reject "playground moves") and similar signifiers that identified black ball as a less than worthy alternative to white baseball, Negro Leagues players and owners pushed for public recognition for their sporting achievements.

Even with the end of the segregated era of baseball, "sandlotter" continued to persist as a derogatory term leveled at African American ballplayers. Larry Doby, a former Negro Leaguer who played with the Cleveland Indians after Jackie Robinson broke the color line and who was the first African American player in the American League, encountered the term during his first season in major league baseball. Critics referred to Doby as a "sandlot performer," emphasizing both his perceived athletic shortcomings and his background in the Negro Leagues.[179] As African Americans entered the era of integrated baseball, they still had to counter the major league perception that they were not as talented as their white counterparts because of their color and their time in the Negro Leagues.

African American baseball players also had to contend with the vagaries of Jim Crow travel. Like African American musicians and actors, black baseball players traversed both the North and the South. As they traveled the country, they encountered regionally-specific types of segregation. Based on these experiences, black ballplayers were uniquely qualified to speak to the ambiguity of racial practices as well as to promote successful strategies for dealing with Jim Crow.

Travel, especially interstate travel, was a significant site of contention in Jim Crow era America. Public transportation was often segregated, either by law or tradition. Similarly, hotels and restaurants operated under codes of segregation, particularly but not only in the South. Travel across and around racial boundaries could be a dangerous undertaking for early twentieth century African Americans, especially in the years prior to the publication of *The Negro Motorist Green Book* in 1936. African American travelers, unfamiliar with towns and regions they passed through, had little way of knowing how to successfully navigate local, unwritten customs of segregation.[180] The black press devoted a great deal of coverage to Negro Leagues travel, reflecting the anxiety and interest regarding travel on the part of their readers. Throughout the first half of the twentieth century, the *Defender* and the *Courier* published detailed accounts of spring training trips to destinations in Texas and Louisiana.[181]

In Jim Crow America, securing safe and reliable transportation was a crucial racial and political issue.[182] The freedom to travel was culturally significant for African Americans. As Angela Y. Davis has noted: "for people of African descent who were emerging from a long history of enslavement and oppression during the late nineteenth and early twentieth centuries, sexuality and travel provided the most tangible evidence of freedom."[183] Even as African Americans exercised this new freedom, segregation placed increasing limitations on how blacks could travel in the United States. Racial tensions and ambiguous racial policies also brought increasing danger for those who traveled without local knowledge of racial customs.[184] Frazier "Slow" Robinson recalled the inherent difficulties in negotiating regional differences throughout the United States:

> The hardest part about my time with the Blackballers was being away from home and facing strange racial situations. In Okmulgee, I knew where I could and couldn't go. The high school was segregated, but the movie theater wasn't. That sort of thing. It never made sense to me why I could sit next to the white

kids in a movie theater but not in a classroom, but that's the way it was. On the road with Tulsa in 1927 and 1928, I never knew what to expect.[185]

For Robinson as well as ordinary black folks, travel under Jim Crow was complex. Travel became both a way to assert one's freedom and a test of one's ability to navigate American racism safely.

Negro Leagues players and teams struggled with transporting themselves through the country during their barnstorming tours. These tours involved constant travel, with stops in a different town or city each night, when stops were possible. For black baseball teams, segregated railroads and buses limited their options for getting from one place to another with ease and comfort. Instead, team owners had to arrange for transportation that would be both safe and cost-efficient.

Black fans and sportswriters were acutely aware of the many difficulties faced by Negro Leaguers in their attempt to play their scheduled games. The *Defender* highlighted not just the results of Negro Leagues games but also how the team traveled and how they were treated on the road. In 1910, the Chicago Giants began a road trip through the South, and the *Defender* noted that team officials had provided for the team's security and well-being by arranging for a private Pullman car for the duration of the trip. Moreover, the article pointed out that having the Pullman car would ensure "that they may have nothing but the best comforts."[186] This reassurance of the safety and "comfort" of the traveling players symbolized hope for a more promising, less restrictive future for African American readers and fans.

That future was a long time coming. More than 20 years later, the *Pittsburgh Courier* printed weekly reports on the 1932 Crawfords' spring training and exhibition tour through the Southern states. These reports highlighted the exuberant reception the teams received from Southern black fans while carefully avoiding mention of any difficulties encountered by the clubs. The *Courier* accounts even applauded the status of black-white race relations in cities like New Orleans and Monroe, Louisiana, noting that in Houston "Negroes are employed as detectives. Taxi lines and service stations are operated by members of our race."[187] The report from Monroe did hint at potential problems, but quickly glossed over them to present a more pleasant picture. "Although a visitor to Monroe might say that no compliment should be passed on to the way Negroes are huddled together, they seem to get along alright, and enjoy themselves."[188] By underplaying the racial tensions in the South, the black press and its readership could construct a narrative in which black performers were not subject to the indignities of Jim Crow travel.

In one respect, the Crawfords were shielded from some of the less pleasant aspects of travel through the 1930s South. After initially purchasing "seven passenger Lincolns for the team," Greenlee decided to invest in grander transportation. The Crawfords and Greenlee traversed the country in a new team bus, emblazoned "Pittsburgh Crawfords, World Colored Champions."[189] Eye-catching and attention-grabbing, the bus served two purposes for Greenlee and his team. First, it provided Crawfords players with a safe and comfortable means of transportation, limiting their interactions with segregation. Crawfords player Buck O'Neil described the bus as "big and luxurious" and it certainly gave some protection to its black passengers.[190] Second, it demonstrated the wealth and pride of the Crawfords, in a manner meant both to intimidate opposition teams and to inspire black fans. The Crawfords extended the importance of their bus by advertising Greenlee Field on the vehicle's body. In one picture or viewing, a fan could immediately link the Crawfords' independent transportation with their renowned and black-owned baseball park. Through this bus, the Crawfords were able to subvert at least one of the most visible forms of segregation and discrimination in twentieth century America.

Similarly, the Newark Eagles maintained a team bus in the late 1930s and 1940s, a large vehicle that prominently featured the team name on the side. Other Negro Leagues teams, aware of the prestige that accompanied the acquisition of club-owned transportation, highlighted their own vehicles in posters and flyers. The Washington-Philadelphia Pilots, a barnstorming team, compiled a poster that prominently mentioned that the team would be "traveling in their own bus with a great aggregation of base-ballers."[191] In the case of the Pilots, who were attempting to interest booking agents in addition to fans, the importance of having independent transportation was immense. Booking agents felt that teams that could control their methods of travel had a much greater chance of successfully meeting all barnstorming commitments.

The Kansas City Monarchs also utilized buses to circumvent both segregated transportation and lodging while on the road. Under owner James "J. L." Wilkinson, the Monarchs traveled around the country on a bus with two trailers. Wilkinson could thus access towns too small to have a railroad station and take advantage of untapped markets. As a bonus, the Monarchs employed the trailers as lodging for players in towns where it was impossible for black men to rent a hotel room. One of the trailers also had dining facilities, eliminating the need to find food in areas of the country where businesses often refused to serve African Americans.[192] In their bus, the Monarchs were slightly insulated from the problems that African Americans encountered traveling through Jim Crow America.

For fans of the Monarchs and other Negro Leagues teams, these buses symbolized an effective strategy against segregation and discrimination as well as an effective advertisement. Even if they themselves could not utilize similar strategies to escape the difficulties of racism while traveling, they could appreciate the potential indignities that made bus travel so attractive for black baseball players. Much as Negro Leagues fans applauded the construction of black-owned ballparks and lighting systems, transportation that subverted Jim Crow represented a small victory against racial injustice. Thus, as Negro Leagues owners alerted potential customers to their presence, they also traded on the positive political implications of transportation ownership.

Other teams, lacking the financial resources of Greenlee and the Crawfords, relied on less reliable and much less comfortable forms of transportation. In his memoir, Buck O'Neil recalled an instance when all 11 teammates had to share one car to get to their next game.[193] Other players had similar recollections of crammed automobiles and long, dangerous drives between ball games.[194] When even cars were not an option, players "hopped freight train[s]" to keep up with the demanding schedule.[195] Buck Leonard recalled an instance when his team was forced to sleep in the baggage car of a train because of overcrowding and an unsympathetic conductor.[196]

Unsurprisingly, Satchel Paige employed a means of transportation that circumvented almost all of the difficulties of segregation and reinforced public perception of Paige as a trickster. In 1946, with the support of Monarchs owner J.L. Wilkinson, Paige turned away from team buses and Pullman cars in favor of using an airplane to travel to games. Even though the great pitcher was wary of air travel, the status gained from an airplane dedicated to his personal use was too good to pass up. To travel during the 1940s on an airplane rather than on a team bus reflected Paige's determination to prove his financial and athletic status to all observers, and once again applied greater pressure to white baseball to acknowledge and include black ball players. The photographs of Paige and his airplane signified to the black community Paige's ability to circumvent and literally rise above the limitations of Jim Crow.[197] The plane travel was short-lived, as Paige was unable to overcome his fear of flying, yet the public notice of the plane was widespread, with an article about Satchel and the plane appearing in the *New York Times*.[198]

Finding lodging and food was extraordinarily difficult during barnstorming tours. Players recalled long bus stretches, from Chicago to Cleveland, during which they were unable to stop because of Jim Crow policies.[199] Even when lodging was available to the players, it was often substandard. Buck Leonard, Negro Leagues first baseman, described the accommodations as dreadful:

> Sometimes we'd stay in hotels that had so many bedbugs you had to put a newspaper down between the mattress and the sheets. Other times we'd rent rooms in a YMCA, or we'd go to a hotel and rent three rooms. That way you got use of the bath.... All those players would change clothes in those three rooms, go to the ball park and play a double header.[200]

With difficult economic times of the Depression, teams like the Monarchs could no longer afford Pullman cars or private trailer buses. Without a means of portable lodging comparable to that of a Pullman, the team "relied on a loose network of black boardinghouses and private homes on their rounds."[201]

This experience of finding informal lodging on the road was common in the Negro Leagues. "Wild Bill" Wright described the usual options as nothing less than a constant struggle: "In small towns there weren't any black hotels and you had to either sleep in the bus or someone would take you to their home."[202] When they were unable to secure this type of lodging, players made due by erecting makeshift campsites near their destination, at times "even on the ball field on which they would play the next day."[203]

For the local black fans, the uncertain accommodations of the barnstormers had important implications. Although many black fans viewed the traveling players as superstar athletes, they witnessed the indignities of travel for African Americans regardless of status. For ordinary black folks, the sight of well-known baseball players forced to erect temporary tent lodging in fields because of a lack of accommodation underscored the power of segregation in the United States. No exceptions were made for black baseball players, musicians, or boxers. Black theater groups reported similarly limited accommodation options during their tours. An all-black cast of *Macbeth* "slept at the YMCA, at churches, at schools and in private homes. There were a few boarding houses, and some 'fourth-rate flea bag [hotels].'"[204] Black female entertainers also suffered through difficult traveling situations as American chivalry and protection of "womanhood" had a clear racial boundary in the Jim Crow Era. According to historian Sherrie Tucker's study of black all-girl swing bands in the 1940s, the musicians relied on similar networks of informal lodging through friendly locals.[205] Aware of the indignities endured by black celebrities, African Americans closely identified with the plight of the traveling performers and united against the unfairness of Jim Crow. Within this context, those who could somehow circumvent segregation and discrimination were greatly admired.

Memphis Red Sox outfielder Cowan "Bubba" Hyde recalled "a lot of places we were turned down" when asking to purchase food, consequently "we would make it our business to not stop."[206] Some teams relied on their light-skinned players to procure food for the entire team.[207] Buck Leonard recalled this practice as commonplace. "Most teams had a player who could pass for white and could go into restaurants and buy sandwiches for the rest of the team."[208] In some instances, Negro Leagues teams took advantage of the fact that non-native English speakers could pass through the color line. Latino players at times were served in establishments that refused African American patrons.[209] Leonard and his Homestead Grays teammates observed this exception to the color line during a barnstorming tour.

> One time, Luis Marquez, who was about my color, said he was hungry and that he was going to go in a white restaurant and get something to eat. We all laughed and walked on down the block, waiting for him to get put out. After a

little while, we went back down to the corner and looked in through the window, and he was in there eating. When he came out, we all gave him our orders for him to get us some sandwiches, too. He could do that just because he spoke Spanish, and we couldn't go in there.[210]

Despite the success of some of these ventures, players who tried to "pass" in order to avoid Jim Crow prohibitions risked violent reprisal if an owner or employee realized he or she had been tricked. In these circumstances, black baseball players had to weigh the benefits and risks of exploiting the holes in the color line to procure food, lodging, or gas as they traveled. In general, teams did their best to negotiate within a Jim Crow system that employed threats and overcharges to discourage black patronage, by relying on informal information networks to avoid hostile businesses and to patronize those willing to bend Jim Crow policies.[211]

For African Americans, the ownership of and access to leisure space was immensely important. As the Great Depression diminished their opportunities to work and obtain an income, issues of racial pride and black enterprise became increasingly important to black baseball stakeholders. African Americans supported and encouraged baseball ventures that not only provided a social outlet and diversion, but also reflected their racial politics and invested in local black communities and businesses.

On a larger geographical scale, African American players and fans also grappled with the very real difficulties of negotiating the physical space of the United States. Reliant on road trips and barnstorming tours for their financial well-being, Negro Leagues players encountered and confronted the local ambiguities and difficulties of Jim Crow while traveling through the southern, northern, and western United States.

In the first half of the twentieth century, black baseball fans, players, writers, and owners negotiated the issues of physical space within a segregated sport and country. Yet ballparks, trains, and diners were not the only problematic sites within segregated baseball. The black Negro Leagues athletes, their bodies and their behaviors, were the subject of public debate and concern during the first half of the twentieth century. As black baseball became more prominent and profitable, African American reformers, leaders, sportswriters, and fans developed a number of expectations for the public comportment of black baseball players. Black observers and scholars longed for their ball players to function as "race men" who would uplift the race as a whole. The players themselves became a battleground in the public discussion of civil rights in the Jim Crow Era.

Two

"A man and a gentleman in every respect"[1]

Negotiating Black Manhood and Respectability in a Segregated Sport

In 1926, Harlem Renaissance poet Langston Hughes composed an article for *The Nation* in which he reflected on class divisions among African Americans. Hughes was particularly concerned with the denigration of "folk" cultural productions: jazz, spirituals, and dialect poems. Hughes observed two types of people: the "high-class Negro" and the "low-down folks." The "high-class" people came from the economic "middle class: people who are by no means rich yet never uncomfortable nor hungry." In contrast, the "low-down folks" were

> the majority ... who have their nip of gin on Saturday nights and are not too important to themselves or the community ... or too learned to watch the lazy world go round ... they do not particularly care whether they are like white folks or anybody else. Their joy runs, bang!, into ecstasy.... They furnish a wealth of colorful, distinctive material for any artist because they still hold their own individuality in the face of American standardizations.[2]

A year earlier, a sportswriter for the *Pittsburgh Courier* had bemoaned the lack of colorful players within organized black baseball. At the time, "Colorful Ball Players [were] scarce.... A few years back all clubs had one or more players in their lineups who were box office attractions." The writer identified an exception, Oscar Charleston, and posited that Turkey Stearnes could become a colorful player "with just a little more polish."[3]

African American ballplayers faced new expectations following World War I. Thanks in part to Jack Johnson's influence (both positive and negative), black athletes' public performance of manhood had become a political and cultural concern for many African Americans. At the same time, the emergence of the New Negro, as personified and illuminated by Harlem Renaissance writers and artists, provided black baseball players with a new model of modern manhood.

In *Manning the Race: Reforming Black Men in the Jim Crow Era*, scholar Marlon B. Ross has distilled the three key components of the New Negro's manhood: "clean living and Yankee Christian temperance in the Bookerite mold are bonded to physical duration and mental cunning from the folk mass, then the two together are enhanced by Du Boisian and Lockean concentration on arrogant mastery of the highest classics of European learning."[4] During the interwar period, some, though certainly not all, black baseball players tried to construct their manhood in a manner consistent with the first two aspects of New Negro manhood. Although black sportswriters trumpeted the academic accomplishments of black athletes when appropriate, the learnedness of the New Negro was not a central concern for black baseball players. Instead, players completed the triad of New Negro manhood by establishing their skill and athletic prowess on the field.

The *Courier* writer's call for "colorful players" emphasized two of the three aspects of contemporary manhood. The desire for colorful players spoke to the need for men who exhibited "folk" tendencies, i.e., Hughes's "individuality." Displays of such "colorfulness" improved attendance at games and distinguished black baseball from its white counterpart. On the other hand, "colorfulness" without skill was insufficient, according to the writer. Singling out Turkey Stearnes, he noted that Stearnes could only serve as a truly colorful player if (and only if) he performed with skill on the field. It is this desire for both skill and "colorful" entertainment that both allowed clowning teams to thrive during the period and led to its public disavowal by a number of black baseball players and advocates. Teams that clowned for the sake of clowning were frequently denounced as damaging to the race.

In this chapter, I examine the multiple ways in which black baseball players negotiated their public manhood in light of shifting expectations and the continued pressures of Jim Crow. Because of the complex ways in which black men performed gender during this era as well as the dynamic shifts in gender expectations during the Jim Crow era, I use "manhood," "manliness," and "masculinity" in three distinct ways. "Manhood" denotes the general category of male-gendered characteristics and performance. In contrast, "manliness" and "masculinity" both reference specific, historical conceptions of manhood. As delineated by cultural historian Gail Bederman, "manliness" refers to the Victorian ideal of gentlemanly comportment and was the dominant ideal from the 1880s until the turn of the century. Manly men represented the pinnacle of white manhood; they were self-controlled, morally upright, and of exceptional character. "Masculinity," in contrast, developed as a desirable characteristic male power and encompassed aggressiveness, physical force, and more explicit sexuality. These two competing ideals functioned in relation to each other. The development of a "masculinity" ideal did not mean the wholesale abandonment of "manliness." In a way, "masculinity" built upon the belief that white men had already proved their "manliness," and thus could assert their manhood in more explicit and aggressive ways. According to Bederman, by the 1910s, men were defining masculinity as the primitive lusts and passions of their primordial ancestors. But they did this with the belief that white male Americans had already reached the apex of civilization, and they were merely reinvigorating their prowess through an infusion of savagery. These notions of manhood were explicitly and implicitly raced and classed. African Americans and members of the working class, regardless of race, were excluded from the ideals of both "manliness" and "masculinity."[5]

This unstated exclusion did not prevent African Americans from promoting the attainment of these ideals as a prerequisite for racial and social equality. Both manliness and masculinity acquired a distinctly racialized meaning when performed by African Americans. In particular, adherents of a Washingtonian philosophy of accommodation and respectability championed manliness as an important goal for African American men. New Negro masculinity built upon black manliness (and gentlemanliness) but allowed for a more explicit expression of physical prowess. Moreover, the New Negro man contested the color line whenever possible, performing what Ross has called the "cool pose of racial trespassing."[6]

First, I briefly discuss the transitional notions of manliness within black baseball. As performed by early Negro Leagues stars such as Andrew "Rube" Foster and "Gentleman" Dave Malarcher, this conception of manhood rested upon notions of racial uplift, respectability, and accommodation.[7] Yet this manhood was increasingly challenged by the ascension of the New Negro sensibility. The politicization of African Americans that accompanied World War I and the Great Migration provided an ideal setting for the transformation of black manhood. I then turn to the performance of black masculinity during the inter-war period. Although a number of scholars have specifically addressed the ways in which African American men (especially middle and upper class men) shaped and were shaped by conceptions of masculinity from 1880 to 1920, full-scale examinations of black masculinity during the 1920s and the Great Depression are scarce and usually have taken the form of individual biographies and studies of the Harlem Renaissance intelligentsia. In particular, more work is needed on African American working-class manhood.[8] To this end, I analyze newspaper accounts and oral interviews to uncover public displays and critiques of black masculinity in the 1920s and 1930s. In particular, I address the question of how African American baseball players met, and, conversely, at times rejected, the demands of New Negro manhood.[9] Through their on-the-field performance of stylized baseball and their public activities, a number of black baseball players challenged the gentleman model of the African American athlete. Instead they often functioned as New Negroes and, at times, as bad men.

* * *

Negro Leagues founder Rube Foster straddled the line between the turn-of-the-century gentleman-athlete and the burgeoning (and masculine) New Negro. In the years immediately preceding and following his founding of the Negro National League in 1920, Foster cultivated a reputation as a "gentleman" and "race man." Both identities would prove to be advantageous for Foster, allowing him to gain the loyalty and cooperation of a supportive black press and to promote his league partially through the force of his own personality and reputation.

Foster's ascent to black celebrity status occurred during a time when popular magazines and periodicals increasingly included sports in their pages, a trend that had begun in earnest around the turn of the century. For example, *Harper's Young People* started a regular and expanded sports column in 1893. *Harper's Round Table* instituted their sports column in 1898. Sports coverage in the *New York Times* increased significantly between 1880 and 1916.[10] Magazines such as *Munsey's* and *Scribner's* dedicated multiple pages to sport coverage and featured baseball-themed illustrations. Similarly, black periodicals like *Half-Century* also incorporated sporting news into their publications. The illustrations used by these magazines reflected contemporary conceptions of sporting manhood, both white and black; thus shaping the cultural expectations of manhood that Foster simultaneously supported and challenged.

In particular, three cover illustrations published in the 1910s illuminated the ways in which the African American and white press perpetuated an ideal manhood that incorporated baseball imagery. In 1914, *Collier's* featured a cover image of an older man and a young boy poised at home plate. The boy, as catcher, excitedly awaited the pitch, while the man assumed a batting stance. The older man was dressed in a suit, as if he had spontaneously decided to join in the game after work (Figure 2.1). This image underscored the more salient aspects of 1910s manhood, as the man and boy were participating in an approved form of leisure, baseball, thus finding an outlet for their masculine energies. For the boy, in particular, such sporting activities were meant to be instructive and beneficial in shaping his manhood. Progressive Era reformers encouraged young men to channel their excess energy into innocent and healthful pursuits, like baseball. In particular, the Muscular Christianity movement held that through athletic participation, young men would learn the skills and values that were necessary for future American leaders.[11]

Three years later, the Chicago-based *Half-Century Magazine* printed a

Figure 2.1: *Collier's Magazine*, June 1914. This cover illustration highlights an "All American" scene: a white father and son grin as they engage in the national pastime. Baseball's role as a generational unifier and signifier of American identity is highlighted.

remarkably similar cover illustration (Figure 2.2). *Half-Century* undoubtedly sold itself to predominately elite blacks, it was the most "upmarket of the new [1910s/1920s] publications."[12] Founded by black beauty industry and banking entrepreneur Anthony Overton, *Half-Century* targeted both male and female readers, advertising itself as a magazine for "the Business Man and the Home Maker," bringing together Overton's two main consumer groups.[13] Through its portrayal of sporting events that required at least a nominal financial outlay, the magazine glamorized sports that were out of the reach for many African Americans, particularly newly arrived migrants from the Deep South. By emphasizing fashionable elite black sporting figures, *Half-Century* prioritized participation in organized sport rather than the informal recreation enjoyed by many black migrants.[14]

In *Half-Century*'s version, the man was older, appearing to be more of a grandfather type than a fatherly type, and also less athletic-looking. Otherwise, the two illustrations were almost identical, down to the excited expression on the catcher's face. Both illustrations supported the contemporary notion of manhood as a product of wholesome, athletic diversion as well as the expectation that amateur sporting contests would promote the maturation of young American men. None of the key figures appeared to be overly masculine or sexualized in any way.

In contrast, a subsequent *Collier's* cover would reinforce the notion of the hypermasculine and potentially dangerous black man. In 1915, *Collier's* featured a cover image of an obviously enraged African American man wielding an ax (Figure 2.3). The artist placed evidence of a card-game gone awry in the foreground, thus suggesting that the man's violence stemmed from a gambling disappointment. This image, with its juxtaposition of vice and assault, perpetuated the racial stereotype of the violent and degenerate African American man. In a different context, such as a black magazine or novel, this image could have suggested the bad man folk heroes of African American culture, men who challenged power and authority but in doing so also claimed power on behalf of the oppressed. However, its employment by a white periodical and its lack of context or explanation reinforced white readers' commonly-held negative image of black manhood. Within this environment, Foster and his fellow black ballplayers were at a disadvantage from the start. To craft a positive public image in the contested terrain of racialized black manhood ideals required careful negotiation and foresight, as well as the cooperation of the black press.

In the 1910s, Foster was undoubtedly the most well-known of the early twentieth-century black baseball players. As pitcher-manager of the Leland Giants in the first two decades of the century, Foster's name was synonymous with professional black baseball. Frequently, Foster was the only player men-

Figure 2.2: *Half-Century Magazine*, July 1917. *Half-Century Magazine* emphasized the ways in which the black middle class could achieve status and respectability through adherence to white American values and ideals. In this cover, an African American grandfather and grandson play baseball together and make a visual case for their claim on the national pastime.

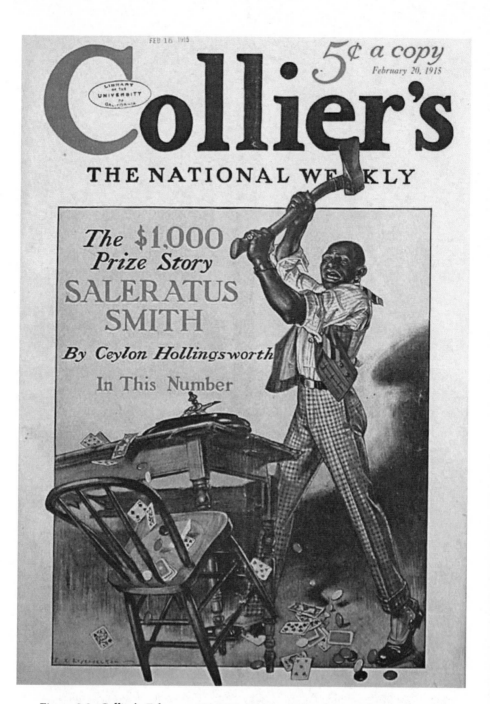

Figure 2.3: *Collier's*, February 20, 1915. In contrast to the nostalgic image of the white father and son in the earlier cover illustration, the visual depictions of black men in white publications were often negative and reinforced stereotypes about African Americans.

tioned by name in newspaper articles promoting and reporting on black baseball games. Foster functioned as the public face and most important attendance-drawing card in early black baseball. White newspapers like the *New York Times* not only announced any local appearances of the Leland Giants but also made specific note of Foster's role on the team and in the sport.[15]

On the sport pages of black newspapers and magazines, the coverage was much more extensive. Certain black periodicals, especially those targeting the middle class and promoting racial uplift, identified Foster as the embodiment of manliness and race success. Magazines like *Half-Century* and *The Competitor* published laudatory articles that praised Foster's moral character and success within a segregated sport.[16] In these articles, the sportswriters highlighted Foster's adherence to the values expected of an early twentieth-century gentleman and race man.[17]

In a *Half-Century* profile of Rube Foster, Howard A. Phelps underscored his moral character, concluding: "I wonder at him, not so much as a player now but more for his gentlemanly bearing and conduct."[18] Moreover, Phelps repeatedly praised Foster for his ability to navigate the Jim Crow South, remarking that "Foster has played in all the Southern states using a Pullman all the time and has yet to have any trouble even of minor importance. His ball team has traveled more than all the Colored Clubs combined; as much as any white club."[19] In a seemingly odd turn, yet one that was consistent with Washingtonian philosophy, the author presented Foster's ability to avoid racial conflict as a testament to his good character and respectability rather than to any other external factors. Phelps also noted that white Southern writers expressed a great deal of admiration for Foster's athletic prowess on the baseball diamond. In essence, Phelps applauded Foster's skill at negotiating a segregated system without altercation, while simultaneously demonstrating his superior baseball abilities. Phelps went on to describe Foster as "a man of unquestionable race identity."[20] For many elite blacks, then, Foster was the ultimate "race man," avoiding controversy, displaying prodigious talent, and courting interracial approval.

In his article, Phelps also alluded to actions that were more consistent with the burgeoning New Negro ethos than with the earlier black gentleman model. Phelps highlighted Foster's athletic skill and the triumph of Fosters' Lelands over "an aggregation of big leaguers," during which Foster "pitch[ed] four games and [won] them all." This discussion of Foster's victory over a white major league All-Star team established Foster's (and black baseball's) athletic superiority for the readers of *Half-Century Magazine.*[21]

Moreover, Foster's use of a Pullman car for his travels in the South revealed his willingness to subvert Jim Crow conventions to claim access to manhood.[22] "The Giants' access to a Pullman car sent a public message about status and exceptionality. Discussing the travel habits of Booker T. Washington in a 1916 hagiographic biography, Emmett J. Scott (aide to Washington) and Lyman Beecher Stowe (grandson of Harriet Beecher Stowe) noted that "Pullman cars in the South are not as a rule open to members of the Negro race. It is only under more or less unusual conditions that a black man is able to secure Pullman accommodations."[23] Booker T. Washington, according to Scott and Stowe, labored under these unusual conditions as "[t]he work he was compelled to do ... made it necessary that he conserve his strength as much as possible."[24] According to scholar Marlon Ross, the concluding message of Washington's use of a Pullman was that "only the singular leader of the race, because of his unique martyrdom, can afford to evade Jim Crow restrictions as an essential comfort of his self-sacrificing service."[25] Scott and Stowe's insistence that Washington "never believed he was defying Southern traditions" with his travel placed his choice within his own accommodationist principles and send the message that ordinary African Americans should accept "Southern traditions."[26] Within this context, Foster's rental of private Pullman cars symbolized a subversion of Southern segregation. A respected race man but not a leader of Washington's stature, Foster claimed "comfort" and protection from Southern travel. Foster's Giants traveled through the South by using a form of transportation intended only for whites as passengers, but that employed only African Americans as porters.

With the establishment of the Negro National League in 1920, black magazine writers linked baseball players' behavior with the success of black baseball as a race enterprise. Ira F. Lewis, writing for *The Competitor*, predicted that the future of the new league rested upon the "boys themselves." According to Lewis, "[a] strict observance of training rules, and gentlemanly conduct on the part of the players will do as much towards making the league a success as any amount of money put into the project."[27] In the first two years of the League's existence, sportswriters with *The Competitor* and *Half-Century* (as well as the owners and managers they interviewed) continued to stress the importance of players presenting themselves as gentleman. C.I. Taylor, owner-manager of the Indianapolis A.B.C.s, proudly reported that he had "never ... had the pleasure of preparing a bunch of players who were more gentlemanly ... or who more readily absorbed the all-important things required of baseball players."[28] The same article highlighted a "high-class performer" on the Detroit Stars and the "new and classy material" on the Dayton club.[29] Of course it was certainly in Taylor's best interest to promote his team by commending both the skill and the character of his players. Regardless of the actual behavior of the players, team owners knew that the best way to gain the support of fans and community leaders was to present a public image that was beyond reproach. By doing so, they could secure a reputation for themselves and their players as "race men" worthy of patronage.

As the Negro National League worked to establish itself as a viable baseball league in the 1920s, team owners tried to regulate the public behavior of the players. Foster and his counterparts employed various measures to control their players off the field. Foster established curfews for his players and implemented a dress code to ensure that the public image of his Giants was beyond reproach. When those measures failed to curb his players' appetite for illicit and immoral pastimes, Foster would hold players' pay so that they could not spend it on alcohol, gambling, and women.[30] Kansas City Monarchs owner J.L. Wilkinson kept "a tailor ... on call to make sure everyone had a nice set of clothes."[31] Wilkinson also prohibited players from shooting "craps on the bus or in the hotel" and "fined or fired those who preferred parties over a good game."[32] These regulations indicate that the actual activities of many Negro Leagues players were less than consistent with the choirboy image that Taylor and others sold to the black press.

Homestead Grays owner Cum Posey publicly admonished his players for what he considered problematic behavior and explicitly tied players' conduct to fan attendance. In a 1925 column in the *Pittsburgh Courier*, he chastised black ballplayers for their behavior. Posey warned Negro Leagues players that their fans would only tolerate so much: "The public is beginning to sympathize with the owners; they are sick of seeing a bunch of good-timers merely putting in a few hours on the ball field between drinks."[33] Posey, like Taylor, Foster, and Wilkinson, was well aware that black baseball players' status as "race men" was necessary for the continued profitability of the Negro Leagues. He also was using the press to pressure his players into adhering to team rules by threatening their livelihood and the support of their fan base.

According to Posey and his fellow owners, the public would only patronize sports that featured "gentlemanly" athletes. Within this context, one particular Negro Leagues player (and eventually manager) came to exemplify the lifestyle that team owners desired for their players. Dave Malarcher, a third baseman for the Chicago American Giants, embodied all of the personal attributes inherent in the older model of black manliness. Dubbed "Gentleman Dave," Malarcher expressed a distaste for unsavory pursuits such as drinking, gambling, and womanizing. Once he succeeded Foster as manager of the Giants in 1926, he expanded Foster's code of conduct by requiring his players to attend church services.[34]

Not all of Malarcher's contemporaries would craft similar gentlemanly public images. Two of the most notable sporting celebrities of the 1920s embraced the excesses of fame, indulging in "dissipations" rather than moderation. White baseball star Babe Ruth enjoyed a rabid following despite his now notorious appetites Ruth was a heavy drinker and flagrant womanizer, albeit one who was aided by reporters in covering up his vices.[35] Historian Richard Bak noted that Ruth suffered physically on at least one occasion due to his sexual relationships, contracting a venereal disease that sidelined him for a significant portion of the 1925 season.[36] Moreover, black prizefighter Jack Johnson continued to attract fans and considerable attention (some negative and some positive) despite his conviction on Mann Act charges and his loss of the heavyweight championship in 1915. The Mann Act, passed in 1910, was a federal legislative response to overblown societal fears about white slavery. The Mann Act criminalized the act of transporting women across state lines for "prostitution or for debauchery, or for any other immoral purpose." The vagueness of "immoral purpose" allowed officials to wield the Mann Act as a tool against men like Johnson who threatened the status quo. In 1920s feature articles about the boxer, writers for the *Pittsburgh Courier, Half-Century Magazine*, and *The Competitor* mentioned Johnson's travails and legal problems but faulted Johnson only for his "indiscretion," not his actions.[37] Johnson faced more direct criticism from black civil rights leaders like W.E.B. Du Bois and Walter White who saw his very public legal trouble as detrimental to racial progress. Even Johnson's black critics, however, emphasized the ways in which his conviction was a symbol of a flawed and racially biased justice system and federal government.

The 1930s and 1940s witnessed the flourishing of black baseball and the ascent of black baseball players as true celebrities for many African Americans. Most information regarding player behavior during from the 1930s and 1940s has come from the former players themselves. Numerous players commented on the behavior of their Negro Leagues teammates in oral interviews. With few exceptions, most of these former players claimed to have been observers, not participants, in the less than savory activities, but their descriptions provide a window into the social life of black baseball players.[38] The interviewed players still struggled with the importance of maintaining a clean and moral public image despite the passage of years and decades. Most of the interviews took place in the 1970s and 1980s, and many players had an interest in promoting their play and accomplishments to gain the recognition that they had been denied because of segregation. The timing of these interviews also means that the majority of the interviewees participated in black baseball in the 1930s or later. Many of the men who ended their careers in the 1910s or 1920s had already passed away by the time the Negro Leagues were "rediscovered."[39] It was not only baseball historians who were suddenly interested in former Negro Leagues players. In the 1970s, the National Baseball Hall of Fame began inducting Negro Leagues players through special committees, an attempt to begin righting the wrongs of racial discrimination that barred black superstars from competing in the major leagues and becoming eligible for ordinary admission. Understandably, players being considered for inclusion were anxious to make the case for induction and present themselves as "clean living." Of course, these motivations do not indicate that the players were lying to the interviewers or discount the honesty of their recollections. It is likely that the ones who recalled exercising moral restraint did indeed avoid the bad behavior of their teammates. Yet their ambivalence in describing the antics of other players and their emphasis on their own morality reveals the degree to which these players still strove to live up to the ideals of "race men."[40]

Particularly for the young players at the start of their careers, black baseball opened the door to a black urban social and cultural milieu that exceeded their expectations.[41] Those players who competed on the well-established clubs experienced a greater financial independence than they had ever known. As Negro Leagues shortstop Pee Wee Butts recalled, "the Kansas City Monarchs were very good at picking up guys in little small towns in Texas and Arkansas." The Monarchs would then sign the young players and procure a new set of clothes for them. Consequently, "those guys could step out of the clubhouses Sunday sharp as a tack, good dressers, good times, no curfew."[42] Well-dressed Negro Leaguers took advantage of the exciting social scene in cities such as Pittsburgh, Chicago, Kansas City, and New York. The Great Migration had fostered immense growth in terms of leisure opportunities in black urban neighborhoods. In these metropolitan areas, the players patronized well-known black nightclubs and restaurants, often interacting with local black musicians.[43] As black celebrities, well loved by the community, they enjoyed the perks of fame. According to jazz scholars Frank Driggs and Chuck Haddix, the Monarchs were an incredible source of pride for black Kansas City residents, bringing "the community prestige and respect."[44] The price for indulging in urban nightlife was often paid at the ballpark the following day. Catcher James "Joe" Greene recalled the detrimental results of such behavior: "[s]ome guy would get a little money in his pocket, go out and stay out all night" then he couldn't "play ball the next day."[45] Although late-night carousing did not always guarantee a long and productive career and often hindered one, the young men seized upon the chance to experience a vibrant social scene, one in which they played a central role.

A significant number of players, both married and single, capitalized on the availability of attractive young women who flocked around the Negro Leaguers. Negro Leagues players recalled the necessity of reaching an "understanding" with their wives. Under this arrangement, Negro Leagues wives had little expectation that their husbands would remain faithful during road trips.[46] Ted "Double Duty" Radcliffe, one of the league's more notorious (and self-confessing) ladies' men, described the ease with which he entered into romantic relationships as a black ball player. "I didn't drink or smoke but I was a lady's man. I always like nice clothes and I ain't never had enough women—I was just like a cat. When I went into a town I was a good ballplayer and I could get the pick of the girls."[47] Radcliffe took full advantage of his celebrity and the ways in which his on-the-field skills could result in off-the-field success with women. Interestingly, Radcliffe made sure to distinguish between vices, denying that he indulged in alcohol or smoking but happily admitting to womanizing. This disclaimer, in some ways, reinforced the manliness of his actions by emphasizing his powerful masculinity as demonstrated by his athletic achievement and sexual success.

Ted Page related a similar story, with a similar disclaimer, about how women could heal rifts among teammates. Page recalled playing "a lot of years with Dick Seay. I was his type: no cussin',' no drinkin.' Those other guys would get a bottle of whiskey and they'd go out to the race track."[48] Despite Page's reticence to partake in alcohol and gambling, other risky behaviors held an appeal. After getting in a fight with George Scales and spending a tense night sharing a room (both men slept with weapons that evening), Scales remedied the situation by extending an olive branch to Page. "The next night George rounded up two girls, one for him, one for me, and we took them to our room. One was a waitress, the other one, I guess she was a nurse. We had a party.... I say this to show how we lived and how we settled things."[49] Both Radcliffe and Page described themselves and their teammates as active and interested participants in the black urban social scene of the 1930s and 1940s.

This privilege was limited in certain important ways, however. While adultery and extramarital sex was not encouraged by the black press, community leaders, or team owners, it was tolerated as long as it was sex between two African Americans. Interracial sex was taboo for many, especially in light of the Jack Johnson controversy and conviction. A large number of African Americans (and Johnson himself) believed the boxer had been punished for breaking the sexual color line. In terms of sexuality during Jim Crow, white men had access to white and black women, while black men had access to black women. In the 1930s and 1940s, black female musicians and artists, living a lifestyle of travel and performance similar to that of the Negro Leagues players, could not enjoy even the racially limited sexual freedom of black ballplayers. To ensure their respectability, black female performers were expected to repress their sexuality.[50] During World War II, white female baseball players in the All-American Girls Professional Baseball League faced similar limitations on their conduct and sexuality.[51]

The winter trips to Cuba and other Latin American countries provided even more of a respite for players weary of the constant scrutiny of both the black press and anxious team owners. Traveling without their wives, black baseball players seized upon the opportunity to expand their social life without fear of negative repercussions. According to historian Donn Rogosin, those who participated in international winter ball used their distance in order "to sow wild oats away from unsympathetic parents and wives."[52] What Rogosin failed to mention was that for African American ballplayers, trips abroad allowed them space from the scrutiny of the larger black community as well.

At the same time, players found that being colorful could bring rewards in the form of larger contracts and larger crowds. Answering the call of poet Langston Hughes and the *Pittsburgh Courier*, Negro Leagues baseball players acted the part of tricksters to add color to the game. Satchel Paige, in particular, performed as an athletic trickster on the field. According to scholar of African American studies Gerald Early, in his work on black boxing, "the Trickster, inasmuch as he is represented by the slick accomplished boxer, does not need to fear another formidable Trickster ... for in the brutal pantomime of the prize ring the Trickster's technique masks the fact that he is the personification of anarchy."[53] To take this idea further, scholar Gena Dagel Caponi has discussed at length the aesthetics of black sporting performance and the way in which "'hotdogging' becomes "community building." For Caponi, "the virtuousic individual performance is a social act, inspiring the team and the community."[54] Trickster athletes, therefore, provide value to their community through their "colorful" athletic displays, especially in light of Jim Crow segregation.

Paige used his stylized skills to tremendous financial advantage. It was Paige's on-the-field prowess and showmanship that allowed him to command such extraordinary treatment.[55] Paige, in an oral interview with James Banker, recalled calling in his infielders before facing a hitter.[56] Paige would then strike the batter out on three quick strikes. Teammate Quincy Trouppe told a similar story but described the stunt in a different manner. According to Trouppe, at least on one occasion, the infielders and outfielders themselves decided to sit down and forced Paige to strike out the opposing batter.[57] This action was not meant as a pure "stunt," or an opportunity to embarrass the opposing batter; instead it was intended to increase attendance. Word would quickly spread to the next town, where Paige would play to a capacity crowd. Baseball historians Larry Lester, David Marasco, and Patrick Rock have recently investigated this story about Paige and found documented evidence in an *L.A. Times* news article describing him performing this "trick" in 1935.[58] The 1935 date places the story in the timeframe during which Trouppe and Paige played for the Bismarck Churchills, lending further credence to Trouppe and Paige's recollections.

Paige biographer Lawrence Tye documents a 1933 occurrence of this trick, one brought on not by a desire to procure more fans but because of team tension. Paige was not getting along with his teammates at the time and chastised the outfielders for what he believed to be sloppy play. In response, the outfielders sat during the next inning and Paige was forced to strike out the side without defensive support in the outfield. The result was the same, however. Bismarck fans thrilled at what they believed to be Paige's audacity in sitting his outfielders, and it flamed the already oversized mythology of Paige.[59]

At times, even this trickster stunt had larger political and racial implications. In interracial contests, the stakes were symbolically higher for both teams. For Negro Leagues professionals, a victory over a white team served as another attack against the racial prohibitions of major league baseball. Paige was particularly cognizant of the consequences of such competitions, both for himself and for his fellow players. When Paige traveled to Bismarck, North Dakota, to play on an interracial team, he noted the importance of his move. "I was going to be playing with some white boys.... It looked like they couldn't hold out against me all the way after all. I'd cracked another little chink in Jim Crow."[60] While pitching for the Bismarck club, Paige once again demonstrated his supreme confidence and showmanship flair. Paige, up 14–0 against a white semipro team from Kansas, called in both his outfield and infield. In front of a contentious crowd, Paige then struck out the side.[61] In yet another instance, while facing white major leaguers in an exhibition, Paige raised the stakes even higher. Angry with Chicago Cub Frank Demaree for derogatory comments about his team, Paige seized an opportunity for revenge. Paige intentionally walked enough batters to load the bases when Demaree came to bat. Paige once again called in his outfielders before pitching to Demaree, but this time he also ordered his infielders to sit down. In a one-on-one battle, Paige struck Demaree out on three straight pitches.[62]

Buck O'Neil told a similar story in his memoir. O'Neil recalled that in a game against a semipro Coors Brewing team, Paige overheard one of the Coors players "shouting from the dugout. 'He's nothing but an overrated darkie. Let's beat him.'" At that point, Paige, who had been wild that day, called in the entire team. "So there we were, seven of us, all kneeling around the pitching mound. Satchel struck out the next three batters on nine pitches. The fans gave him a standing ovation, and the guys on the other team apologized for what one of them had said." According to O'Neil, "[f]or Satchel, making believers out of doubters was sweeter than winning any ballgame."[63] In O'Neil's view, the stakes were always high for Paige and always about more than baseball.

Under these circumstances, Paige's trickster actions had more significance. By triumphing in such an outrageous manner over white players who had access to the major leagues, Paige contributed yet another "chink" to the color line that prohibited African American big league ball players, undermining the often specious arguments about white supremacy that formed the basis of Jim Crow.[64] Perhaps just as significantly, these actions also empowered Paige in terms of his own manhood. By triumphing over his opponent with only the assistance of his catcher, Paige asserted his own masculinity and established his prowess.

In addition to the outrageous on-the-field stunts, Paige demonstrated his trickster tendencies in his pitching movements. One of the most famous photographs of Paige documents his unusual style. Paige leans back, his right leg planted on the ground and right arm, ball in had, stretched out far behind him. As Paige winds up, his left leg extends in a high kick. Paige then delivers the ball, using the entirety of his long body, to home plate. To increase the drama of his pitching movement, Paige developed the "hesitation pitch," in which he would briefly stop in mid-motion before releasing the pitch.[65] When this pitch was effective, Paige's erratic movement would thoroughly distract the opposing hitter, causing him to strike out. The hesitation pitch was Paige's most famous "trick" pitch, but he had a number of others in his repertoire, including the "be ball," "submariner," "trouble ball," and "bat dodger."[66] All of the pitches and their evocative names contributed to the trickster legend of Satchel Paige.

Larry Brown, a catcher for the American Giants, also capitalized on similar "trickerations."[67] In the Negro Leagues, "trickerations" encompassed any baseball move or strategy that was not considered common practice in the white major leagues. Everything from clowning (catching in a rocking chair, calling in the infield) to extraordinarily aggressive strategies (long lead-offs, stealing home, unexpected bunts) fell under the umbrella of trickerations and fall into the category of Caponi's "hotdogging." In a larger sense, black ballplayers' employment of a more stylized form of baseball was in itself a "trickeration."[68] For Brown and Paige, the stylized performance of baseball served both as a competitive and audience-drawing strategy, as well as a public demonstration of their athletic skill. As a catcher, Brown's "trickerations" centered on challenging and ridiculing the opposing team's baserunners. "I could throw pretty good. The crowd used to roar to see me throw the men out. And I used to miss the ball and let it roll about eight or ten feet and go get it and then throw the guy out. Make him run."[69] By employing his "trickerations," Brown, like Paige, played the trickster and brought anarchy and disorder to a game that insisted upon order. These unique strategies and alternative style of sport brought additional suspense and excitement to the game, increasing their fan base. Thus, they helped shaped Negro Leagues baseball into a new, more stylized type of baseball, one that reflected a larger African American cultural tradition of the trickster.

Sportswriters rarely documented the off-the-field misdeeds of black baseball players. As active stakeholders in the promotion of the game, members of the black press had little to gain from spotlighting Negro Leaguers taking advantage of the local nightlife by drinking, gambling, and having affairs. Instead, the black press actively refuted charges of misconduct by white periodicals and white baseball officials.[70] This advocacy role was consistent with the larger political ideology of the black press as well as with the standard operating procedure for sportswriters in general. White sportswriters labored to keep Babe Ruth's more problematic behaviors under wraps as well, anxious to protect him as a valuable commodity for newspaper sales. Black newspapers, under the direction of civically minded owners, functioned as promoters of black racial progress and as watchdogs guarding against civil rights violations. From heralding the Great Northern Drive that symbolically began the Great Migration to marshaling support for the World War II Double Victory campaign, papers like the *Chicago Defender* and *Pittsburgh Courier* were active participants in the fight against Jim Crow.[71]

It was not only the press that had a vested interest in masking the misbehavior of black ball players. In the 1930s, the financial demands of the Depression meant that Negro Leagues team owners could not afford to alienate paying customers. To ensure attendance, the owners marketed their ability to "guarantee good order" at the ballpark and within their teams, and profited from the willingness of black sports writers to gloss over player misconduct when possible.[72]

In one instance, a sportswriter tried to counteract Paige's public reputation as a partier, womanizer, and trickster. Al Monroe, in his *Chicago Defender* column, remarked upon Paige's apparently unremarkable social life. According to Monroe, Paige "was one of the quietest man in baseball." Monroe also praised Paige for being "[t]he best dressed man in baseball, owner or otherwise."[73] Perhaps undercutting his own conclusions regarding Paige's demeanor and behavior, Monroe noted that despite occupying the room next to Paige, he had "yet to hear or see him in his room." Monroe claimed that Paige's quiet reserve explained this lack of notice. Yet accounts by his teammates (and by Paige himself) suggest that Paige was probably out on the town and occupying night clubs instead.[74] In this manner, Monroe was able to report truthfully if superficially—Paige, by all accounts, was a snappy dresser and there was little noise emerging from his room, without delving into the deeper truth of Paige's after-hours activities.

Only in rare instances did black sportswriters report on players' misdeeds. Wendell Smith, for instance, took Satchel Paige to task for "loll[ing] around in the dressing room while his mates were out on the field taking a shellacking from the Homestead Grays."[75] Yet even though Smith implied that Paige was lazy, disinterested, and perhaps distracted by other, more exciting diversions, he did not directly accuse him of immoral behavior. Instead, Smith attempted to shame Paige into straightening up his act.[76] When Smith wrote, in 1943, the possibility of baseball integration was becoming more immediate. Afraid to derail the progress that was slowly being made to challenge the color line, Smith and his fellow sportswriters sought to establish the strong athletic and moral credentials of Negro Leagues players to persuade the white major leagues to open the door.

Throughout the Negro Leagues period, black baseball received a great deal of public scrutiny. White opponents of integration frequently invoked a "character clause" when defending segregated baseball, arguing that black players and fans lacked the necessary character to qualify for the white major leagues. Yet there is no evidence that the white major leagues released players because of character or morality deficiencies. This reasoning, which easily fit into contemporary racialist stereotypes of African American men as physically strong but morally inferior, was pervasive during the Jim Crow era and was repeated by former Negro Leagues players. Buck Leonard made this argument in an oral interview. "There was one requirement in the major leagues that we didn't have, and that was your character. If you don't have good character, you don't stay in the major leagues long. But if you could play ball, regardless of your character, you could come in our leagues."[77] Even Leonard, a star of the Negro Leagues, had absorbed this incredibly common and racially-biased logic as a truth.

A contemporary joke flipped this notion of moral superiority by inverting the stereotype. *Life* reprinted the following (as originally printed in the *New York Evening Graphic*) in 1930 and claimed it was "Harlem's favorite joke."

> [A] Caucasian gent ... remarked to his negro valet, "Washington, I dreamed last night that I went to the Negro paradise. It was very dirty and full of rubbish. And just packed to the heavenly gates with your people in rags." "That's nothin', sah!" chuckled the colorado-maduro lad, "Ah dun dreamt I went to de white folkses' heaven. It shoh was nice dere. Flowers and pretty smells and trees everywhere. But, Lordy, it was empty!"[78]

The clear message of spiritual superiority for African Americans (presumably when and where it really counts—when eternity is on the line) challenged the various restrictions that couched racial discrimination in terms of moralism.

To challenge this (hypocritical) claim of moral superiority, black sports writers highlighted the "gentlemanly" nature of African American players and advised fans to avoid any problematic pursuits or behaviors during their attendance at games. Both sportswriters and Negro Leagues officials publicized the need for strict rules of conduct. Al Monroe addressed both the behavior of fans and of players in a 1934 *Chicago Defender* column. Monroe praised Chicago American Giants owner Robert Cole for his commitment to respectable behavior. Noting the Giants' strong attendance numbers, Monroe attributed fan support to the fact that "Cole and his associates have promised that there will be no misgivings in conduct tolerated on the ballfield." In addition, "they have majored in an attempt to keep all promises as to attractions and courtesies to patrons."[79] Chicago area fans then could expect to witness clean ball playing in a respectable environment.

Similarly, at least two Negro Leagues managers also expressed concern over players' behavior. In 1936, journeyman manager James "Candy Jim" Taylor advised League players and owners that they could survive and thrive in the Depression only if players were closely constrained. Taylor observed "[i]n the last few years the ball player has been allowed to do as he pleases with no one to demand his living clean. There was a time when we were told to be in bed at a certain hour every night and the manager was instructed ... to see that you were."[80] Taylor also spoke to attendance concerns and underscored the need to protect "lady fans" by keeping parks "clean." "Very often some of our lady fans go to our parks and have to go to the cleaners on Monday."[81] While a portion of Taylor's complaint can likely be chalked up to the nostalgic longing that so often colors the comments of those who were at the end of a decades-long career, Taylor gave voice to a common concern among Negro Leagues owners, managers, and sportswriters.

Three years later, another manager argued that player conduct could impede successful integration. In a *Baltimore Afro-American* article, Elite Giants manager Felton Snow cautioned that integration might be difficult due to players' attitudes and habits. According to Snow, "there are so many men that get three of [sic] four dollars in their pockets and right away want to tell 'the man' where he can go."[82]

It was not just black baseball players who were subject to intense public scrutiny over their behavior. In 1941, a *Chicago Defender* sportswriter published a highly critical article about the Harlem Globe Trotters, in town for a championship tournament. According to the article, the Trotters had been guilty of "sloppy" play that disappointed their fans. The writer decided to set the record straight as to why the Trotters had not lived up to expectations. When their opponents were resting, the Trotters were out taking advantage of the Chicago night life, "enjoying themselves at the Gay Octette's cabaret party ... until the rays of the morning sun were breaking over Lake Michigan."[83] With their high profile, the Trotters were somewhat easy targets for the vigilant black press, anxious to police the behavior of black athletes who could have an outsized influence on matters of national race policy.

As race heroes, black baseball players struggled with the demands of two competing roles.[84] The black sporting press and black elites encouraged the players to serve as models of behavior and integrity, to function as positive race representatives in the minds of both blacks and whites. At the same time, fans and journalists clamored for the cool and "colorful" performances of baseball tricksters. This behavioral ideal reflects both the black elite's desire for public respectability as well as the African notion of maintaining cool. Art historian Robert Farris Thomspon has defined "the cool" as the overall principle that allows communities to function and thrive in a orderly, cohesive manner. In the West African communities studied by Thompson, the performers of the "dance of derision" communicate to their audience the idea that cool should be maintained despite "those who would break the rules of society." Thus,

> [t]he dance of derision attests that although most West African dances exist as concrete metaphors of right living, some Africans do cheat, steal, and kill. Terrible events occur in West Africa not because the inhabitants lack moral control (their dances make this clear), but because thus far no society on earth has ever completely satisfied or embodied a definition of ideal behavior.[85]

In the fraught environment of racial discrimination, African Americans struggled to define what that "ideal behavior" would be for their public representatives, including Negro Leagues players. The inconsistencies and contradictions of the ideal fostered continual public debate over the behavior and character of black ballplayers.

Wendell Smith once equated black baseball players to race "ambassadors," elaborating that "[e]very Negro in public life stands for something more than the role he is portraying ... whether he likes it or not."[86] Smith's pronouncement was a continuation of long-standing rhetoric regarding African American athletes. In 1920, *The Competitor* praised track star Sol Butler, noting that "he always considered the fact before a vast audience where he was usually the only colored man competing, that he was representing his race, and the people could rest assured that his personal conduct would certainly reflect no discredit on his race."[87] Rube Foster often earned similar praise from the black press. Butler and Foster exemplified the race ambassador model based on the ideal of a race gentleman.

Yet their performance as heroic badmen was also significant. As badmen heroes, they employed strategies of resistance designed to critique white authority and to effect change in race relations. By performing the role of badmen rather than sanitized race heroes, black athletes provided a more relatable, and at times more satisfactory, public model. Unlike the traditional nineteenth-century folkloric badmen, the twentieth-century badmen often escaped without the condemnation of the law.[88] Utilizing the quick wit of the trickster, these "new" badmen often avoided imprisonment and becoming the victim of extralegal violence. Jack Johnson was a good example of a badman who was not able to escape punishment of white authority. Likewise, Muhammad Ali would later be subject to criminal persecution and the loss of his boxing license due to his challenge of an army induction order and his outspoken stance against the Vietnam War.[89]

Working-class blacks delighted in the stories of the badmen, while the black elite, fearful of any negative repercussions, condemned the badmen's behavior as subversive and problematic. Chicago sociologists Drake and Cayton dubbed this character the "bad Negro" and documented his significance for African American life in the 1930s.[90]

One such story (originally told about Jack Johnson) had Paige speeding down a highway when he was stopped by a white sheriff. The sheriff informed Paige that he owed $25 for a speeding ticket. Paige quickly pulled out a $50 bill and told the officer to keep the change because he was going to be coming back the same way. Perhaps reflective of the Depression-era context of Paige's story, the amount of money is half that mentioned in the World War I–era Johnson version.

> It was on a hot day in Georgia when Jack Johnson drove into town. He was really flying: Zoom! Behind his fine car was a cloud of red Georgia dust as far as the eye could see. The sheriff flagged him down and said "Where do you think you're going, boy, speeding like that? That'll cost you $50." Jack Johnson never looked up; he just reached in his pocket and handed the sheriff a $100 bill and started to gun the motor; ruuummmmm, ruuummmmm. Just before Jack pulled off the sheriff shouted "Don't you want your change?" and Jack replied, "Keep it, 'cause I'm coming back the same way I'm going!" Zooooom.[91]

This same story was also told with a gender reversal, making the protagonist a woman. Mark S. Foster relates an account of a black woman being pulled over in the South while driving a luxury car. The woman easily paid the extravagant fine demanded by the white officer, leaving him dumbstruck. "When Naomi counted out enough cash money to pay the fine, the policeman's eyes popped out.... There was nothing left for him to do but take all that money from a 'nigra' and let her go."[92] Mamie Fields, the cousin of the woman in the story, expressed the great delight that always met the retelling of this tale. "My Lord, how we used to laugh when Naomi told that story."[93]

Another version of this story removes the sheriff as the antagonist. "Double Duty" Radcliffe, Paige's teammate on an integrated North Dakota club, the Bismarck Churchills, related a tale of Paige's challenge to a white judge in Kansas. According to Radcliffe, a police officer had stopped Paige, in a fancy new Lincoln, for speeding. Brought before the judge and fined $40, Paige "pulled eighty dollars from his wallet and said 'Here you go judge, 'cause I'm coming back tomorrow.'"[94] In this telling, Paige is able to subvert a more powerful figure by getting the best of a judge.

Frank Duncan, Jr., however, offered the ultimate twist on this frequently repeated tale. Duncan claimed that he accompanied Paige on a barnstorming trip through Wyoming. The story proceeded like the other iterations with a significant difference. Instead of merely handing over the $50 bill and taking off, Paige "got outta the car and was walkin' down the side of the road with the guy, arm around him…. When Satchel got back to the car, he … showed us the $50 bill."[95] Finally, in this last version, Paige plays the ultimate trickster, he flaunts his wealth, speeds, and evades even what would have been to him an insignificant fine.

In the multiple versions of this tale, Paige assumes a dual role as hero and trickster. The hero of the tale, Paige counters the stereotype of the poor African American. Not only can Paige afford the fancy car he is driving, he also has enough cash to pay the speeding fine twice. As a trickster, Paige escapes from a potentially dangerous situation, being pulled over by a white sheriff. In some iterations of this story, including the initial Jack Johnson version, an explicitly Southern setting increases the dangerous tone of this tale. Paige's and Johnson's black audiences were well aware of the vulnerability of a black traveler in such a situation. As a result of being pulled over, both men were vulnerable to physical harm from the officer and incarceration into convict labor had they been unable to pay. 1920s and 1930s journalists and more recent historical scholarship on the abuse of the legal system during Jim Crow highlighted the ways in which Southern jurisdictions exploited the legal system to sentence African Americans to periods of forced labor and virtual enslavement.[96] *Competitor* writer Herbert J. Seligmann detailed the horrific use of peonage to virtually enslave and physically abuse African Americans in Georgia. The author was responding, in part, to the murder of an African American man by the white farmer for whom he toiled in peonage.[97] Similarly, editors at *The Competitor* argued that the state of Georgia was complicit in maintaining peonage, and called on state officials to remedy the situation to no avail.[98] Historian Leon Litwack described various incidents of peonage and forced labor throughout the South. "All too often, peonage operated with the full connivance and encouragement of state and local authorities. Convicted of a crime, the black offender would have to pay both a fine and court costs, more than he or she could afford. But an employer would then intercede to pay the fine, requiring the offender to work for him until the debt had been settled."[99] Douglas Blackmon, in his study of forced labor, has called this era the "Age of NeoSlavery" and has documented the ways in which farmers and corporations used this system to acquire cheap laborers, often paying a monthly fee to the state in exchange for a steady stream of convicted black men.[100]

Rock and roll great Chuck Berry lyrically immortalized this all too common outcome in the song "Brown Eyed Handsome Man." In the 1956 Berry song, the protagonist faces "charges of unemployment" and the possibility of jail time or peonage.[101] Instead of either of those dire outcomes, Satchel Paige turned the situation to his advantage, using his wit to outsmart the sheriff. And, in the most fantastical of the tales, he emerged completely unscathed, having convinced the sheriff to refund his fine.

Paige's tale has special significance because of the relationship between African Americans and white law enforcement in the early twentieth century. According to folklore scholar John Roberts, in trickster tales following Emancipation the white law authorities took the place of the slave master.[102] In essence, both Paige and the white sheriff are symbolic in this folktale. Paige represents resistance and civil disobedience against the white sheriff, who represents all of the potential inequities of law enforcement during Jim Crow.[103] Particularly for African Americans familiar with the badman folk hero tales of the early twentieth century, Paige's actions are significant as part of a much larger tradition. Paige's disobedience is a heroic, trickster-like action that fulfills the desire of African Americans to outwit a police officer without violent repercussions or enslavement.

Paige fulfilled the role of trickster by overcoming not only the white law enforcement authority but also the economic barriers faced by African Americans, particularly in the Depression-era South. Throughout the tale, signs of wealth were emphasized. Paige drove an expensive vehicle, carried a large amount of cash for the time, and the tale's turning point centered on Paige's casual ability to pay double the amount required. In the story, and in reality, Paige's ability to flaunt his wealth as superior to the majority of whites demonstrated his vast economic success despite the obstacles of Jim Crow. James "Joe" Greene described Satchel thusly: "Satchel liked the fast life. He always had fast cars, Lincoln Continentals, tailor-made suits, and plenty of women."[104] Paige was not alone in his desire to demonstrate his wealth through his clothes and cars, other Negro Leagues players displayed their status similarly. Quincy Troupe recalled his father, catcher Quincy Trouppe, as follows:

> My father was a tall man, six-foot-three, strong and handsome. He was brown-skinned, a very dapper dresser, and wore the latest and best of fashions—wide-lapel suits and sports coats, oversized, with two buttons; loosely draped pants and "bad to the bone," two-toned Foot Joy shoes; wide-brimmed Panama hats and gold Rolex watches. He always drove a new Cadillac or Chrysler. Only the best was good enough for my father.[105]

Within most of the renditions of this trickster tale, by emphasizing his wealth to a white police officer, who at the time usually would have been from a lower class background, Paige proved his economic superiority over a man who generally would feel most threatened by the economic success of a black man.[106] Especially in the time of the Depression, Paige's ability to perform as a consumer, provider, and participant in the display of wealth signified a special and masculine achievement. Because of his race, Paige's financial success symbolized a direct attack against the limitations of Jim Crow and helped to define him as a true economic threat to the racial system of the time.

This type of economic threat was often incredibly dangerous to the black men who challenged the socio-economic hierarchy of Jim Crow. Historian Leon Litwack has argued that African American economic success posed the greatest threat to whites and the Jim Crow system in the postbellum United States.[107] Whites enraged by African American economic success at times punished black men through targeted violence and lynchings. White manhood's reliance on economic superiority made it fragile and subject to dismantling when small numbers of black men attained a degree of financial security or means.

Moreover, the tale's symbolic power is increased by the disconnect between the events of the tale and the everyday experience of African Americans. Travel was an especially dangerous undertaking for African Americans in the early twentieth century. For black observers, accounts of how African American celebrities dealt with the same issues and "racist conditions" that were a part of daily life for ordinary black folks were particularly applicable. As film studies scholar Arthur Knight noted in his essay "Star Dances," "Black stars ... embodied African American social and cultural history, connectedness, courage and the expressive freedom possible within the racialized limits of sociopolitical freedom in the United States."[108] In essence, African Americans viewed the triumphs, challenges, and failures of black athletes and entertainers as leading indicators of their own "freedom" within Jim Crow America.

One of Paige's encounters with Southern white law enforcement illustrated the ways in which African American ballplayers struggled to walk the line to maintain a public image as badmen without ending up in jail. In 1928, on Paige's trip home to Mobile to visit his family, a white sheriff spotted him driving down the Alabama interstate "[i]n his shiny red roadster, looking as fly as a man in a blue suit, straw hat, and spats could look." The sheriff pegged Paige as a car thief, unwilling to believe that Paige was the rightful owner of the vehicle. Deaf to Paige's insistence on his innocence and his athletic fame, the sheriff arrested Paige. After spending a long night in the Mobile county jail, Paige was released after a reporter from the *Chicago Defender* vouched for his character. This story may have been apocryphal, a search of the *Defender* did not reveal any accounts of this event and clearly, as a reporter with access to this story would have published it. That this story was repeated by Paige's daughter and at least one other source speaks to its veracity or at least to its circulation.[109] Other African Americans, familiar with similar incidents, found in Paige's folktale retribution for years of false incrimination by white law authorities.

Paige's two disparate encounters with white law enforcement also speak to the tenuous line walked by black celebrities under Jim Crow. Both too little notice and too much attention could result in potentially dangerous situations for black celebrities like Paige. The most well-known black stars (particularly non–Hollywood celebrities) were unknown to certain segments of the white population, thus placing black stars like Paige in situations like the one described above, trying desperately to prove their status to disbelieving (or disinterested) white authorities.[110] When black celebrities engendered a great deal of attention from whites, they were also the target of suspicion and potential legal repercussions. Jack Johnson served as the most potent example of a black celebrity, despised by whites, brought down by trumped-up legal charges.

After Johnson's arrest on white slavery charges under the Mann Act, black stars attempted to negotiate the precariousness of African American celebrity status with greater care. Jesse Owens and Joe Louis were especially diligent about cultivating public images that fit with the expectations of whites and the black elite. Owens and Lewis served as the ultimate race ambassadors, avoiding public scandal and cultivating a respectable public reputation. Louis's status as a race ambassador was immortalized in the 1953 Hollywood biopic made about his life, *The Joe Louis Story*. The biographical film employed a narrative that highlighted his hard work and dedication while avoiding notions of class conflict, black agency (white managers and authorities are given credit for much of the athletes' success), and individuality.[111] The story is even framed by a white reporter who gets to define Louis and the significance of his life and career.

During the cold war, "race ambassador" became an official position for a number of black musicians. In 1956, the U.S. State Department instituted a jazz ambassador program through which artists like Dizzy Gillespie and Louis Armstrong traveled to other countries and performed. The government hoped that these "ambassadors" would convince members of the international community that the United States was making progress in terms of civil rights and win the goodwill of other nations through this sharing of the arts. Most importantly, government officials intended for these ambassadors to further the U.S.'s Cold War goals. In actuality, these jazz ambassadors did not always tow the government line by painting a positive picture of United States race relations, but they did not explicitly denounce U.S. racial policies during their tours abroad, as Josephine Baker and Paul Robeson did.[112] Paige, on the other hand, never fit the role of ambassador. Nor did he embrace Johnson's brash disregard for the social-cultural norms under Jim Crow. Instead, he fashioned himself as a subtle badman, a resistant hero made all the more potent by his fool's clothing.

Some of Paige's contemporaries took a more direct route, embracing the role of bad man. Having survived years of frustration and racial discrimination, these players were unwilling to tolerate further abuse by hostile whites. Thus, when they had the opportunity to strike back, they did.

One such player was Quincy Trouppe. He recalled touring Arkansas as manager of the Cleveland Buckeyes. Because Trouppe served as manager from 1945 to 1947, the following encounter would have occurred within that time period. While the team bus was stopped, two white men approached the team and expressed their disapproval of African Americans from the North traveling through the South. The two men threatened the players and two of the Buckeyes responded physically. According to Trouppe, "My two players lit into them and planted knuckle sandwiches all over their heads. When it was all over two Southern white men were laying stretched out cold in the hard, sun-baked ground of Arkansas." Trouppe then gathered the team and quickly left, "headed for the Missouri line." [113] After the team traveled 50 miles away from the site of the incident, a highway patrolman stopped the bus. The patrolman suspected that the players had attacked the white men and left them, but Trouppe convinced him that he was targeting the wrong men. The bus then departed and the team safely arrived at the next stop. [114]

Trouppe and his players functioned as "badmen" and outlaw folk heroes in the above story. By performing their retaliation against the white men outside of public view, Trouppe and the Buckeyes were able to respond in kind to the violent threat of the men and do so without legal repercussions. The players did commit an illegal act, in terms of the law, qualifying them as "badmen" or "outlaws." Yet they also fulfilled the role of hero, by partaking of "justifiable retaliatory action" in an arena outside of white authority. [115] This story and the players' actions are perhaps less surprising due to the historical context. In the aftermath of World War II, racial tensions were heightened. The presence of uniformed black soldiers was met with hostility by white southerners and those same soldiers were increasingly unwilling to accept the indignities of Jim Crow passively. As a result, some African Americans began to reject segregated seating and accommodations, often resulting in violent confrontations. [116] The confrontation between the Buckeyes and the white men was emblematic of a more widespread conflict over the enforcement of segregation. When the patrolman questioned the players, their manager, Trouppe, persuaded the officer to search elsewhere for the assailants. These men successfully performed their role as heroic badmen, by not attracting general public notice and negative publicity, while still achieving a means of racial justice. [117]

Throughout the Jim Crow era, African Americans struggled to define manhood on their own terms. The conception of the New Negro manhood provided an outlet for individuality that had been missing under previous conceptions of black manliness. Limitations still existed, though. As black baseball advocates strived to ensure the profitability of their black enterprise and to pave the way for integration, the public behavior of African American fans and players came under scrutiny. In the interwar period, owners and writers promoted black baseball players as respectable men, even while those players tested the limits of acceptable public morality.

In the 1930s and 1940s, sportswriters glossed over any unsavory conduct on the part of players and instructed fans on how to behave at games. At the same time, many African Americans were unwilling to revert to the "gentleman" model of the early twentieth century to please elite reformers. Instead, they continued to gamble, flirt, drink, and carouse within the confines of local black communities, a strategy that would keep such behavior an open secret. More explicit challenges to white supremacy and the color line manifested themselves in newspaper editorial art, photographs, and advertisements. Likewise, African Americans capitalized on a vernacular expressive culture to circulate trickster tales; tales that celebrated black baseball players' masculinity and their performance as "badmen."

THREE

Representing Race
Black Baseball and Visual Images

In the nineteenth century, Currier and Ives produced a number of prints that featured baseball. In 1882, as part of their Darktown series, Currier and Ives produced a print entitled *A Base Hit*, depicting a group of African Americans ineptly trying to play baseball (Figure 3.1). The artist, Thomas Worth, was a freelancer who specialized in comic/caricature prints and was responsible for Currier and Ives's Darktown series as a whole. Worth would sketch a scene and then submit it to Currier and Ives. If they deemed it acceptable to print, they would compensate Worth for his work.[1] In the print, three African American players dive and stumble for the baseball. At the same time, a passerby is hit by that baseball and knocked off his feet. Examining the background of the print, four players are simultaneously occupying first base, while three players in left field are lounging rather than playing. Additionally, Worth drew the players in the foreground of the picture in a way that exaggerated their facial features and reflected nineteenth-century stereotypes about African Americans.

Other Darktown comics devoted to baseball played upon the same racial imagery of "A Base Hit." In one such print, published in *Harper's Weekly*, the baseball diamond is the scene of complete chaos (Figure 3.2). The artist crowded the print with caricatures of African Americans, none of whom can successfully participate in the game. The players seem to have little if any understanding of the rules of baseball, lacking even the knowledge of where or how to stand on a diamond. A player in what would roughly be considered the shortstop position has adopted a catcher's crouch, while the entire right side of the field (first base, second base, right field) appears to be devoid of fielders. The artist also portrayed the athletes as unable even to follow the sporting action as they all are looking in different directions. Adding to the confusion, the batter is not in a proper stance, but instead is attempting to hit the ball off of his own face, presumably because no one has taken on the role of pitcher.

In this print, the artist also reproduced minstrel stereotypes.[2] The stereo-

A BASE HIT.

BASE-BALL AT BLACKVILLE—THE "WHITE STOCKINGS" AGAINST THE "BLACK LEGS"—FIRST BLOOD FOR THE "BLACK LEGS"—[DRAWN BY SOL. EYTINGE, JUN.]

types include that of the lazy black man, as many of the men in the foreground are reposed, and the black dandy represented by the overdressed umpire with hat, long jacket and cane. It is important to note, however, that Worth's depiction of the clothing choices of the baseball umpire reflects more than a stereotype. From the days of slavery to the present, African Americans have embraced stylized clothes to challenge presumptions about their wealth and status, and those choices have often become a source of controversy and conflict in larger American society. In the Jim Crow era, black men like the umpire both contradicted stereotypes that conflated class and race and expressed their own vision of how a man should dress by employing the sartorial signs of the rich.[3]

In contrast, Currier and Ives prints of contemporary white baseball emphasize a serene, well-organized game, in keeping with white baseball's claims to be a dignified and truly American sport (*The American National Game of Base Ball*, Figure 3.3). The white baseball print depicts a professionally played game on a well-maintained and manicured diamond. The players are in proper position. All is orderly and calm. The players are amateurs, yet they approach the game in a serious and even reverent manner. The white umpire, unlike his black counterpart, is dressed in an unremarkable, staid gray jacket.

These Currier and Ives prints helped to spread and reinforce the public opinion that African Americans were not qualified to play the "national game." In the first half of the twentieth century, African American publications challenged such prevalent negative stereotypes through the valorization of black athletes and recreational sport. In particular, major black newspapers such as the *Chicago Defender* and the *Pittsburgh Courier* highlighted Negro Leagues baseball in their news coverage, devoting regular column space and resources to the coverage of black baseball.

This chapter interrogates mass-media published images of black baseball that were produced and disseminated in the 1915–1946 era, the golden age of the Negro Leagues. As discussed in the previous chapters, larger societal moves to support black enterprise and to facilitate progress toward integration marked this time period, particularly the latter half of the era. Within this context, one

Opposite, top: **Figure 3.1: Thomas Worth, "A Base Hit," Darktown Comics, Currier and Ives, 1882. Worth's Darktown series was popular in the late nineteenth century. Meant to tickle the fancy of whites, these comics traded on then-popular ideas of the inferiority of African Americans. In this image, the exaggerated facial figures and the farcical actions of the black subjects align with contemporary arguments that African Americans were animalistic.** *Bottom:* **Figure 3.2: Thomas Worth, "Base Ball at Blackville," Darktown Comics, Currier and Ives, 1882. Another of the Darktown Comics, this drawing promotes the idea that African Americans are inept in the sporting realm.**

THE AMERICAN NATIONAL GAME OF BASE BALL.

Figure 3.3: Currier and Ives, *The American National Game of Base Ball,* **1862. In contrast, Currier and Ives's prints of Elysian Field memorialized white baseball as pure, organized, and pastoral (courtesy Library of Congress).**

can analyze these images to answer the following questions: How did African American newspapers and magazines portray black baseball? What implications did these images have for the readers of these periodicals? What do these images communicate about societal and cultural ideals of African Americans during this time period? Finally, how did these images reflect contemporary expectations regarding race, class, and gender?

Black press images challenged the implicit and explicit racist assumptions inherent in negative white depictions of black athletes. For the readership of publications like the *Courier, Defender,* and *Afro-American,* the dignified portraits of sporting stars granted their athletic idols the respect they had earned at the ballpark, on the gridiron, and in the boxing ring, and still were often denied by the white press and white sporting fans. Contemporary pieces of editorial art on the pages of black newspapers attacked the hypocrisy of segregated baseball and proclaimed the moral and athletic superiority of the Negro Leagues. These visual images reflected black fans' observations and beliefs about the athletic talent possessed by their favorite Negro Leagues ball players. As such, pos-

itive visual images performed a crucial function in an era when widely disseminated images of African Americans at play reinforced the exaggerated racial
stereotypes common in minstrel shows. Through these images, African Americans could visualize a different type of reality and perhaps a different future,
one in which talent trumped skin color.

* * *

The Darktown prints, as part of a larger late nineteenth/early twentieth
century trend, used visual images that depicted African Americans as primitive
and oafish. With the wide dissemination and popularity of the prints, they
helped to spread and reinforce the public opinion that African Americans were
not qualified to play the "national game."[4] In the first half of the twentieth century, with the influx of black migrants to industrial cities, African American
publications challenged such prevalent negative stereotypes through the valorization of black athletes and recreational sport.

Among white papers, the *Chicago Daily News* was unusual in its early and
positive depiction of African American baseball players. By 1903, the *Daily News*
began to cover black baseball occasionally and the few local integrated high
school level baseball teams. Chicago public schools had an official policy of integration. In reality, however, white citizens and officials worked to ensure that
schools had sufficiently imbalanced racial makeup. As a result, Chicago high
schools were frequently disproportionately white or black. African American
students were permitted to compete on public school athletic teams but "did
not share in social activities." Private and Catholic schools in the city did enforce
segregation.[5]

Daily News photographers documented members of the Chicago black
baseball clubs in a variety of shots. The initial 1903 photographs showed an
integrated high school baseball team in Chicago.[6] By 1905, the white press's
limited coverage of black ballplayers featured segregated semi-professional baseball teams competing in the Chicago area. Many of these photographs were
group shots, with the team aligned and posed in a way familiar to any reader of
the sports pages. These pictures had the same composition as those made of
contemporary white baseball teams.[7] In addition to the familiar team shots, the
Daily News photographers also captured individual players in posed configura-
tions. These poses were meant to suggest live action shots (the players are in
motion, batters in stance, pitchers in wind-up), but the backgrounds of the photographs betray their artificial nature. In one picture, a batter is shown in stance,
but without a catcher or umpire.[8] Likewise, in the photos of the pitcher, the
field is devoid of any other players.[9] In a 1909 series of photographs, most of the
pictured show the players on the sidelines, clearly outside of the playing field,

again in mock-motion.[10] The *Daily News* also published photos from a 1907 interracial game between the Leland Giants and a squad of white all-stars.[11]

While one would expect a white newspaper to cover the meetings between a white and black squad, the *Daily News'* attention (although limited) to black baseball within Chicago demonstrates both the importance of black baseball to Chicago during the early part of the twentieth century and the short-lived, more fluid racial lines that characterized industrial cities like Chicago in the years preceding the Great Migration. The posed nature of the picture and the similarities to those of contemporary white teams suggest that the photographers for the *Daily News* made little distinction between white and black baseball teams and players during the first decade of the twentieth century. Indeed, the fact that the *Daily News* bothered to cover black baseball, particularly outside of interracial contests, indicates that the newspaper was either trying to reach out to a black readership and/or that the white readers of the paper were interested in black baseball.[12] While it was not unusual to see coverage of black ball in other white newspapers of the time, most of these papers were in smaller markets devoid of professional baseball and merely reported on any traveling baseball team that made a local stop. Chicago, on the other hand, had a thriving major league baseball scene, with both the Chicago Cubs and Chicago White Sox competing regularly in the city. In either situation, the presence of these photographs indicates a less restrictive racial climate in Chicago during this time period, at least as it applied to sport and leisure.

This more benevolent treatment of African Americans would be short-lived. Before World War I and the attendant increased need for labor in urban centers, African Americans residing in the North did not generally encounter widespread, explicit segregation and racially based violence. The growing black population had a significant impact on racial relations in northern cities. With the advent of World War I, confluent concerns of ethnic nationalism and black migration created very regimented ethnic neighborhoods within cities like Chicago.[13] According to historian Allen Spear, "many whites ... felt threatened by Negroes. They responded by attempting to tighten the color bar in housing, schools, and public accommodations. Failing that, some resorted to terrorism. The occasional skirmishes of the prewar period gave way to organized guerilla warfare."[14] Recreational spaces frequently served as flash points as black and whites fought to carve out public spaces for leisure.[15] This hardening of de facto segregation within Northern cities, particularly in regards to leisure space, resulted in a more strict racial division in public recreation.

Black visual images of sport during World War I and the early 1920s greatly ranged in tone depending on the periodical. Magazines like *Half-Century* published largely positive photos and drawings of baseball players and games.

Posed pictures like the ones in the *Chicago Daily News* were common in *Half-Century*. These photographs, featuring a player in batting, pitching, or catching stance, accompanied laudatory articles celebrating the athletic achievements of the subject. Despite its location in the urban center of Chicago (and perhaps because of it), *Half-Century* published cover drawings that reinforced the mythical pastoral nature of baseball. These images were much more aligned with the *National Pastime* print by Currier and Ives, than with the Darktown Comics. The May-June 1923 cover, for example, depicted a young boy sitting at a fence, watching a baseball game through a knothole in the fence (Figure 3.4). Above the fence line, the hats of the various spectators were visible, while the background showed a rural setting for the game.

The editorial choice to romanticize baseball as a rural, gentrified event reflected *Half-Century*'s focus on promoting respectability. *Half-Century* downplayed the masculinity of black men by featuring male black athletes only within the interior sporting pages. *Half-Century* did sometimes run covers with African American adult males. These pictures, however, generally featured black soldiers, who seemed less threatening to the black elite community due to their added legitimacy and authority as members of the military. Black soldiers, particularly during World War I, symbolized hope and promise for many African Americans.[16] The young baseball fan on the cover was a non-threatening youth, while the baseball field itself was free of gamblers, hustlers, and the encroachment of urban settlements. Thus, the fence obscured the social baseball scene with which most Chicago baseball fans would have been familiar, and the generic rural setting divorced Negro Leagues baseball from its normal urban, industrial environs.

In addition, the use of the knothole iconography traded on a well-established American image of the young, innocent boy watching a game through the hole in the wooden fence surrounding a ball field. Periodicals like *Sporting Life* printed sentimental prose and poetry that celebrated the knothole gang. In 1904, sportswriter Ren Mulford, Jr., waxed nostalgic about his days as a young man watching a baseball game through a knothole and claimed that he "loved the old game with the same intensity that marked [his] youthful adoration."[17] Likewise, a 1910 poem romantically immortalized the knothole:

> It was narrow,
> It was small,
> But 'twas big enough
> Every youngster took his turn if he had sense.
> There in brotherhood they came,
> There they learned the nation's game,
> At the little, jagged knothole in the fence.[18]

The twinned emphasis on the Americanism of baseball spectatorship and the wholesomeness of a young boy's love of the game reinforced the intercon-

Figure 3.4: "Baseball Fans," *Half-Century Magazine*, May-June 1923. In this cover illustration, a young African American boy takes in a game through the "knot hole," an undertaking that was often glorified in nostalgic prose by white male writers of this age.

nection of baseball and American life. White baseball fans and sportswriters used the trope of the knothole gang to create a common identity, one that marked them as upstanding American men and citizens. The absence of African Americans as players from the national pastime also excluded them from claiming those markers of manhood so crucial to the early twentieth century ideal of the American man.

Half-Century Magazine's employment of this much loved iconography of white Americana allowed African Americans to assert their own connections to the American pastime and, hopefully, to the privileged status of male citizenship. At the same time, the illustration romanticized the African American childhood with the same tones of nostalgia and innocence found in the poetry and prose of white journalists.

Despite their general absence as cover models, black male athletes appeared within the pages of *Half-Century* with some frequency. In 1919, *Half-Century* began to include a section entitled "Sporting News." These one-page articles generally discussed a particular black athlete who had achieved national fame for his athletic achievements. Although these athletes came from a variety of sports, including football, baseball, basketball, boxing, and track and field, their photographic images shared a great number of commonalities. Photographs of the athletes often accompanied the text and depicted them dressed in proper uniform while assuming a serious pose and looking directly into the camera. In these photographs, the black athlete claimed additional authority through his association with organized sport and recognized teams.

In contrast, the major black newspapers, like the *Courier* and *Defender*, used visual images not only to promote black baseball but also to challenge segregation and white supremacy. The *Pittsburgh Courier* published one of the more arresting images countering the racist arguments against the integration of the major leagues. In this editorial drawing, the central image is a depiction of a black baseball player in a "Negro Base Ball" uniform. The player points at smaller figures representing white baseball and signs saying "bribery," "more scandal 1924," "organized baseball—I'm glad they bar me!"[19]

This image represented a strong counterargument to the prohibition on African American players in the major leagues. The small signs referenced white baseball's embarrassing scandals. The "White Sox 1919" referred to the Black Sox scandal, in which eight Chicago White Sox were found to have accepted money in exchange for throwing games during the World Series.[20] The Black Sox scandal resulted in the establishment of a major league baseball commissioner to maintain the integrity of the game. Kenesaw Mountain Landis vehemently yet unofficially opposed integration during his long tenure as commissioner. Even under Landis's notoriously iron grip, gambling scandals plagued the major leagues. The 1924 scandal highlighted by the artist refers to a game-throwing scheme by New York Giants Cozy Dolan, Jimmy O'Connell, and Phil Douglas. Hal Chase, one of the players mentioned, was involved in throwing numerous games through the 1910s. Bennie (Benny) Kauff, the other player included in the illustration, stole a car and was implicated in a gambling scandal.[21]

By referencing the scandal-plagued days of major league baseball, the artist clearly asserted the superior position of black baseball players. During a period when the term "organized" baseball referred only to white baseball and implied inferiority on the part of the Negro Leagues, the cartoon inverted the language. Members of the black press highlighted the moral shortcomings of the white major leagues to provide a counterargument to the assertions that the Negro Leagues were unorganized and black players lacked character.[22] Subsequently, the black readership witnessed a reversal of terms and morality. Black baseball had not suffered the public humiliation of thrown games and therefore was superior to the "organized" game. Negro Leagues players, therefore, were fortunate to be "barred" and spared an association with a tainted game. African Americans, frequently bombarded with admonitions to behave in a way consistent with racial pride and progress, had role models in black baseball stars who were metaphorically (and visually in the image) above the fray.

In the 1930s, as the Negro Leagues expanded and more teams began barnstorming around the country, black baseball gained wider attention in the white press. Depression-era owners, promoters, and sportswriters recognized the added significance of interracial games that lured fans anxious to see their race prevail on the field. Concurrent with this trend, white press coverage of the Negro Leagues increased. This coverage was often limited to short notices announcing an upcoming game or short recaps of previous competitions. At times, however, these white papers would include additional information about certain star players and their performances.[23]

Satchel Paige, the most famous of all Negro Leaguers in the 1930s and 1940s, often found himself as the subject of these white newspaper articles and the accompanying visual images, which frequently played upon the racial stereotypes of the time. Quotes from players like Paige were printed in dialect rather than in proper English, to underscore both the Southern origins of many of the players and the assumed inability of a black man to speak in anything other than dialect. This type of implicit racism has an incredibly long legacy. African American athletes still struggle with these stereotypes. Sportswriters and broadcasters frequently praise particular black athletes as "articulate," implying that most black athletes lack eloquence. The same commentators rarely if ever remark upon the speaking abilities of white athletes.[24]

A Chicago article announcing Paige's appearance at Comiskey Park portrayed Paige as a buffoon without intellect to match his physicality. Entitled "He's Just a Big Man from the South," the article referred to Paige as "Mistah Paige"; the other ballplayers in the story deferred to the author as "suh"; and the author noted that Paige's athletic prowess, especially his pitching practice of "throwing baseballs at those stuffed cats at carnivals," had allowed him to keep "himself in cigars and his girl friends in kewpie dolls."[25] Throughout the article, the author, Bob Ray, described Paige as little more than an overgrown child who just happened to have a talent for baseball. In an attempt to diminish Paige's significance and originality, Ray claimed that Paige's stunt of pulling in his outfielders before facing a batter "was a trick Rube Waddell made famous."[26] He also solidified Paige's reputation among white observers as an entertainer who embraced both the Jim Crow system and racial stereotypes rather than as a professional baseball player. Even though Ray's editorial noted that "Satchel is quite a pitcher and if it weren't for his color he'd be in the big leagues," the reporter's glorification of racial stereotypes and his unwillingness to fault the white major league's color line revealed a paternalistic and dismissive attitude toward the athletic achievements of Paige and the Negro Leagues.[27] Moreover, his overall portrayal of Paige reinforced negative racial stereotypes that conceptualized black baseball as a diversion and white baseball as a truly skilled sport.

In 1935, when Paige played for the North Dakota–based and interracial semiprofessional Bismarcks, the *Bismarck Tribune* devoted a great deal of press to Paige and his teammates. Interracial baseball in North Dakota had a short and intense period of success in the mid–1930s. In 1934, an integrated Jamestown, North Dakota, semiprofessional team undertook a barnstorming circuit that included several games against a white team with members such as Jimmie Foxx, Jimmy Dykes, and Tommy Bridges. The Jamestown club managed to win several of their contests against the barnstorming major leaguers. Inspired by their success, Neil Orr Churchill, owner of the rival semipro Bismarcks, lured Satchel Paige and a significant number of Jamestown's black players to his club. With black stars like Paige and Ted Radcliffe as well as highly competent white semipro players, the 1935 Bismarcks drew large crowds and attracted national attention when they won the *Denver Post* semi-pro championship. Semipro fans, players, and owners recognized the Denver tournament as the ultimate test of a team's quality.[28]

In the 1930s, race relations in the upper Midwest were complicated. Residents readily welcomed black ball players and supported interracial baseball. Yet, seemingly without contradiction, local papers advertised Ku Klux Klan meetings in concert with interracial games.[29] These types of racial tensions also extended to black baseball experiences in Canada. Black American baseball players competing on barnstorming tours in the Canadian Maritime provinces encountered tensions. The black touring teams were popular with Maritime residents, yet "to attract fans, they often had to cultivate an image of 'otherness' that played upon white racial theories about the different characteristics of the races."[30] In essence, Maritime and Midwestern fans fetishized and embraced what they viewed as the exoticism of black baseball rather than supporting a less racially restrictive world.

This unease with aspects of integration would bring about the end of integrated semipro baseball in North Dakota. After a successful 1935 season and alleged interracial romances between Paige and local white women, the North Dakotans started to turn against the players. According to Mark Ribowsky, "[c]heering Paige on the mound as his team went for the town's first championship of any kind was one thing; offering up their daughters to a black man's bed was another."[31] Sources from the time recall that Paige had been warned to at least be discreet in his interracial romances while in Bismarck, but the absence of his wife and the desire to enjoy himself proved irresistible for Paige.[32] Shortly after the accusations of illicit romances, Paige fled North Dakota and joined the Kansas City Monarchs.[33]

Toward the end of Paige's tenure in Bismarck, the *Tribune* printed a cartoon illustration announcing that Paige had signed with the Kansas City Monarchs. The illustration seized upon numerous racial stereotypes and derogatory racial images (see Figure 3.5).[34] Accompanying the large rendering of Paige's face (which exaggerated the size of his lips) are four smaller pictures meant to portray Paige's athletic abilities and his pitching position. The smaller illustrations portray African American men in an animalistic mode. In particular, the rendering of the black boxer that describes Paige's delivery as possessing the "dynamite in a Joe Louis Punch" depicts a black man who resembles a gorilla more than a man. This illustration exaggerates the torso and minimizes any facial expression. Similarly, the depictions of the track stars (Jesse Owens and a hurdler) are elongated and devoid of facial features. The smaller drawing of Paige himself obscures all but the contrast between the blackness of his skin and the white of his uniform. The caption on this drawing cautions "no Elmer, not an Ethiopian War Dance—just Satchel Paige winding up" and prompted the reader to associate Paige as an exotic native African tied to strange tribal traditions, rather than as an accomplished African American man and athlete.

These images and accompanying text diminished Paige's success by questioning his claim to be a skilled and trained athlete. They also reinforced the notion of racialized otherness that marked the interest of and appeal to many white fans in places like the upper Midwest where African Americans were a rarity. By dehumanizing and emphasizing the exoticism of African Americans, black players like Paige were once again separated from larger society. In this

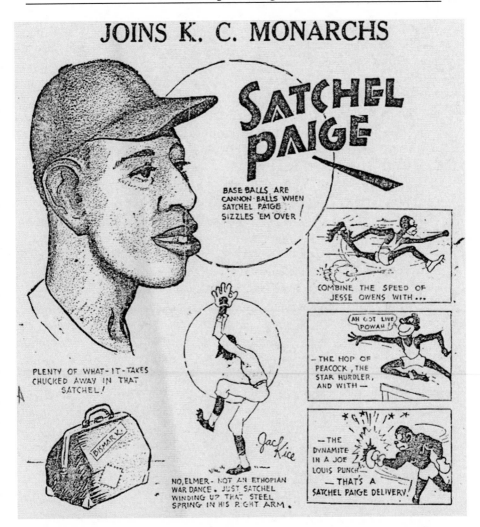

Figure 3.5: "Joins K.C. Monarchs," *Bismarck Tribune*, August 28, 1935. This illustration by the *Bismarck Tribune* advertises the great athletic achievements of Satchel Paige, while undercutting that message with stereotypical renderings of black men in the side images (courtesy *Bismarck Tribune*).

instance, it was not strictly through Jim Crow segregation, but by the denial of black humanity.

Skill was an important commodity within black baseball. All of the stakeholders for black baseball benefited from the skilled performance of black players. The black elite and black press used the public display of skill in the Negro Leagues to push for increased recognition of racial success and to lobby for integration, while Negro Leagues owners highlighted the skill of their players to sell more tickets and fill the stadiums.[35] The *Chicago Defender* published a series of illustrations by George Lee that emphasized the skill and accomplishments of black baseball players.[36] Lee's illustrations centered on a realistically drawn portrait of the player in question surrounded by smaller blocks of cartoon-style illustrations and text. The text and sub-illustrations highlighted the accomplishments of each player. The cartoons retain a caricature-like style but do not trade on the animalistic stereotypes of black men common in white visual media at the time. Lee also employed a more vernacular speech style in his Melvin Powell illustration, in particular, yet does not resort to the exaggerated dialect used by white sportswriters to denigrate the intelligence of black players.

For the players themselves, attaining the label of "skilled" athlete reinforced their claim to manhood. A number of players noted with some pleasure that baseball success was predicated on skill and a keen mind for strategy. As Bill Foster recalled, "It was a long time before they found out that he [the black athlete] could actually think technically. They thought we could think just generally, but they didn't think we could think things out in detail. They didn't think we could think and remember a set of signals."[37] In an era when racially-biased intelligence testing was used by eugenicists to prove black racial inferiority, a black athlete's intellectual prowess challenged the prevailing stereotype.[38] Success in baseball, a sport that emphasized strategy, refuted the idea that black athletes succeeded only through "brute strength" or speed.[39] Black boxing and track stars could be, and were, dismissed as impressive physical beings who won because of their bodily gifts rather than with strategy. Baseball's reputation as a more thoughtful game meant that it was more challenging to minimize black baseball success.

Thus, the stereotypical images of African American athletes as buffoons were all the more distressing to black advocates of sport. Two of the more well-known white New York baseball writers, Dan Parker and Jimmy Powers, repeatedly employed derogatory imagery. Similar depictions appeared in contemporary comics as well. In the first half of the twentieth century, cartoonists capitalized on derogatory stereotypes, such as "sambo," "mammy," "savages," and "pickaninny" in their portrayal of African American characters.[40] Caricatured illustrations of African Americans in sport frequently accompanied Powers's and Parker's columns, sending an unmistakable message to their readers. These illustrations echoed Currier and Ives's Darktown Comics in tone and racial insensitivity.[41] The artists portrayed both players and umpires as incompetent and drew the subjects as dark and animalistic. The captions and the dialogue in the cartoons used dialect and played upon racial puns. A player being chased by an umpire calls to the chaos of the Darktown comics and transforms black baseball into a sideshow. The dialogue attributed to the player includes interjections like "Yowsah!" and reinforces the stereotype of the uneducated, unsophisticated black man.

In one cartoon included in a Parker column, the umpire declared to a fan that the game "was called on account of darkness." This text referenced an older, racial joke that also had a baseball setting. In 1916, a New York–based magazine called *The Independent* included the joke in a humor column, reprinting it from *Harper's Weekly*. This version of the joke was even more problematic and mean-spirited as it was told at the expense of an elderly African American woman. "The boys of Wallace University Schools were playing baseball on an empty lot in Nashville, Tennessee, when the game was interrupted by an old negro woman crossing the lot, and a small boy called out, 'Game called on account of darkness.'"[42]

Within his column, Parker compared Negro Leagues outfielders to "infants chasing balloons." Parker also made disparaging comments about the fans and the marching band, comments that seized upon popular racial stereotypes of the time. Parker described the band members as having "huge, flat feet" that "trampled" the grass in a way that had never before happened and argued that the band wanted to play the "blues" rather than the traditional march they performed. He also claimed that the band members were "aping the white folk who are always out of step" despite the fact that "Colored brethren" were "ordinarily blessed with a fine sense of rhythm."[43] Later, Parker took the fans to task for a lack of "jollity" and attributed the sedate nature of the crowd to the number of white people in attendance.[44] Black attendance was down, Parker noted, because the same teams planned to play a doubleheader the next day "to take advantage of the bargain bill."[45] Parker was implying that it was finances keeping black fans from the park on Saturday, May 18, 1935. What was more likely is that, like so many other African Americans in the 1930s, black baseball fans were working Monday through Saturday, and Sunday (the day of the doubleheader) was their only day of leisure. Although finances were certainly an issue for many black fans, it was leisure time that was the limiting factor and as a result, Sunday games were the most well-attended.

Despite their use of derogatory images and language, both Powers and Parker approved of racial integration of the major leagues. Parker publicly called for the breaking of the color line as early as 1933 in response to a *Pittsburgh Courier* inquiry. Parker declared, "I don't see why the mere accident of birth should prove a bar to Negro baseball players who aspire to places in organized baseball."[46] The 1935 illustrations in his column demonstrate that even supportive members of the white press saw no harm in publishing stereotypical images of African Americans. Moreover, Parker concluded his 1933 letter by stating his fear that integration might cause the Yankees to "lose their great mascot ... 'Bojangles' Robinson." Within this phrasing, Parker patronizingly reinforces an African American star's subordinate role in white society.[47] Bojangles is not a fan or supporter in the mind of Parker, he is a mascot, a pet, clearly inferior to the white players and fans.

Jimmy Powers published his column from 1935 to 1957, during the very time when desegregation was the crucial issue facing both white and black baseball. Powers, like Parker, in at least once instance supported the integration of the white major leagues. The *Defender*, in a note preceding a reprint of a Powers column, compared him to William Lloyd Garrison and John Brown and praised "his campaign for admittance of Race baseball players into the big leagues."[48] The article was triumphantly titled "White Sports Writer, Backed by N.Y. Daily, Fights for Race Players in Major Leagues!" With this title, the *Defender* reshaped Powers into an activist reformer. Powers did not quite live up to the Garrison and Brown comparisons in much of the rest of his writing. In addition to the racially offensive cartoons embedded in his column, Powers voiced negative opinions about black athletes in general. Powers launched particularly virulent attacks on Joe Louis, calling the boxing champion "a vain kid, or dumb" and referring to a 1939 Louis fight as a "pre-conceived pig-sticking" event.[49] Perhaps unsurprisingly, considering the negative stereotypes perpetuated in his columns, his support of the campaign for integrated baseball proved short-lived. In a 1946 "Sports Beat" column, Wendell Smith noted Powers' continued objection to integrated baseball as well as his dislike of Branch Rickey due to Rickey's decision to "break up the lily-white policy of organized baseball."[50] Smith also reported on a racially offensive skit performed by New York sportswriters. In this skit, Jackie Robinson was portrayed as a butler and white baseball commissioner Happy Chandler was Robinson's "massa."[51] The similarities between Powers's and Parker's racist visual images and the slavery-themed skit that stripped Robinson of his agency underscores the pervasiveness of racial stereotypes in the 1930s and 1940s.

The black press countered the offensive images published by the white media through its use of editorial art. These images do not rely on panels or storytelling and thus are more akin to political cartoons than to comic strips. At the same time, a number of these drawings instruct or describe instead of providing a satiric look at a current event. Frequently these illustrations utilize a much more realist style of art than their cartoon counterparts although the artists sometimes combine realistic sketches with smaller comic drawings in the same panel.[52]

The black press published caricatures that challenged the stereotyped images of African Americans as minstrel-like characters. In contrast to the depictions of Satchel Paige, Joe Louis, and Jesse Owens published by the Bismarck, North Dakota, paper, papers such as the *Baltimore Afro-American* presented dignified photographs and artistic renderings of black athletes. The sport-themed editorial art celebrated the achievements of African American sport celebrities. In instances when these images were critical of black sport, they generally attacked the infighting among Negro Leagues owners rather than individual players. In other critical pieces, the artist was prescriptive and cautioned fans to exercise restraint after important victories by African American athletes to prevent racial riots.

Photographers of the Homestead Grays and Satchel Paige presented their subjects in a dignified manner in fitting with the respectable public image sought by black baseball. These photographs clearly contradicted and challenged the more prevalent comic illustrations of black athletes as popularized in the Darktown comics and comic strips like *Felix the Cat*.[53] A 1938 photo of the Grays featured the team members in alignment, dressed in clean, matching uniforms under the headline "Here They Are! Baseball's Kings of Swat!" Notably, the *Courier* headline writer felt no need to specify that the Grays were black baseball's "kings of swat." For *Courier* readers, the Homestead Grays were baseball, so no differentiation was needed. Individual portraits took a similar approach, with the player either in a subdued motion or standing still, looking into the camera. The headline typically proclaimed the outstanding athletic ability of the man in question and the caption provided further information about the individual's background and accomplishments.[54]

The editorial art featured in the sporting pages of the black press underscored the important accomplishments and abilities of men like Joe Louis. The artists used a more naturalistic approach in some cases, attempting to capture the subject accurately. In addition, these images communicated what the black press believed were important messages about conduct. With the memory of the riots that followed Jack Johnson's victory over Jim Jeffries still fresh, black periodicals warned their readership to avoid any confrontations in the days leading up to Louis's 1937 title bout against James Braddock (Figure 3.6). A *Baltimore Afro-American* cartoon cautioned its readers that their behavior could have dire consequences both for the community as a whole—"Louis will be the last colored man to get a crack at the title if you guys start painting the town"—and potentially for their own sons in particular: "A scrap in your neighborhood may keep your boy from a chance at the title when he grows up." Both of these warnings were designed to prevent violent outbursts or overly exuberant public celebrations in the aftermath of what many believed was the inevitable outcome—a Louis victory. Notably, Francis Yancey, the cartoonist, includes a figure in the brawl who represents potential white antagonists. A suited man is being held

Figure 3.6 "Joe Louis Fight Bulletin," *Baltimore Afro-American*, June 19, 1937. Prescriptive warnings like this one in the *Afro-American* were common in the lead up to major fights that feature Joe Louis. Black papers not only sought to report on stories of interest to African Americans but also aimed to use their influence for the betterment of their communities (courtesy *Afro-American* Newspapers Archives and Research Center).

back, but continues to shout "[b]low your top, son." This man encourages the younger African American man to fight as the rest of the image warns against engaging in such altercations. Through this character, Yancey implies that there would be those white men who would try to lure black men into a fight, knowing that ultimately the black man would be harming himself and his race. The white man becomes a sort of devil-like seducer, baiting young men into action that could have long-term negative repercussions for all African Americans. As predicted, Louis did win the bout and became the first black heavyweight champion since Jack Johnson.[55] African Americans celebrated in their homes, the streets, bars, and clubs, cheering for their hero, mindful both of the title's significance and the repercussions of any public violence.[56]

Similarly, two 1937 cartoons in the *Baltimore Afro-American* poked fun at the administrative and contractual difficulties in the Negro Leagues. Because the leagues were frequently in flux and the owners were often at odds over the best way to run the league, Negro Leagues politics provided an easy target for a sports-minded humorist. This pleased black baseball fans frustrated by chaos and inconsistency within the leagues that often resulted in teams folding and players jumping from team to team. Even in these critical pieces of editorial art, the artists were careful to preserve at least a basic level of dignity and respectability for their subjects. As these artists took satirical aim at the mismanagement of the Negro National and American Leagues and the willingness of black athletes to seek their fortune elsewhere, the figures were mostly devoid of stereotypical features for their African American subjects.

In Figure 3.7, the players, though sketched rather crudely, did not reflect any of the animalistic or minstrel-like characteristics of the Darktown comics or the North Dakota–Paige cartoon. Instead the artist created a retrospective of the 1937 season for his readers. That was a significant year for Negro Leagues baseball. It marked the beginning of a nine-year streak of championships for the Homestead Grays, led by Buck Leonard and Josh Gibson. A new Negro American League was established in 1937 as well.[57] The *Baltimore Afro-American* cartoon provides the sporting press's view on these major events. The National League is depicted as a giant, blown-up creature, subjugated by the trim and superior Homestead Grays. The American League, on the other hand, is beset by squabbling, particularly between the two most venerable league members, the Chicago American Giants (the deceased Rube Foster's team) and the Kansas City Monarchs (still under long-time owner J.L.Wilkinson). In the end, both the cartoonist and the rest of the American League are left to wonder at the infighting and to bemoan the "bad breaks" that kept them out of championship contention. The cartoon critiques the internal conflicts that variously threaten to destroy or blow up the professional black baseball leagues in the late 1930s.

Figure 3.7 "Negro National League," *Baltimore Afro-American* July 17, 1937. Sports-writers and editorial cartoonists for black papers walked a fine line between advocating for black sport and criticizing its management. Here, the *Afro-American* shines a light on fundamental problems with the Negro National League (courtesy *Afro-American* Newspapers Archives and Research Center).

Additionally, Yancey makes sure to remind his readers of the always-present economic struggles of black professional baseball. Sitting astride the bloated National League, the Grays figure advises that they should "save the plate" to "use at the end of the season," a reminder to fans and Negro Leagues stakeholders of the potential financial instability.

One of the threats to the stability and profitability of black baseball in 1937 is pictured in a second *Baltimore Afro-American* cartoon. Entitled "Money Shouts Even When It Whispers So Soft and Low" (Figure 3.8), this editorial art also relied on quick sketch-type images to adhere to the cartoon-like style of illustration. In this image, the players once again escaped visual denigration, while the artist showed a symbolic figure representing Negro National League owners in a more negative light. With one exception, the owners were collectively represented as a large angry man with exaggerated facial features, clearly under duress and a bit confused by the actions around him. This portrayal emphasized the degree to which the black press often depicted Negro Leagues ownership as out of touch and lacking control. This critique was an internal but important one, and functioned as a warning of sorts to Negro Leagues ownership. Black sportswriters continually pushed, cajoled, and demanded professionalism and competency from black owners and players. To many in the black press, racial progress would arrive only with black achievement that fit with the ideals of respectability so prized among African American reformers. As often was the case, these rebukes were meant to be kept within the community whenever possible. In the national conversation on segregation, black leaders and writers worked to present the best possible public image of their athletes and owners and served as de facto public relations officers for members of the race, selling their achievements and respectability to an often skeptical white power structure.

The other major figure in the image was that of "Santo Domingo," a stereotypical portrait of a wealthy Hispanic-Caribbean man. This mystery man clearly represents Dominican Republic dictator Rafael Trujillo and his agents. In 1937, Trujillo, through intermediaries and donations, sponsored a baseball team known as the Dragones de Ciudad Trujillo. Looking for the best talent for his roster, the manager of the Dragones, a dentist named Dr. Jose Enrique Aybar, secured the services of Satchel Paige with a substantial salary and money to recruit other black ballplayers to join the team. Paige was successful in luring away star players like James "Cool Papa" Bell and Josh Gibson from other winter ball commitments.[58] Many of the players who joined the Dragones came from Gus Greenlee's Pittsburgh Crawfords. In the cartoon, Greenlee sits on a chair and wonders if he "will ever get [his] nine back." Greenlee was hit doubly hard by the defections of the players. Not only did he bear the brunt of most of the

Figure 3.8: "Money Shouts Even When It Whispers Soft and Low," *Baltimore Afro-American*, June 12, 1937. The 1937 defection of Satchel Paige and other Negro League All Stars was a matter of great concern for black baseball owners, sportswriters, and fans (courtesy *Afro-American* Newspapers Archives and Research Center).

player losses on his own team, at the time of their departure he was serving as president of the Negro National League, and thus bore responsibility for the health of the league as a whole.

The experience of Paige and his compatriots in the Dominican Republic was quite mixed. Paige, Bell, and others returned to the United States with stories of playing under the threat of imprisonment if they were to lose. In reality, these threats were likely mere rumor and innuendo spread among the team and inspired by measures taken by team officials to disincentivize late-night carousing on the part of the ballplayers.[59] Rafael Trujillo was a dangerous and deadly dictator, however his energy and interest was directed towards the elimination of Haitians and the solidification of his own iron rule rather than towards ensuring victories on the baseball field. In 1937, the year that Paige and his teammates played in the Dominican Republic, Trujillo engineered the massacre of more than 10,000 Haitians in what became known as the Parsley Massacre and was clearly a campaign of genocide.[60] The black baseball players were seemingly unaware of the genocide and enjoyed most of their time in the Dominican Republic. Likewise, editorial art like what ran in the *Baltimore Afro-American* focused on the lure of money from the Caribbean rather than on the horrors of life in the Trujillo dictatorship. "Santo Domingo" was drawn as an island paradise with easy money meted out by local businessmen, rather than as it was in 1937. No longer Santo Domingo, in 1936 it had become Ciudad Trujillo, the namesake of the ironfisted ruler and a symbol of his ruthless and overwhelming power.[61]

Within African American communities, especially in urban areas like New York City with both substantial black and Latino migrants, attitudes toward Latino baseball players varied.[62] The Negro Leagues teams had a substantial number of Latino players on their rosters as major league baseball's prohibition against black players extended to dark-skinned Latino athletes as well.[63] Black sportswriters generally spoke of Latino ballplayers in favorable terms, viewing them as fellow victims of Jim Crow. Yet, in some instances, black writers employed racialized language to differentiate African American players from those of Latino descent. For example, a *Chicago Defender* sports writer described the players on the Cuban Stars as "little brown men" and singled out one of the Stars' pitchers by calling him a "cool little islander."[64] Two years later American sportswriters used the same designation "little brown men" to describe Japanese athletes competing in the 1932 Olympics.[65] Sport historian Mark Dyreson has highlighted instances during the 1932 Los Angeles Olympics in which members of the local population conflated Japanese athletes with Mexican residents, forbidding the Japanese representatives from entering segregated businesses.[66] To at least some Americans, people who did not fit into either a black or white racial category were dismissed as some sort of "brown" other.

During Jim Crow, Latinos, Asians, and American Indians challenged the bifurcated racial system in the United States, as their liminal status as neither white nor black could not easily fit into a system of segregation designed to separate white from black. The presence of Latino athletes from diverse racial, ethnic, and cultural backgrounds complicated a system that required simplistic racial identification. As historian Adrian Burgos, Jr., has pointed out in his study of Latino baseball players, "Latinos were the main group used to test the limits of racial tolerance and to locate the exclusionary point along the color line."[67] Indeed, Latino players' liminal racial status in the United States had implications for their media depictions in both the black and the white press. The black press was alternately welcoming and dismissive of Latino players participating in the Negro Leagues.

Black newspapers' editorial art featuring Negro Leagues players was not always positive and celebratory of black achievement. As previously mentioned, black cartoonists used the platform of editorial cartooning to critique and rebuke behavior that they found problematic and detrimental to the larger cause of racial success. In other instances, the artists reflected on the inherent vulnerability of black sporting stars, particularly in the age of Jim Crow and white supremacy. Black reformers and sportswriters had born witness to the rise and fall of African American athletes as a result of racial problems. The foremost example of the fallen black athlete and the cautionary tale for those who followed him was the heavyweight champion, Jack Johnson.

Johnson's legal woes and conviction on Mann Act charges fueled the fears of African Americans, who quite rightly understood that their athletes would be held to a much higher moral standard in larger American society than their white counterparts. Extramarital dalliances, late-night partying, and excessive drinking would not be laughed off or dismissed as a colorful character flaw. Instead, many black sport stars who dared to violate moral norms, especially the legal and de facto American prohibitions against interracial romance between a black man and a white woman, strived to uphold a squeaky clean image for the good of their reputation and their race. Advisors, coaches, mentors, and sportswriters encouraged black athletes like Joe Louis, Jackie Robinson, and Jesse Owens to marry young, cultivate an image as a family man, and avoid public relationships with white women.[68]

The black sporting press and public were especially concerned about the perceptions of black athletes as symbols of the race as a whole. A piece of editorial art in the *Baltimore Afro-American* documented the perceived vulnerability of black sport stars in the 1930s (Figure 3.9). In the cartoon, track and field stars Jesse Owens and Eulace Peacock stand on Kings' Row alongside other black luminaries. Alongside Olympics gold medal winner Owens and his main rival

Figure 3.9: "King's Row," *Baltimore Afro-American*, July 10, 1937. African American sports fans and writers, having witnessed the public disgrace of black sporting stars like Jack Johnson, cheered new heroes at the same time they feared a misstep that would result in their fall from grace (courtesy *Afro-American* Newspapers Archives and Research Center).

Peacock (who was unable to compete in the 1936 Olympics due to an injury), the visible members of the pedestaled group included light heavyweight champion boxer John Henry Lewis, featherweight champion Henry Armstrong, and high jumper Ed Burke.[69] The "kings" wait to welcome Joe Louis, who was climbing the steep and winding path to black celebrity. Louis had won the heavyweight title just a couple of weeks earlier. This achievement had allowed him to ascend to the higher pantheon of black sport stars and had resulted in a metaphorical crowning in the cartoon. As Louis reaches the peak, the contemporary black baseball champions, the Pittsburgh Crawfords, are trailing behind him. The Crawfords had not yet achieved the same sort of overwhelming fame and success that Louis had, but were making a name for themselves with their impressive summer showing in 1937.

At the bottom, just beginning his journey on the "comeback trail," was boxer Kid Chocolate. Chocolate, born Eligio Sardinias-Montalbon, was a Cuban boxer of African descent who had once held the junior lightweight and featherweight titles. In 1937, Chocolate's fans held out hope for a comeback, that he might regain the titles that he had lost starting in 1933. The artist of the cartoon clearly shared that hope and considered Chocolate a still viable enough candidate for black sport superstardom in 1937. Chocolate spent 1937 in a flurry of fights, 24 in all, anxious to regain some of his previously held titles.[70] At the time of the drawing, Chocolate is still at the bottom of the path, but carries a suitcase of 16 wins, indicating his early success in his attempt to regain his title. Alas, it was not to be. A year later, in 1938, Chocolate retired from boxing, having failed to climb that "comeback trail."[71]

Most notably, the artist depicted Jack Johnson as part of the tableau. Johnson can be seen off to the side of the image, sliding down the hill to ultimate disgrace, having fallen from Kings' Row. In this image, as in life, Johnson was an ever-present shadow that lurked at the edges of black sporting life, a reminder of the cost of indulgence and what passed as impudence in an age of white supremacy. Owens cautioned Louis, "If you think it's hard to get up here, Joe, wait'll you see how tough it is to stay up here." Having achieved the almost impossible in becoming only the second black heavyweight champion, Louis still had to face danger and instability. His obstacles in maintaining his status were clear: he must not succumb to his boxing rivals (like Kid Chocolate vainly climbing the comeback trail) or any external temptations and inner demons (both represented by Jack Johnson's free-fall). In this illustration, the artist underscored the competing demands African American athletes faced and the immense vulnerability of those who made it to the top. The most potent underlying threats in these cartoons were firmly in the hands of the white power structure in 1930s sports: the potential denial of boxing licenses, the continuation of the color line, the indignities of Jim Crow. Were these men to transgress the racial and moral codes, they expected banishment, loss of income, and denial of opportunity.

The other major threat to those on Kings' Row was that of financial instability and continually changing structures. This threat is the one that would topple the Crawfords on their march to Kings' Row and the one that had already pushed Eddie Tolan from the heights of athletic stardom. Tolan won two gold medals in the 1932 Olympics in Los Angeles and was justly celebrated by American sports fans, especially African Americans.[72] Dubbed the "World's Fastest Man," Tolan returned from the Olympics, not to glory but to a quick and steep fall from grace. The Olympics movement's insistence on amateurism made it challenging for athletes to establish a career and to gain a significant salary. There were relatively few opportunities for athletes like Tolan to make a living, especially during the Great Depression. At the time of Jesse Owens' triumphs in the 1936 Berlin Olympics, Tolan had been stripped of his amateur status because of his participation in vaudeville acts with Bill "Bojangles" Robinson. He also had failed to make progress toward his lifelong dream of becoming a physician. Unable to pay for further education and barred from further athletic competition, Tolan was trapped by the difficult economic realities for African Americans in the Depression.[73] By the time of the publication of this cartoon, the Crawfords had already fallen off the path, having been lured to the Dominican Republic with promises of generous salaries.

Even those securely ensconced on the lauded Kings' Row found their careers curtailed and complicated by Jim Crow and financial limitations. Cartoonist Francis Yancey could not have predicted that many of the "Kings" would fall victim to the same fate and disappointments that plagued Tolan and Kid Chocolate. Henry Armstrong would struggle with booking bouts due to segregation policies in certain arenas and fought against the overwhelming media interest in Joe Louis, which left him a sidelight at best.[74] Jesse Owens struggled to find sufficient employment and participated in many of the vaudeville performances that Eddie Tolan had engaged in to make ends meet.[75] Ed Burke's greatest obstacle came not from other high jumpers or racial discrimination, but from timing. In 1937, the sporting press had identified Burke as the most promising high jump prospect for the 1940 United States Olympics squad. The outbreak of World War II forced the cancellation of both the 1940 and 1944 Olympics, dashing Burke's prospects for Olympics success.[76] John Henry Lewis's boxing career (under the management of Gus Greenlee) would come to an end in 1939 after a defeat by fellow race man and boxer, Joe Louis.[77] Louis himself would fall victim to economic mismanagement and tax violations after his ascension to the pinnacle of black sporting success with his 1938 defeat of German

Max Schmeling, in a fight that was viewed by Americans and Germans as a proxy fight for the two belligerent nations as they moved toward war.[78]

Other promising black athletes never had the chance to finish the climb towards Kings' Row. Ozzie Simmons, a talented, sophomore running back at the University of Iowa, had been favorably compared to football legend Fritz Pollard and was being lauded as the next great player in college football within many sports pages. During an October 26, 1934, game against a rival squad from the University of Minnesota, Simmons was knocked unconscious multiple times in the first half of the game and was unable to compete meaningfully.[79] Commentators at the time were conflicted about whether or not the Minnesota Gophers players had targeted Simmons because of his race or, alternatively, if Simmons' own Iowa teammates had neglected to block for him, leaving him open for violent hits. In the *Chicago Defender*, a sportswriter offered a dissent, claiming that Simmons was targeted as the best player on the team; race was not a factor. Even if the violence against him was not racially motivated, Simmons would experience other limitations in his sporting career due to his race. Despite his accomplishments, Simmons was not named an All-American or awarded any post-season honors; he was not elected captain; and he was unable to join the NFL due to professional football's 1934–1945 color line.[80] For Simmons and others like him, the uphill path to Kings' Row was both treacherous and insurmountable. One can imagine another version of Yancey's cartoon, this one with large fissures and chasms that the athletes would fall into as they vainly tried to ascend.

Yancey's use of a cliff as the pedestal was visually arresting and, more significantly, incredibly apt in terms of capturing the great fall that was not just possible, but likely, for black athletes who made it to the top. Having ascended to the height of fame as African American sporting stars, the strategy to maintain that status was not as clear as the path to it. What was one to do to maintain the delicate status quo? For most of these athletes, financial issues (made all the more pressing because of Jim Crow racism) caused the foundation of their success to crumble and resulted in their loss of stature. Their supremacy would be fleeting and, regardless of their willingness to conform to the standards of race respectability, many would fall due to larger issues of racism and its attendant lack of economic opportunity.

Regardless of these obstacles and challenges, all of which Yancey makes clear in his drawing, the artist maintains a real sense of pride and optimism regarding black athletic achievement. Even as he highlights the pitfalls of sporting fame and the vulnerability of black athletes, Yancey expresses his (and by extension the black community's) great joy at the national and international achievements of black athletes. Yancey draws himself into the frame, commenting "if these guys keep up this championship stuff, I'll get crownitis." In this statement, the artist demonstrates optimism and hope for the future (couched in the slightly crotchety persona of a put-upon journalist), while acknowledging the difficult racial climate for black athletes. Yancey was not alone in maintaining this balancing act within the black press. Black sportswriters also tried to walk a fine line between a realistic account of the indignities and obstacles of Jim Crow while at the same time celebrating the accomplishments of African Americans and promoting a progressive narrative that presumed a gradual improvement in American race relations.

Yancey, thus, was attempting to put forth two competing yet often complementary narratives in many of his cartoons. Starting with the Joe Louis championship cartoon, continuing through the cartoons of the Negro Leagues, and finishing with his Kings' Row image, his readers could conclude that although black athletes had provided the community with much to celebrate, danger still lurked on the horizon. Individual battles may have been won, as their race men emerged victorious from title bouts and Olympic Games, but the war itself—a war of racial discrimination—was far from won. And, as is frequently the case in war, the black press was calling on both the front line athletes to continue their valiant fight but also on the home front, the black fans, to do their part by battling racial misconceptions in the stands, around the ring, and on the streets.

To counter the potential negative forces in the national media, the black press emphasized the professionalism and respectability inherent in the Negro Leagues. Unsurprisingly, given his fame within black baseball, a number of papers highlighted Satchel Paige in their editorial art, illustrations, and photographs.

For instance, in 1941, the *Chicago Defender* portrayed Paige in a much different manner than the white papers, emphasizing his skill and making a direct point about the inherent inequality of the prohibition against black players in the major leagues. The image printed in the *Defender* depicted Paige in mid-wind-up, in a naturalistic manner. Significantly, Paige was drawn true-to-life for the main picture, rather than as a caricature, in contrast to the coverage in the Bismarck paper's cartoon in the mid–1930s (Figure 3.5). Making a political point about segregation, the *Defender* artist chose to show Paige's opponent and audience as white men. In the lower corner of the block, Paige successfully gains another base while a white infielder waits in vain to receive the ball. In the upper right hand corner, three white men (explained to be major league pitchers) appear perplexed with questions marks over their head. These men are shocked at Paige's remarkable pitching speed and are literally blown away (they are drawn as pushed back in shock and surprise). According to the caption, "[b]ig time pitchers from the major leagues sit up and take notice when Satch starts tossing the ball around."[81]

The *Defender's* illustrator thus attacks the fundamental rationalizations for the major league color line through the depiction of Paige's athletic prowess. Throughout the illustration, Paige triumphs over white baseball figures, be they fans, scouts, or players. Each is stymied by his abilities, which negate the argument that major league teams barred only those who were insufficiently talented. Within this editorial cartoon, the artist argues not for mere equality or sufficiency of talent, but for Paige's overwhelming dominance. The cartoon shows Paige to be vastly superior to contemporary major league pitching, not just "chinking" Jim Crow but directly attacking the underpinnings of white supremacy.

In witnessing Paige's pitching, his observing white counterparts are also moved to assert his manliness. Remarking "whotta man," these major league pitchers affirm Paige's (and in turn other black athletes') claim to manhood. A successful claim to American manhood was a fundamentally necessary step to gain civil rights and respect during Jim Crow. The *Defender's* depiction of Paige emphasized both his success and his aptitude as one of the main arguments against the continued segregation of major league baseball.

As Negro Leagues attendance increased with the start of World War II, the potential integration of the major leagues became a pivotal issue on the sports pages of the black press.[82] Black sportswriters continued to utilize Paige as a major tool in the fight for integrating major league baseball. Paige's high profile among both black and white baseball fans made his image one of the most easily recognizable in black baseball and the most powerful symbol of black baseball success and ability. In a 1942 *Opportunity* article, William Brower argued that it was "time for baseball to erase the blackball," supporting his contention with examples of the "Negro players whose skills qualify them for major league play, but are boycotted because of their skin."[83] The article included a few photographic illustrations, highlighting the most renowned Negro Leaguers of the time: Josh Gibson, Willie Wells, Ray Dandridge, Henry Williams, Mule Suttles, and the omnipresent Paige. Paige's picture stood out among the rest, however. The first two photographs were traditional and mostly unremarkable. The photograph of Gibson depicted him in motion, and the picture of Wells, Dandridge, Williams and Suttles was a posed group shot. Paige's photograph, however, made a pointed argument against segregation, while bolstering claims of the white establishment's acknowledgment of his baseball prowess.[84]

In the photo, Paige, dressed in New York Yankees pinstripes, appeared to be in conversation with three well-dressed white men: Joe Williams, Grover Cleveland Alexander (famed white major league pitcher), and New York mayor

Fiorello La Guardia (Figure 3.10). The picture communicated a great deal to the readers of *Opportunity* magazine. Paige's pinstriped uniform recalled the most famous and well-regarded franchise in major league baseball, the New York Yankees, underscoring both his qualifications for such a team and the color line barrier that prevented him from joining such a team. The picture was taken before a Black Yankees game at Yankee Stadium, the figurative center of the white baseball world. Once again, Paige's restricted access to major league facilities, and Yankee Stadium in particular, underscored the hypocrisy of white baseball's policies. Paige could appear at Yankee Stadium under rental agreements that shuttled profits to white park owners, but could not compete there as a major league player.

Figure 3.10: William A. Brower, "Time for Baseball to Erase the Blackball," *Opportunity 20* (June 1942). New York in the 1940s was the geographical center for discussions of and action toward the potential integration of baseball. In this press photograph, a white politician, Fiorello La Guardia (center, in stands), and a baseball star, Grover Cleveland Alexander (to La Guardia's left), are photographed with the most famous man in black baseball, Satchel Paige.

On a basic level, the mere presence of these men at a Negro Leagues game lent legitimacy to black baseball in the mind of white baseball fans and bolstered black fans' and players' desire for access to the major leagues. Even for those advocates of black baseball as a truly black enterprise, the ultimate goal was the elimination of the color line in the major leagues, achieving integration.

La Guardia, in particular, made a powerful statement by appearing in the photograph. As a supporter of baseball integration and mayor of a city with three major league franchises, La Guardia's presence symbolized to black fans that some progress was being made toward integration. In 1944, La Guardia appointed a ten-person commission "to study racial discrimination in professional baseball." The committee, which included New York Yankees president Larry MacPhail, Brooklyn Dodgers' president Branch Rickey, and tap dancer/entertainer Bill "Bojangles" Robinson, recommended "that the major leagues lose no time adopting a policy whereby Negro Players would receive equal opportunity for advancing."[85] This report publicly and formally addressed the issue of the unwritten color line. Nine years before the 1954 *Brown vs. Board of Education* decision, this committee acknowledged that separate was not and could not be equal.

La Guardia threw out the first pitch at Negro Leagues games at least twice in the 1940s, in May of 1941 and September of 1942. In fact, the picture in Figure 3.10 may be from the May 1941 game, at which Paige pitched the first game of a doubleheader. Despite these seemingly progressive actions, La Guardia had a mixed record on race during his tenure as mayor. In 1935, La Guardia "commissioned ... but refused to publish" E. Franklin Frazier's "report on the 1935 Harlem uprising." La Guardia presumably objected to the findings of Frazier and his committee, who concluded that "the white police camped in Harlem" were "the enemy," and that problems of "discrimination, health, jobs, housing, crime, police brutality..." were "brought on not by the African American residents but by racial oppression."[86] Unwilling to confront the more insidious and institutional racism within his city, La Guardia was anxious to mollify African American voters when possible. Throwing out ceremonial first pitches and forming nonbinding committees to study segregation in baseball were easy ways to curry favor with his black citizens without having to effect real change or alienate white voters.

Regardless of La Guardia's mixed record on civil rights, Paige's presence among powerful white men, in both the political and athletic worlds, reinforced the common knowledge among black baseball fans that Paige was known as a prominent athlete outside of the Negro Leagues, among the very men who could influence the segregationist policies of white baseball, if they so desired. Paige's demeanor in the picture was equally noteworthy; he stood tall, smiling, looking Hall of Fame pitcher Grover Cleveland Alexander directly in the eye. In fact, La Guardia was the only subject seemingly aware of the camera lens. The framing of the picture and the expression of the subjects implied an equality not often found in contemporary depictions of interracial groupings.

Scanning the crowd in the background of the photo, readers would have noticed the integrated crowd that had gathered to watch Paige and the Black Yankees compete. In the audience, African American patrons occupied choice seats directly behind La Guardia. Consequently, black baseball fans, inspired by wartime calls to institute racial equality on the home front, would have viewed the favorable seating for black attendees as an important shift. Not only did this picture indicate that Paige and his fellow players might earn a chance to break the baseball color line, but also that black fans could more fully participate in the consumption of baseball as a leisure activity.

World War II and the service of African American soldiers in the war effort increased the pressure on major league baseball to integrate and provided important visual imagery that the black press used to intensify media attention to the disparity between the treatment of African Americans at home and the ideological basis of U.S. involvement in World War II. The black press seized on World War II as a potential turning point for home race relations early on. Much like DuBois had with World War I, black journalists argued for increased rights and equality for black servicemen. Most notably, the *Pittsburgh Courier* launched what it dubbed the "Double V Campaign" on February 7, 1942. The two Vs represented two victories, one abroad against fascism and one at home against racism and inequality. The black press lost few opportunities to point out the hypocrisy and disconnect between American political rhetoric of freedom and equality and the lack of fundamental civil rights for African Americans.

The 1944 *Negro League Yearbook* seized on wartime imagery to expose the hypocrisy of the color line in baseball. The cover artwork showed an African American soldier throwing a grenade superimposed over the image of a Negro Leagues player throwing a baseball (Figure 3.11). On the cover, both men are in the same stance and have similar facial expression. Particularly within the context of the Double V campaign of the World War II era, the cover sent a clear message. How could the United States deny black men, who willingly served in the military, the same rights and opportunities as white men? The published images of the World War II era employed a similar strategy as that undertaken by black periodicals during World War I. By invoking the powerful imagery of a black soldier, the *Yearbook* spoke to African Americans angered by the injustice of living in a segregated society and to the increasing numbers of sympathetic white Americans who felt that men who were willing to die for their country should not be denied opportunities in the major leagues.

In choosing to highlight a black soldier throwing a grenade, the editors of the *Yearbook* seized upon a visual image that would have disturbed a number of white Americans. During World War I, the black press was careful to de-emphasize the underlying potential for violence and armed resistance inherent in black soldiers. Yet, at the time, even a photograph of an unarmed black soldier in uniform could be viewed as a subversive and dangerous act. Portrayals of armed black soldiers, therefore, served as a potent symbol of the potential power and strength of black men.[87] Black soldiers participating in the violence of war were exerting their masculinity in a noble, patriotic manner, thus adhering to the ideal of (white) American manhood. According to scholar Patricia Turner:

> The anti-black rumors that circulated during wartime reflect the ambivalence, insecurity, and uneasiness felt during a time of crisis. The dominant culture did not embrace the idea of training black men to shoot, but the idea that they

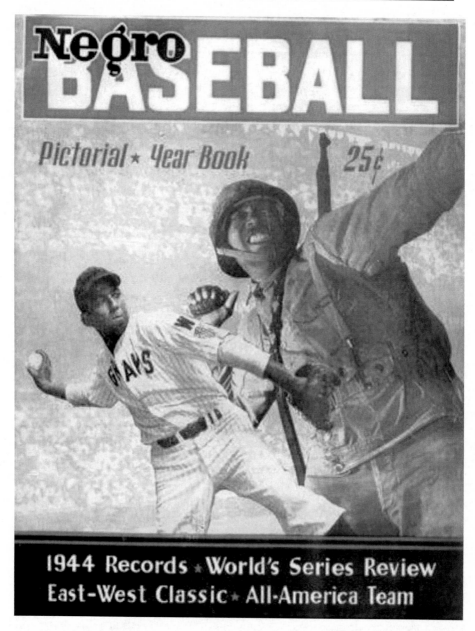

Figure 3.11: *Negro Baseball Pictorial Yearbook*, 1944. Allusions to the valiant wartime service by African Americans were often used by black institutions during World War II to claim legitimacy and civil rights. The Negro Leagues effectively employed the mirrored images of a pitcher and soldier as a visual reminder of African American participation in World War II.

share the risk of being shot at was perfectly acceptable. Blacks were empowered, in short, by America's need for them. A nation that had always tried to limit black access to weapons suddenly needed to train black soldiers. Few roles reinforce masculinity more than that of soldier. Whites knew, moreover, that they could not easily ask blacks to be soldiers while denying them the full rights of citizenship and increased access to the American dream.[88]

By claiming access to manhood, these men were also claiming a degree of power within American society that had heretofore been denied to them on the basis of their skin color. The editors of the *Yearbook* thus sent a message of equality and civil rights to their readers, one that highlighted the underlying strength of black soldiers and the potential rewards of patriotic service.

Similarly, weekly black newspapers highlighted the inequities of racial discrimination during a time when black soldiers were serving their country in the armed forces. The black press published photos of integrated army baseball teams, noting that major league baseball had failed to integrate while the army allowed its soldiers to participate as part of integrated teams. Photos such as the one published in 1943 underscored African Americans' desire for the end of segregated baseball and reinforced the symbolic importance of black army service in the fight for increased civil rights on the home front.

Happy Chandler, who became commissioner after Kenesaw Landis's death in 1944, reportedly made arguments similar to those of the black sporting press. Chandler pushed open the closed door in telling black sportswriters, "If a black boy can make it in Okinawa and Guadalcanal, hell, he can make it in baseball." The sentiment spread in popularity and in 1945, the "League for Equality in Sport and Amusement" held a protest at Yankee Stadium on Opening Day. Protesters carried signs proclaiming "If We Can Stop Bullets, Why Not Balls?"[89]

A number of Negro Leagues officials and players also viewed World War II as a time of great opportunity for domestic racial progress. Effa Manley, business manager of the Newark Eagles and wife of team owner Abe Manley, became very involved in the war effort on the home front, seeing the connection between successful black soldiers and the improvement of racial conditions for African Americans. Manley was one of the most fascinating and controversial figures in the Negro Leagues. A white woman who grew up in an interracial family and married an African American man, Manley spent her life "passing" as a black woman. Because of her unusual circumstance, Manley was acutely aware of the power of the color line and used it to her advantage when possible, gaining access to whites-only spaces when it could further her interests, but identifying as black.[90]

At the same time, she was deeply entrenched within her black community, serving as a very public figure and, at times, as a symbol of black womanhood.

To this end, Manley was involved with a significant number of efforts to promote racial advancement and progress. Along with the Newark NAACP, she organized a concert by Hazel Scott in response to the D.A.R.'s refusal to allow Marian Anderson to perform at Constitution Hall in Washington, D.C.[91] Manley arranged numerous fundraisers to benefit soldiers and actively promoted the Double V campaign.[92]

Within her personal files, Manley kept a copy of a musical piece given to her by a composer, Andy Razaf. Most well known for the hit "Ain't Misbehavin'," a collaboration with the famed African American pianist and composer Thomas "Fats" Waller, Razaf was an African American lyricist who protested racial discrimination and celebrated African American achievement in his musical creations.

Razaf had a history both with black baseball and with protest music. In 1920, having difficulty finding work as a lyricist, Razaf spent a year playing for the Naco Giants in the Cleveland, Ohio Semi-Pro League. Not a strong enough player to continue, Razaf returned to New York after the season and began to have better luck with music. Returning to music, Razaf found work and eventually success in his collaborations with Fats Waller. Notably, Razaf and Waller published (and staged) a song considered one of the first racial protest songs, "Black and Blue," which played with the idea of racial identity and reflected the growing anger and discontent among black New Yorkers by the end of the 1920s.[93]

At times, Razaf's radical race politics, expressed in his music, put him at odds with his own colleagues and with the music industry at large. His song "We Are Americans Too" had been written for inclusion in a comic musical, *Tan Manhattan*, that Razaf and pianist Eubie Blake were putting together in 1940. In the original lyrics, the song functioned as an overt challenge to Jim Crow racism. According to his fellow collaborators, the song was so incendiary that it had the power to completely sink the entire musical. They insisted it be left out of *Tan Manhattan* when it debuted.

Left with a song and idea without an audience, Razaf repurposed the lyrics to appease World War II Bond Drive officials and his collaborators. After he downplayed some of the more direct attacks on white racism to emphasize the contributions of African Americans to American society in a less aggressive way, "We Are Americans Too" became one of the more successful compositions in the Bond Drive campaign.[94]

The cover to the sheet music depicted black soldiers marching off to war while the lyrics recalled the history of black soldiers in America, highlighting the contribution of African Americans to the Revolutionary War, the Civil War, the Spanish American War, and World War I. The cover illustration gave visual life to that history, showing dignified black soldiers marching stoically to war under an American seal that noted "For Distinguished Service." The music and the image traded on the long history of black servicemen whose bravery and commitment to their country endured despite segregation and racially-motivated mistreatment.

The song continued on to connect the success of the black soldier with other accomplishments of African Americans. At its conclusion, the song noted the place of sport in African American history.[95] Even after the song had been revised, the critique of racism and segregation and the celebration of black historical achievement remained. Razaf had repackaged, but not truly changed, his message for America—black soldiers, artists, and others had sacrificed for their country and were not yet included as real or true Americans in the minds of many. In the South, these same men lacked basic rights of citizenship, most crucially the right to vote.

Prominent African American leaders were making similar arguments about the need to fully involve African Americans in the military and the defense industries. Walter White, then the powerful secretary of the NAACP, published an article in a December 1940 edition of the *Saturday Evening Post*, in which he used many of the same points. In "It's Our Country, Too," White noted that military service and success was based on many of the same characteristics held by great athletes—a line of reasoning that sports enthusiasts and proponents of Muscular Christianity had trumpeted in the first few decades of the twentieth century. Singling out black sporting heroes like Joe Louis, Jesse Owens, and Henry Armstrong, White concluded that "the qualities which make a good athlete are required of a flier. Of course he should have physical and moral courage as well. In all of these qualifications Negroes have given ample demonstration of their fitness."[96] Also, as in the song, White highlighted the numerous contributions of African Americans to the country's military, reminding his readers that "Negroes have fought in every war in our history and have been lauded for their bravery by commanding officers from Andrew Jackson to John J. Pershing."[97] By capitalizing on patriotic imagery, a history of athletic success, and historical examples of black military bravery, both Razaf's song and White's article made persuasive arguments for the acceptance of racial equality within the United States, especially within the armed forces. White concluded his piece by noting that "the average Negro ... is, therefore, hanging on to his faith in democracy and going grimly ahead, determined to carry on his shoulders a fair share of the burden of its defense."[98] The illustration on the sheet music provides the visual counterpart to White's word, showing those black soldiers marching off to give their all for a country that did not fully accept them as citizens or men.

In addition to its emphasis on past military service and black sporting achievement, the song also made a direct connection with African American accomplishments in the arts. The music's title, "We Are Americans Too" and its subject (the continued racial inequality of the United States) echoes the famous poem by Langston Hughes, "I, Too, Sing America." In the poem, Hughes claims his part of the American dream and story, regardless of white Americans' unwillingness to acknowledge it. He describes the American experience as a dinner party, one in which black Americans are sent off "to the kitchen." Despite this lack of respect and inclusion, he can "laugh, and eat well, and grow strong," confident that in the future, he "will be at the table ... and they'll see how beautiful I am ... I, too, am America."[99] In both Hughes's poem and "We Are Americans Too," African Americans celebrate and acknowledge the beauty and success of the race, while anticipating a future in which they, too, can claim access to both the American dream and American identity. An even more direct link can be found in a poem Razaf wrote titled "Negro Volunteer." In the poem, Razaf echoes Hughes's lines, repeating the image of the table as the United States.

> As long as men, steeped in hypocrisy
> Reserve the table of Democracy
> For just the chosen ones, to wine and dine
> While only crumbs are left for me and mine.[100]

Razaf's take on the possibility of racial progress is much less hopeful than Hughes's and underlines his intense ambivalence toward the war effort and African American involvement in World War II. His bleak poem and challenging but more celebratory song capture the multitude of positions African Americans took regarding the War as well as the ways in which these two almost contradictory messages could co-exist within an individual. World War II, many (including songwriters) believed, was to be the opening of a door for African Americans. They held out great hope that the patriotism and service of black men would finally be enough for white Americans. Their participation in the American military victory would allow them to claim the privileges of American manhood and womanhood. For others, the war was just another crisis in which African Americans would courageously fight and serve, to be rewarded with a continuation of Jim Crow policies. In the latter instance, black men and women would continue to wait for their seat at the table that they had secured.

Within Negro Leagues baseball, officials and players capitalized on wartime changes to increase attendance numbers. Kansas City Monarchs owner J.L. Wilkinson specifically considered the implications of the war effort in his attempts to draw larger crowds for his team. Wilkinson took advantage of the increasing number of workers who migrated to Kansas City to find defense work during the war by scheduling games in accordance with their work schedules.

Wilkinson also approved advertisements in the *Kansas City Call* that portrayed Uncle Sam as a promoter for the Monarchs. Moreover, Wilkinson made charitable overtures that emphasized his commitment to the war effort by admitting uniformed soldiers without charge to Monarchs games.[101]

Satchel Paige also seized upon World War II as a platform by which he could gain further publicity. Unsurprisingly, Paige's motives were not purely due to his commitment to racial uplift and progress. Throughout the late 1930s and 1940s, Paige battled with Negro Leagues owner and officials over the extraordinarily profitable East-West All-Star Game. Paige and his fellow players were well aware of the financial windfall that the All-Star Game represented and were also conscious of the fact that their pay paled in comparison with the profits of the owners.[102] In 1942, Randy Dixon, writing for the *Pittsburgh Courier*, noted that "players of each squad were paid but 50 dollars apiece and the umpires received a puny $15 for their labor," which is "why Negro baseballers regard their owners as Shylocks and Chiselers" considering that the "game draw [was] 48,000 spectators with a gross of better than $50,000."[103] Particularly with the record attendance at the East-West game in the early 1940s, players' longstanding frustration with what they saw as insufficient compensation bubbled to the surface.

Determined to get a larger share of the take, Paige participated in numerous ploys to persuade owners to compensate the players more generously. In 1943, Paige teamed with Josh Gibson and threatened to boycott the game unless his financial conditions were met. The owners, anxious to hold on to the two marquee names of black baseball, acquiesced.[104] The following year, Paige made a similar attempt to increase the players' share. When he negotiated alone, however, the owners decided they could hold the game without him. Paige then forced the league's hand by making the negotiations into an issue of patriotism. Claiming that all he wanted was for the league to donate its profits to a charity for World War II soldiers, Paige publicly claimed he would refuse to play unless the All-Star Game was staged as a benefit game. Biographer Ribowsky has noted, however, that Paige only requested the charitable donation after being refused a greater percentage of the gate.[105] Paige ultimately failed to convince the league officials to more equitably split their profits, but this crusade was indicative of an already established Paige strategy. Paige seized upon the imagery of World War II for self-promotion throughout the era. During an earlier 1940 contract dispute with the league, after he had once again jumped to a better paying opportunity after signing with the Manleys' Newark Eagles, Paige compared the league's treatment of its players to "Hitlerism" in an interview with the *Richmond Afro-American*.[106] The quip was certainly hyberbolic, but Paige was aware of the power of the Hitler image, particularly in the African American community, and was unafraid to deploy it for his own purposes.

With the wartime decimation of white male baseball, increasing numbers of fans, especially white fans, turned to black baseball and the new (and all-white) All American Girls Professional Baseball League. "Club owners have both the pace hastening ramifications of World War II and the unprecedented publicity accorded Paige ... by white writers to thank as being directly responsible for this box office renaissance."[107] The Kansas City Monarchs attracted large biracial crowds, averaging almost 7,000 fans each game. Bruce notes that the Monarchs consistently attracted a larger crowd than the local white minor league team, the Kansas City Blues, despite the Blues' ties to the Yankees, and consistently successful seasons.[108] Restrictions on wartime travel and gasoline rations also increased attendance in the home cities of many Negro Leagues teams. Starting in 1943, restrictions by the Office of Defense Transportation (ODT) limited the amount of barnstorming undertaken by black baseball teams. They were only allowed to travel a maximum of 700 miles in a one-month period, players needed to use their gas rations for bus travel, and both Negro Leagues were advised to use train travel when possible. After extensive lobbying, Negro Leagues owners managed to gain concessions from ODT on the basis of difficulties with segregated transportation in the Southern states. Even with these alterations, barnstorming, the lifeblood of Negro Leagues profits, was challenging during the war.[109]

It is important to note that black baseball also witnessed significant player losses due to World War II. According to one contemporary article, "[a]lthough there is no definite way of determining the accuracy of this statement, Negro baseball probably has sent more of its stars to war than any other professional sport of comparative stature." Black baseball remained popular and viable due to the longstanding Negro Leagues tradition of hanging on to very veteran players, at a point at which contemporary white players would have retired or been released. The name recognition of these veterans was too valuable a commodity for black baseball owners to relinquish. Thus, many of the famous black ballplayers who did not serve in World War II were at an age where military drafting was not an option.[110]

Adding to the practical issues of war service was the complicated history of African Americans in the military. Some African American men, particularly young working-class men, did not willingly enlist and instead actively avoided the draft. Malcolm X and Dizzy Gillespie were two of the "hundreds, perhaps thousands of zoot suiters and musicians who dodged the draft" because "they opposed the war altogether, insisting that African Americans could not afford to invest their blood in another 'white man's war.'"[111] The lack of racial progress following World War I convinced some African Americans that their participation in the war would be futile. They feared that once again the second V of the

Double Victory campaign would not be won. Instead, black men would fight, suffer, and die (often in subservient roles) for a country that did little to ensure their civil rights and protection at home. Even after President Truman's 1948 integration of the military through executive order, the heart of the argument, black citizens being asked to serve a country that treated them as second-class citizens, would persist. Muhammad Ali would make a similar argument during his fight to avoid induction in the Vietnam War draft.[112] Even within the Negro Leagues, there was some ambivalence about the drafting process. Effa Manley, publicly an enthusiastic supporter of the black war effort, worked behind the scenes to try to procure special considerations for her Eagles players, so that they might not have to serve.[113] She also in at least one instance attempted to use the threat of war time service to punish players who had jumped contract to play in Mexico. In 1943, she alerted the Selective Service, informing them that Willie Wells and Ray Dandridge had left the country. Manley hoped to have them brought back but was told they were on deferment and could travel freely.[114]

Increased spectatorship in the early 1940s was accompanied by a revival of attention to black baseball on the part of the mainstream white media. Feature articles on Satchel Paige appeared in *The Saturday Evening Post*, *Life*, and *Look*. Although these articles did bring increased white national attention to Paige and black baseball, they also reinforced disparaging racial stereotypes. The *Saturday Evening Post* article, in particular, painted Paige as a clowning caricature, a "Stepinfetchit" character.[115] Consequently, black baseball seized the opportunity to make yet another concerted push for the integration of major league baseball.[116]

Media depictions of black baseball in the first half of the twentieth century were powerful pieces of visual propaganda designed to persuade viewers of particular racial and political views. *Half-Century Magazine*, the *Chicago Defender*, and the *Pittsburgh Courier* employed sporting images, particularly those of black baseball, to advocate a particularly middle-class view of racial uplift. Others, like those in the *Baltimore Afro-American*, made pointed critiques of segregation, fan behavior, and baseball politics. Meanwhile, white newspapers and commentators continued to depict black baseball as an enterprise marked by incompetence and played by minstrel-type characters. Particularly with the advent of the clowning teams of the Depression Era, black baseball players had to negotiate between the extremes of racial pride and profitable marketing campaigns that emphasized "tribalness."

Through the space of visual imagery within the black press, African Americans contested the limitations and presumptions of segregation. With photographs and editorial art, the black community established a distinct counterargument to notions of white athletic and moral superiority. Especially in using editorial art, African Americans refashioned a medium that had previously reinforced and disseminated notions of white supremacy. By explicitly promoting black baseball as a viable (and at times preferable) alternative to the white major leagues, the black press sought to support the Negro Leagues as a race enterprise and build the foundation for the eventual breaking of the major league color line.

Similarly, black baseball players and fans constructed an oral culture that disseminated a similar respect for the Negro Leagues. Through the use of trickster tales and (nick)naming practices, African American baseball advocates would continue to challenge and critique segregated sport and its racist underpinnings.

FOUR

Signifying Baseball
Tricksters and Folklore in Black Baseball

The 1989 documentary *There Was Always Sun Shining Somewhere* opens with former Negro Leagues player Chet Brewer relating a story from the days of segregated baseball. Brewer describes the travails of a young African American athlete who wanted to play baseball for the local white baseball team. Day after day, the boy arrived at the ballpark and tried to persuade the manager to allow him to play with the team. By the third day, the annoyed manager threatened to call the police if he did not leave the field. Unwilling to give up his quest, the boy purchased a ticket directly behind the dugout to continue his campaign. At this point, the manager, no longer able to threaten eviction and willing to do anything to quiet the boy, relented and instructed his coach to find a uniform for the new player. Because the home team faced one of the best relief pitchers in the league, the manager believed that the persistent young boy would strike out and embarrass himself, solving the problem. With the bases loaded, the manager brought the new player in as a pinch-hitter. On the first pitch, the boy knocked a line drive back against the right field fence. As the boy rounded second base, the increasingly excited manager exclaimed "look at that Cuban go!" Brewer then delivered the punchline: "so ... with one swing of the bat, he progressed from a black boy without a job to a Cuban with a job."[1]

Trickster tales such as Brewer's were common during the days of Negro Leagues baseball. Although it is almost impossible to prove the veracity of many of these stories, including Brewer's, and others are clearly untrue, their existence and their dissemination demonstrate their significance to black vernacular culture during Jim Crow. The creation and transmission of these tales provide historians with a valuable and untapped set of texts that present additional layers of the story of black baseball, layers that cannot be found in box scores alone. Thus, these rich, and often overlooked, folkloric and humorous stories provide an opening into the study of larger issues of resistance strategies and cultural identity in a time of racial oppression. Through the use of trickster tales, African

Americans created a counter-narrative that not only damaged the foundational beliefs of white supremacy, but as such was also an important step in the campaign to end the white major league color line.

One way in which these stories functioned was to create an indirect but damaging critique of the white major league's color line. Brewer's story, in particular, presented a clear indictment of major league baseball's racial policies and practices. Under the unwritten gentleman's agreement that sought to maintain an all-white major league, white owners enjoyed enormous discretion in the determination of a prospective player's race. As such, owners signed and played talented, light-skinned Hispanic players while at the same time refusing to employ equally talented dark-skinned Hispanic players or African American players of any complexion. Brewer's tale highlighted both the racist assumptions and demeanors of major league baseball officials and the simultaneous willingness of white managers to bend the color line to win ball games. Brewer's anecdote pithily reflected and redirected African Americans' frustrations with a biracial system that constantly shifted, by exposing the glaring hypocrisy of racial categorization.

It was in this nexus of identity, opportunity, and unwritten codes that most African Americans existed in the twentieth century. Both in the North and South, African Americans had to interpret the racial atmosphere and regulations based on a careful calculation that included past personal experiences, legal codes, and informal informational networks. Decisions, often locally determined, regarding one's racial identity were particularly fraught when it came time for African Americans to choose the right race on a birth certificate, the right seat on a city bus or in a baseball stadium, the right store to patronize, and the right playground for their children.[2] For ordinary African Americans, Brewer's tale rang true to their own experiences with the fluidity of identity and color lines and formed part of a larger vernacular discussion about race that took place in the barbershops and around the baseball fields.

Throughout the Jim Crow era, African Americans employed different strategies within a vernacular expressive culture to challenge the traditional (white) stereotypes regarding black athletes. Through the use of trickster tales, African Americans asserted an alternative to the prevalent notion of white supremacy. Black baseball as revealed in its trickster tales was an organized, sophisticated institution that boasted the very best athletes—men who were quick-witted, clever, and cool.

Because most of these tales were part of African American oral expressive culture, it is difficult to situate them within a time-specific historical context. Some of these stories made appearances in the black press, but not all did. Many were passed by word of mouth, at the ballpark, in barbershops, and on the road.

Consequently, most of the documentation of these tales comes from the reminiscences of former Negro Leagues players. In a number of instances, the details of the story provide enough information to establish at least a general time frame for the events discussed. By decoding the timeline of these stories, broad temporal and thematic themes do emerge.

Generally, the early trickster tales of black baseball (roughly 1900–1920s) played on the theme of passing. A significant proportion of these tales involved African Americans attempting, or being advised, to pass as Latino or American Indian. In many cases, a famous white major league player or manager would praise a black ball player, bemoan the restriction of the color line that prevented him from signing the player, and, in some instances, persuade the player to assume a different racial identity to compete in the white major leagues.

In the 1930s and 1940s, the stories began to shift slightly. Although tales where white officials praised black players still circulated, they often did so with a significant difference. In these stories, the white player/manager often assigned an astronomical dollar value to the player in question and remarked on the player's athletic superiority in comparison to contemporary white players. This shift to an emphasis on superiority also marked the other trickster tales told during this time period. The trickster tales of the 1930s and 1940s frequently espoused the superiority of black baseball through tales that hyperbolically boasted of superhuman speed or strength, that lauded the inventiveness of black baseball, and that emphasized the intimidation of and overwhelming defeat of white (especially major league) teams and players.

Trickster tales of Negro Leagues baseball simultaneously employed two different narrative forms, the direct story and the indirect story. Trickster stories held an indirect message that communicated double meanings to African Americans listeners. Black storytellers intended for any white audiences to absorb the superficial aspect of trickster tales. Taken at face value, these trickster tales functioned as amusing anecdotes, meaningless outside of their delivery of further entertainment from and about popular black athletes. African American audiences, however, could recognize a second layer of meaning beneath the story. In this second layer, the storyteller reveals how a trickster was able to get the better of white authorities.[3]

Scholar James C. Scott, in his seminal work, *Domination and the Arts of Resistance*, termed these two levels of meaning the public transcript and the hidden transcript. According to Scott, the public transcript is clear to both dominant and subordinate groups in a society, while each group has its own additional hidden transcript that only members of the group, be it dominant or subordinate, understand. In analyzing the trickster tales of Negro Leagues baseball, it is crucial to consider both the public and hidden transcript of these tales. By utilizing tales with double meanings and transcripts, the purveyors of black baseball trickster tales infused their stories with political meaning by exposing hypocrisy in Jim Crow America.[4]

A large and important part of the hidden transcript, particularly for African Americans, is the practice of signifying. According to literary critic Henry Louis Gates, a signifying practice is symbolized by the tale of the signifying monkey and involves a series of tropes.[5]

> Free of the white person's gaze, black people created their own unique vernacular structures and relished in the double play that these forms bore to white forms. Repetition and revision are fundamental to black artistic forms, from painting and sculpture to music and language use.... Signifyin(g) ... *is* repetition and revision, or repetition with a signal difference.[6]

Thus, within the hidden transcript, one can signify on someone by playing on their words with a response that utilizes another form of meaning or by utilizing words that have double layers of meaning.[7]

To explore the hidden transcript of trickster tales in black baseball fully, one needs to understand the protagonist's role. Tricksters have a long and storied history among African Americans, taking forms from the signifying monkey to the brer rabbit. "In traditional black culture, Trickster is a material representation of the open mood. Trickster is a transformer; he provokes change. Trickster takes up and redescribes the structural features available at the margins."[8] In other words, the trickster was and is a figure with the ability to call authority and structure into question. Generally, the trickster, throughout history, has signified on racist structures. In the twentieth century, African American tricksters specifically revealed the weaknesses in Jim Crow and challenged those authorities who enforced segregation.

With the presence of its own tricksters and signifying language, Negro Leagues baseball both reflected a long cultural tradition and provided a new arena for the creation of black sporting folk heroes. As Jim Crow policies in both the South and the North externally limited access to a number of opportunities, African Americans found their heroes in institutions like black baseball and boxing, venues where African American men proved their prowess over and against white men.[9] Baseball, in particular, with its intoxicating combination of physical skill and quick-witted chatter, allowed for the development of tricksters and the practice of signifying.[10] The triumph of black manhood in terms of athletic success and verbal one-upmanship reinforced cultural and racial pride and exposed the weaknesses in racialist arguments.

Moreover, these players functioned as heroes within many African American communities. Consequently, their behaviors had significant implications for other members of their race. Folklore scholar John Roberts argued that "[i]n reality, the actions that a group recognizes as heroic are those that it perceives as the most advantageous behaviors for dealing with an obstacle or situation that threatens the values that guide action within specific temporal or social, political, and economic contexts."[11] Thus, in the first half of the twentieth century, black baseball players functioned as heroes because many African Americans viewed them as working towards racial improvement in a conciliatory manner while at the same time refuting stereotypes through their radical and trickster-like performances as celebrity athletes. As novelist and essayist Ralph Ellison noted in *Going to the Territory*, members of oppressed racial groups look to sports heroes to effect structural societal change. According to Ellison, "while the baseball, basketball, and football player cannot really tell us how to write our books, they *do* demonstrate where much of the significant action is taking place. Often they are themselves cultural heroes who work powerful modification in American social attitudes."[12]

Early tales of the Negro Leagues centered on trickster strategies to overcome the racial prohibitions of the white major leagues. In these stories, individual players, aided by sympathetic white baseball officials, attempted to camouflage themselves as Hispanic or American Indian to gain entrance to white baseball. Ultimately, most of the players in the stories rejected the possibility of passing or were thwarted by external factors.

One of the first, and most frequently repeated, tales was the story of Charlie Grant. The basic components of the story were somewhat simple. The most commonly told version proceeded as follows: In 1901, John McGraw, then and briefly manager of the Baltimore Orioles, impressed by the talents of Charlie Grant, an African American, renamed Grant "Chief Tokohama" and claimed that Grant was a full-blooded Cherokee Indian (and therefore an eligible major league player). The opposing team's players recognized Grant and exposed his racial background, thus ending the experiment before it truly began.

In one version of the Tokohama story, it was Charles Comiskey, owner of the Chicago White Sox, who stopped McGraw from playing Grant. According to one historian's account, Comiskey, in a strange game of racial chicken, threatened to play a "Chinaman" if McGraw played Grant. McGraw immediately bowed to Comiskey's countered threat, cowed either by the specter of further racial expansion in baseball or by Comiskey's unmasking of Grant. Although McGraw's and Comiskey's actions seem odd, especially to modern readers, they reveal a great deal about racial anxieties. One of the major concerns of white baseball officials was that individual integration could usher in a domino effect. If one African American was allowed to compete, the doors would be wide open and baseball would be filled with black and non-white players, crowding out white athletes.[13]

The McGraw-Tokohama story maintained its significance throughout the first half of the twentieth century and was told in many different permutations. One of the most intriguing retellings occurred in a 1940 *Saturday Evening Post* article. In a feature article on Satchel Paige, Ted Shane related the following story as told by Oscar Hammerstein, identified by the author as merely the "proprietor of a Harlem hot spot." To fool the opposition, McGraw instructed Grant to yell "wah-wah-wah-wah!" and "grunt, 'Me big black Injun.'" According to Hammerstein, this strategy was successful but Grant's cover was blown because "the Negro world couldn't contain itself. When he arrived in Chicago, he was met by the entire South side and a colored Elks band." This version of the McGraw-Grant story flips the ending and thus places the blame for McGraw's exposure on African American fans rather than white players. It also had a long legacy. A 1960 article in *Sports Illustrated* about black ball players included a similar version of the story in its history of the Negro Leagues. In the *Sports Illustrated* version, Grant passed until the beginning of the Chicago game, when "[j]ubilant Negro fans jammed the stands and waved a banner reading OUR BOY, CHARLIE GRANT."[14] Even after integration, white writers could not resist the Grant story, as long as African Americans took the blame for his unmasking.

Hammerstein's position as a white, Jewish business owner in Harlem further complicates the *Saturday Evening Post* version of the story as does the fact that Hammerstein related it to a reporter for a prominent national publication with a large white readership. One imagines that black Harlemites would have preferred the earlier iteration of the tale. In the Hammerstein version, African American fans exhibit uncontained exuberance and naivete to the apparent detriment of a black ball player. This notion contradicts evidence from a number of black sportswriters that African American fans quietly supported black athletes who were able to pass through the color line without exposing their racial background. Even when fans were anxious to unmask an athlete, they generally accepted the consolation of knowing an athlete had circumvented the color line.

It is also noteworthy that although Shane includes quotes and anecdotes from a number of (mostly unnamed) Harlem residents, Hammerstein's quotes contained only dialect when he was attributing words to Grant. Quotes from Paige and "Harlemites" were written in dialect.[15] Shane's employment of dialect when quoting black subjects or when others were quoting them reinforced racist stereotypes about African Americans. This rhetorical choice allowed Shane to highlight Paige as an athlete without challenging the white supremacy that served as the foundation of the color line. For the readers of the *Saturday Evening Post*, especially white readers, the use of dialect helped transform Paige from athlete to comic figure and undercut the work by Negro Leagues officials and black sportswriters to promote their sport and their players and professional, respectable race men.

Despite the setback, McGraw never completely abandoned his plan to sign other Negro Leagues players by masking or altering their racial identity. In a strategy made famous within Negro Leagues folklore, McGraw attempted to convince Oscar Charleston to move to Cuba, learn Spanish, and return as a Cuban immigrant so that McGraw could sign him.[16] According to Tom Gilbert, when McGraw died, his widow found his list of Negro Leagues players to sign if the prohibition of black players was lifted.[17] Numerous former Negro Leagues players and their contemporaries confirmed McGraw's involvement with black players during interviews, specifically citing him as a white manager who expressed interest in their services.[18] McGraw biographer Charles Alexander argued that his pursuit of African American players was driven by an interest in acquiring the best players. McGraw was "no crusader for racial justice ... though ... always on the lookout for new talent."[19] Unfortunately for McGraw, the Negro Leagues players he targeted were well known as black baseball players. Consequently, his attempts at subterfuge failed miserably.

Negro Leagues catcher Larry Brown told a similar story about a passing attempt in an oral interview with John Holway. In Brown's version, Ty Cobb is the one who is interested in Brown and suggests he pass as Cuban. According to Brown, his 1926 winter baseball performance in Havana impressed Cobb. Brown recalled Cobb asking "How would you like to stay down here [Cuba] and learn the *lingua* and come back to the states and pass as Cuban?" Brown turned down the proposition, reasoning that he, like Charlie Grant, was well known in baseball circles and would be recognized. This story has a major inaccuracy—Cobb played in Cuba only in 1910. At that time, Brown was five years old and obviously not yet a Negro Leagues athlete.[20] Another Negro Leagues player, John Davidson, allegedly was offered a similar opportunity and $10,000 to pass as Cuban for a New York baseball team.[21] The prevalence of this type of tale underscored the contemporary interest in the fluidity of the color line, particularly the line between Cuban and black. Following the logic of these tales and the opening story by Chet Brewer, to change race one needed only to learn a new language or if light-skinned, exhibit base-running talent. Race in these tales was an inherently fluid state of being, one that could be altered by external demands.

In an interesting twist, the substitution of Cobb for McGraw in Brown's story made the tale more provocative. Unlike McGraw, who had obtained a reputation among African American baseball players as fair and relatively free of prejudice, Cobb was known as a virulent and violent racist.[22] Negro Leagues third baseman Bobby Robinson recalled that Cobb "was a personal friend of mine" and that Cobb had praised Robinson's hands. Cobb allegedly told Robinson that "if things were like they should be, you'd be playin' third base for my team." Even at the time, Cobb's racism was not exactly a secret among African Americans or the public at large. Both the white and black press noted Cobb's racism and confrontations with African Americans. The difference in the tone and content of the coverage was telling. When the white sporting press covered Cobb's assaults on African Americans, they used the violence as a basis for jokes and puns and as evidence of the "colorfulness" of Cobb's character.[23] On the other hand, black sportswriters, including Sol White and Rollo Wilson, had reported on Cobb's violent encounters with African American employees in grave terms, humanizing the victim and condemning Cobb.[24] As a result, Cobb's background contributed to the power of the trickster tale. To impress the racist Cobb, Brown and Robinson must have been truly exceptional as Cobb clearly was not predisposed to praise African Americans. In addition, this tale reinforced the concept of the Talented Tenth, by implicitly arguing that an African American could triumph over racism through extraordinary talent.

Many of black baseball's boasts centered on and around Satchel Paige. Paige was the most well-known Negro Leagues player, among both black and white communities. Paige reveled in the attention that accompanied his outrageous statements and actions and was a masterful storyteller, fashioning near-mythological tales of everything from his own upbringing to his athletic success. Consequently, he figured prominently as a trickster character in a number of black baseball tales. Although trickster tales sometimes involved other well-known black baseball players, Paige's fame and outrageous public persona made him the central protagonist for black baseball in the same way that so many earlier boxing tales centered on the equally flamboyant Jack Johnson.

Perhaps unsurprisingly then, it was Paige himself who described an even more fantastical scheme to subvert the color line in his 1962 autobiography, *Maybe I'll Pitch Forever*. According to Paige, in 1926,

> Stan Naglin ... who ran the Chattanooga Lookouts in the white Southern association ... wanted me so bad he tried everything to get me into a game. One day he even came up to me and offered me five hundred dollars to pitch against the Atlanta Crackers. I just had to let him paint me white. When Alex Herman heard about it, he got as mad as anybody I've ever seen.... Alex finally talked me out of it, but I sure hated to pass up that five hundred dollars. And I think I'd have looked good in white-face. But nobody would have been fooled. White, black, green, yellow, orange—it don't make any difference. Only one person can pitch like me. That's Ol'Satch, himself.[25]

Paige's message expanded on the exceptionalism argument made by many of his fellow players in their tales of near passing. In Paige's version, however, it is not just that he was so valued as a player that a white baseball official would want to alter Paige's race to gain him as a player; more significantly, the plan would fail because of his own extraordinary talent. It is a catch–22 embedded with the ultimate compliment, Paige's pitching transcends all other's. In order to truly pass, he would have to perform poorly. If he pitched, even in disguise, his talent would reveal the truth.

In the 1930s, Dizzy Dean, a major league pitcher for the St. Louis Cardinals and a contemporary of Paige, frequently made similar comments about the advantages of making Paige white. In one such instance, Dean suggested that he would like to drop a bucket of calcimine on Paige to turn him white. These comments, suggesting that Paige attempt to employ "whiteface" methods, had particular symbolic meaning in a society inundated with advertising campaigns that focused on skin bleaching and hair straightening for African Americans.[26] These beauty products and their attendant marketing came on the heels of a long tradition of commercial advertisements that made use of similar claims to depict African Americans as "dirty" and inferior.[27] In an environment where consumers, particularly black consumers, were regularly subjected to racist advertising campaigns, Dean's proposal was both unsurprising and reflective of larger societal assumptions about the primacy of "whiteness."

Although the stories became less prevalent as time went on, players continued to recount stories of encounters with white major league officials who urged them to pass as Hispanic in the 1930s and 1940s. Quincy Trouppe described his response to the proposition of passing in his autobiography.

> One Sunday, after I had pitched the first game, a baseball scout came down from the stands and asked me if I was interested in playing in the big leagues. I was amazed at the question. He suggested that I go to a Latin country and learn Spanish, explaining that if I could speak that language I would have a good chance of playing organized ball. The idea seemed so far fetched to me that to tell you the truth I just did not think much about it.[28]

Underlying this story, within the hidden transcript, Trouppe espoused his belief in the fluidity of racial categories as well as the arbitrary nature of major league baseball's prohibition against black players. Yet, at the same time, Trouppe advanced the idea that passing was unacceptable to him and that he was unwilling to consider such a refutation of his identity as an African American man.

In other instances, the trickster tales from this time period stressed an inherent athletic superiority among Negro Leagues players. Judy Johnson recalled such an interaction with famed Philadelphia Athletics owner Connie Mack. According to Johnson, as the two were friends, he asked Mack why he had not signed a black player. Mack responded, "[t]here are too many of you to go in. It would have taken too many jobs away from the white boys."[29] This reported response again had the added benefit of justifying segregation not by claiming insufficiency on the part of African American ballplayers but conversely by crediting those prohibited players with an excess of talent. The trumpeting of this line of reasoning allowed Negro Leagues players to highlight their talent rather than to dwell on the racism that prevented their entrance into the major leagues.

Webster MacDonald also reported a similar encounter with Mack. According to MacDonald, Mack approached him after a game in which he beat Dizzy Dean at the peak of Dean's career. Mack commented to MacDonald that he'd "give half my ball club for a man like you."[30] Mack's son also shared his reported interest in black ball players. According to Cool Papa Bell, Mack's son Earle expressed his admiration for Bell's abilities. "If the door was open, you'd be the first guy I'd hire. I'd pay you $75,000 a year to play ball. You'd be worth it in drawing power alone."[31]

The tales told by Johnson, MacDonald, and Bell signified on the rationalizations offered by white baseball officials regarding the maintenance of the color line. As a counter to the argument that black players were unqualified for the major leagues, Johnson's encounter with Mack provided an alternative interpretation. Instead, it was the Negro Leagues players who were overqualified to play in the major leagues. Additionally, the comment attributed to Earle Mack hit on one of the more popular arguments in favor of integration during the 1930s and 1940s—increased attendance. Negro Leagues team owners and sportswriters often argued that major league teams could improve their attendance numbers and their bottom lines by bringing in black players. With a black player on the team, they reasoned, African American fans would turn out in droves.[32]

As many black sportswriters in the late 1930s and early 1940s pushed for integrated baseball, they also echoed sentiments of black baseball superiority. Ollie Stewart editorialized in the *Baltimore Afro-American* that the color line provided white professional ballplayers with their only assurance of maintaining their employment. According to Stewart, "You really can't blame white big league baseball teams, or white groups of any kind from barring colored entries. When you blame them, you're forgetting the very first law of nature—self-preservation.[33] Under this reasoning, the cessation of the prohibition against black players in the majors would result in a radical shift in the racial composition of major league baseball and thus a significant loss of employment for white baseball players.

This understanding of the color line flipped the traditional interpretation that black baseball players were unqualified for the white majors. Instead, these versions of the narrative made white major leaguers vulnerable to the success and athletic prowess of black ball players. Rather than emphasizing the hypocrisy or unjustness of arbitrary segregation, this tale reinforced the power of black athletes. In Jim Crow America, power was a restricted commodity allocated by race. African Americans could acquire fame and money, but segregation and white supremacy prevented them from gaining or exercising real power in most cases. These stories were significant for allowing African Americans to seize power rhetorically—a radical act considering the context.

A famous subset of the trickster folktales focused on the superhuman feats of the black ball players. One such story described the immense speed of "Cool Papa" Bell, arguably the most prominent center fielder of his time. According to Satchel Paige, who was Bell's roommate while they both played with the 1930s Pittsburgh Crawfords, Bell moved so fast that he could hit the light switch, jump across the room, and get under the covers before the light went out.[34] Obviously, this tale emphasized Bell's remarkable athletic talents, particularly his incredible speed on the baseball field. Bell's speed would be attested to by numerous teammates. Fellow Negro Leaguer Hilton Smith described Bell's speed in baseball terms, though arguably Smith's description was as much hyperbole as Paige's. "Bell was the fastest human I ever saw. I saw him on first base one time.... They bunted past second and by the time the second baseman had retrieved the ball, Bell had scored. In 1937 I saw him get four hits, not one past the infield." The *New York Age* praised Bell for his speed in similar terms, calling him "the game's fastest human."[35] In each of these accounts, Bell becomes a signal figure within the larger tradition of black boasting. In these seemingly simple but actually complex trickster tales, not only was the subject a hero but so was the author of the story. Through the construction of a clever boast, the author trickster used hyperbole to assert his masculinity while promoting (and at times overshadowing) the exploits of his partner, the subject trickster. Thus Smith and Paige assert their own acumen and masculinity in tales about Bell's speed.

Famously, in a case of tricking the trickster, Bell discovered on one trip that the light switch in his hotel room had malfunctioned, causing a pause between when he flipped the switch and when the lights went out. Bell called Paige into his room and told him to sit and watch. "He flicked the switch, strolled over to bed, and pulled the covers up. Bing! The lights went out 'See, Satchel,' he said, 'you've been tellin' people that story bout me for years, and even *you* didn't know it was true.'"[36] Buck O'Neil relates a similar version of this tale in his autobiography. In his version, however, Paige bets Bell $50 that he can't get in bed before the room goes dark. Thus, "[i]t cost him [Paige] fifty bucks to find out Cool Papa Bell was faster than the speed of light."[37] As Paige arguably held the most power among all Negro Leagues players, Bell's alleged trick and wordplay allowed him to subvert the more dominant figure in the relationship and profit from his tricksterism, just as Paige used similar strategies to combat and profit from white supremacy and Jim Crow.

Bell's story would have a long history within and outside of the sporting world. In the 1974 lead up to his famous "Rumble in the Jungle," Muhammad Ali, a master of both the boast and the trickster tale, reappropriated the story as his own. Describing his punching speed, Ali noted "I'm so fast that, last night, I turned off the light switch in my hotel room and was in bed before the room was dark."[38] Ali, a virtuoso with boasting statements, used the description of Bell to increase his own legend. For both Bell and Ali, the story celebrated their immense natural talents. Through the tale, the men could lay claim to superhuman athletic talent. Celebrating their speed, they underscored the abilities of their bodies and hence, their masculinity. Ali, in telling the tale about himself, rather than about another athlete, also assumes the role played ably by Paige, that of a charming, quick-witted, fast-talking, self-promoting trickster. Ali is therefore both author and subject, and wields power in both roles. Most significantly, however, the long history of this hyberbolic story highlights the way in which trickster tales were at their foundation about power relationships and the way in which the oppressed could claim power from an oppressor.

These tales carefully navigated the line between racial stereotypes and documenting achievements in much the same way as white supremacists did. African American advocates of baseball wanted to showcase the strength and athletic ability of black players while at the same time combating the stereotype of African American athletes as animalistic. As such, hyberbolic trickster tales supported the notion that black athletes had superior strength and speed while also emphasizing the acquired skill of African American baseball players in comparison to white athletes. Just as Cool Papa Bell became the symbol of the speed of Negro Leagues players, Josh Gibson represented the strength and physical power of black ball players.[39]

Gibson, a catcher for the Pittsburgh Crawfords and Homestead Grays, made a name for himself through his power hitting. Most stories about Gibson revolved around the incredible distance of his home runs.

> There is a story that one day during the 1930s the Pittsburgh Crawfords were playing at Forbes Field in Pittsburgh when their young catcher, Josh Gibson, hit the ball so high and far that no one saw it come down. After scanning the sky carefully for a few minutes, the umpire deliberated and ruled it a home run. The next day the Crawfords were playing in Philadelphia when suddenly a ball dropped out of the heavens and was caught by the startled center-fielder on the opposing club. The umpire made the only possible ruling. Pointing to Gibson he shouted, "Yer-out—yesterday in Pittsburgh![40]

Obviously exaggerated stories, such as this one, cast Gibson as a superhuman strongman, a hero through physicality for his race. Much like Bell's speed, Gibson's strength symbolized his masculinity and his superior athleticism.

Hyperbole aside, Gibson was certainly one of the most proficient home-run hitters of all time. Various sources estimate that Gibson hit upwards of 70 home runs in a single season, far exceeding the record of white contemporary Ruth, who held the major league record of 60 home runs. The 1944 *Negro Baseball Yearbook* noted that in 1943 Gibson hit more home runs at Griffith Stadium than "the entire major American League players put together."[41] Adding to his already superhuman reputation, some of Gibson's most storied home runs took place in Yankee Stadium, the legendary "House That Ruth built," and thus greatly contributed to the mystique of Gibson, who became known as the "Black Babe Ruth."[42] Even if he did not quite hit a home run that flew from Pittsburgh to Philadelphia, Gibson's power hitting bonafides were impossible to ignore.

In lieu of merely establishing an equivalency of talent, trickster tales involving interracial baseball games promoted black athletic ability as superior to that of white baseball players. Black baseball squads competed against white teams semi-regularly, especially during the off-season barnstorming campaigns. When tensions over race were at a high point, trickster tales and accounts were more likely to emerge and sportswriters were more likely to highlight these competitions. Two decades particularly witnessed high interest in interracial baseball competitions. Interracial baseball games in the 1910s attracted a great deal of attention, largely due to the racial tensions surrounding Jack Johnson's interracial boxing victory.[43] In the 1930s and into the early 1940s, racial tensions escalated within the baseball world as the public debate over the major league color line intensified.[44]

Even the white press acknowledged the high stakes of such matches. Ted Shane, in his profile of Satchel Paige noted: "When Satch's boys tangle with big league barnstormers, there is no foolishness. They play in real earnest. The colored players do their best to show their class, while the whites don't like to be shown up."[45] Though Shane generally portrayed Paige and the Negro Leagues in comical terms, he granted them a degree of professionalism and competency in his description of their interracial game play. A degree of racist judgment still underlies even this more complimentary description of Paige as Shane refers to the other black players as "boys" in a seemingly patronizing manner and implies that during regular play the black players do not "show their class."

Within this context, interracial baseball games had an added significance. According to Jack Marshall, a Chicago American Giants player, teams first utilized batting helmets during a game between a Negro Leagues all-star team and a white semi-pro team from Texas.

> Did you know Satchel Paige is the cause of ballplayers wearing plastic helmets today? In 1936 we had a Negro National League all-star team we took to Denver to play in the Denver *Post* tournament.... We didn't lose a game. We won 7

straight games. And when we came up to play Borger, Texas, a white team—we were the only colored team in the tournament—these boys sent back to Borger, Texas, and had these helmets made to go around in their caps because they didn't want to get hurt with Satchel's speed.[46]

This trickster tale fits in with other stories of black athletic superiority and dominance as well as with the subset of interracial competition folklore. The *Denver Post* tournament itself had a complicated racial history. It had previously functioned as a segregated tournament, barring the Cuban Stars from participating. According to *The Crisis*, "Charles L. Parsons, sports editor of the Denver paper, who invited the Cubans to join the tournament, reneged [sic] when protest came pouring in from the baseball moguls in three of the larger Southern cities."[47] In 1934, the tournament permitted the all-black Kansas City Monarchs to participate as well as an integrated House of David team that featured Satchel Paige.[48] At that point, the *Denver Post* tournament became an open (and highly prized) semi-pro event for baseball squads throughout the 1930s.

Sport historian Leslie A. Heaphy documented a different origin for the batting helmet. "As the story is told Byrd [Bill, pitcher with Baltimore Elite Giants] is also in part responsible for the use of the batting helmet. He beaned Willie Wells, knocking him unconscious. The next time Wells faced Byrd he borrowed a hard-hat from a construction site to protect himself."[49] The Byrd/Wells story may be the more likely (and certainly has been the more documented) origin tale for the development of the batting helmet. However, the Satchel story signified on traditional narratives by constructing a story in which it was white players who feared for their safety while facing African Americans. This flip of the joke not only slipped the yoke à la Ellison, but also flipped the power, putting Satchel in the role of the dominant male figure. In a larger American/Jim Crow context in which early twentieth century carnival sideshow attractions involved throwing baseballs at the heads of African American men, this reversal spoke to the strides being made by the trickster heroes of black baseball.

In the 1940s, with campaigns to integrate baseball becoming more public and insistent, the public, white and black, paid more attention to the outcome of integrated games.[50] For African Americans, a win or a loss reflected upon the skill and prowess of their racial representatives on the field. Advocates for and against segregated baseball could (and did) use the results of such contests in their arguments about the future of the major leagues. Within the sports pages of the black press, a number of news articles documented integrated games, highlighted the athletic prowess of black athletes and questioned the fairness of baseball's racial prohibition.[51] In this context, the Paige version of the batting helmet tale spoke volumes to proponents of the integration of baseball. Paige, as the central figure, symbolized overwhelming power and ability on behalf of black baseball. The opposing team feared Paige to such an extent that they were unwilling to face him without unusual protection. For advocates of black baseball, this tale highlighted the immense ability and athletic prowess of Negro Leagues players as well as the inherent fallacies of arguments for segregation that rested upon a belief in the athletic inferiority of African Americans. On the other hand, for those opposed to the breaking of the color line, this tale implied that black ball players would bring a dangerous element to the white major leagues.

Through the use of trickster tales and the hidden transcript, African Americans constructed cultural and social currency that signified upon the racial hierarchies of the time. By challenging the racial stereotypes and expectations of Jim Crow society, these men and women reinforced notions of cultural superiority and self-sufficiency while also attacking the foundations of racial discrimination. Thus through their selective use of both the public and hidden transcript, African Americans were able to fashion an alternative conception of black baseball.

Trickster tales functioned as a space through which African Americans could negotiate black baseball during Jim Crow. Within these spaces, African Americans encountered and challenged contemporary conceptions of the color line, racial identity, and white supremacy. In questioning the enforcement of segregation in "passing" stories, in countering the very nature of scientific racial categorization in Brewer's tale of racial transformation and the Tokohama story, and in promoting the strategies and strength of black ballplayers in stories of Bell's speed and Gibson's strength, African Americans used trickster tales as an important tool in the fight against Jim Crow–era racial restrictions. Through their performance and discussion of black baseball, as spectators, observers, and participants, African Americans contested the racialist foundations of segregated baseball and racial binarism itself. These seemingly simple and humorous tales, repeated in ballpark stands and barbershops, were in effect radical acts that called into question every aspect of hegemonic white supremacy. Black baseball tricksters used the hidden transcript to raise questions about the existence of defined and categorical races as well as to enter the debates of racial ability, superiority, and power. The resultant texts, by themselves, did not directly open the doors to racial integration, but did greatly aid in exposing the fissures of the hypocrisy that supported segregated professional baseball.

FIVE

Giants and a Gentleman
Naming and Resistance in the Negro Leagues

Radicalism was not found just in trickster tales and in the editorial art of black newspapers. Black ball players also used a fundamental linguistic tool, naming, to combat and challenge white supremacy. The history of naming in African American communities is long and complex. Many historians of slavery, in particular, have documented the ways in which black slaves employed naming strategies to counter the horrifying power imbalance of living in forced enslavement. Similarly, slave owners utilized their power to name in ways meant to demonstrate their complete dominion over their slaves, belittling and mocking the slaves through the naming process to further humiliate and intimidate their human property.[1] Emancipation brought physical freedom to African Americans but also the freedom for former slaves to rename themselves, rhetorically severing the link between their painful past and their more hopeful future. In addition, freemen and freewomen were finally able to name their own offspring, a parental privilege that was just one of the many stripped from them in the inhumanity of the slave system. Understandably then, names—always powerful and meaningful as the public representation of one's identity and family—were particularly significant to African Americans during Jim Crow and were understood to have a great deal of power.

Black baseball players signified upon racial stereotypes and hierarchies through the selective use of nicknames. Nicknames were particularly important to African American players and the larger African American community. In his book, *Baseball Nicknames*, James Skipper asserted the importance of nicknames. According to Skipper, baseball fans equated baseball with innocence, democracy, and pseudo-amateurism in the first half of the twentieth century. Owners paid their players, but the public expected baseball players to compete for the love of the game rather than for material compensation. These expectations, Skipper argues, led fans to transform professional baseball players into modern day "folk heroes"—a designation that helped to cement the identification of the working class with baseball players.[2]

Extending Skipper's argument to the African American community magnifies the importance of this phenomenon. African American ball players were in an even more precarious situation than white players regarding their professional status. Negro Leagues players competed under a system that prohibited them from reaching the major leagues. Although some superstars, such as Paige, eventually achieved significant salaries, the living and playing conditions in the Negro Leagues were fraught with difficulties that white players rarely, if ever, had to encounter. Not only did players have to confront the indignities of traveling through a country that boasted a mosaic of strongly enforced but often unwritten segregation lines in order to practice their livelihood, the precarious finances of most Negro Leagues teams resulted in a instability and vulnerability for players who could not always count on a steady salary or the continued existence of their team.

Unlike the situation with white baseball players, however, African Americans did not expect Negro Leagues players to toil without pay. In fact, black members of the sporting press were more likely to herald large contracts as a sign of black baseball's value and success. Due to a more freewheeling contractual system and the constant addition and deletion of new teams and regional leagues, Negro Leagues players were able to capitalize on one advantage they possessed that major leaguers did not—the ability to push team owners into a bidding war for their services. Like the white major leagues, the Negro Leagues had a reserve clause. Unlike the white major leagues, the Negro Leagues' reserve clause was weak and unenforced.[3] Any reserve clause would have been challenging to maintain in the Negro Leagues given the continual flux as well as the demand for black players from Latin and Caribbean teams. These factors resulted in unprecedented freedom for black ball players, especially compared to their white major league counterparts. These players could quite easily escape an unattractive contract by joining a team outside their league or a team in another country. Attempts by Negro Leagues officials and owners to ban, punish, and fine players who jumped contract were generally unsuccessful.[4] Star players were in great enough demand as gate draws for Negro Leagues teams that punitive measures were ineffectual.

Not surprisingly, the great Satchel Paige was one of the most successful in this type of contractual maneuvering. According to Paige biographer Donald Spivey, Paige "was soft-spoken but tough-minded when it came to making deals.... Paige was determined, long before free agency and mega salaries for star athletes, to negotiate hard and get as much for his services as the market would bear."[5] Paige rarely spent more than one season with a team, and at times even switched among teams during the season. In one of the most infamous examples of Paige's business dealings, he negotiated a deal with Dominican Republic dictator Rafael Trujillo. Paige agreed to head a team of all-star Pittsburgh Crawfords players for a two-month season in the Dominican Republic to boost Trujillo's political popularity. For his services, Paige received a salary of $3,000 for two months of work during the Depression. Paige had been under contract to Gus Greenlee and the Pittsburgh Crawfords at the time. Greenlee was understandably upset that his most valuable players fled to the Dominican Republic at the beginning of the 1937 season, leaving him without much of a team.[6]

Paige was not alone in his savvy business dealings. Numerous players took advantage of the talent-hungry Mexican and Latin American clubs. Owners attempted to enforce rules against jumping by instituting severe penalties. These measures rarely worked, as team owners frequently were willing to defy the league to gain the talents of players like Paige and Wells.[7] If a player felt an owner offered an inadequate contract, he left the team and the country to play south of the border for handsome compensation. Players who played in Cuba or Mexico also benefited from the superior race relations in those countries. Buck Leonard singled out Puerto Rico and Venezuela as being accommodating. "There was not any racial discrimination at all in those two countries."[8] Similarly, Wilmer Fields noted that in Puerto Rico, "Segregation was not an issue.... We went to movies and restaurants freely, and when I was on the baseball field, no unpleasant words were directed at me."[9] African American ballplayers found their new homes to be incredibly inviting. According to Willie Wells, who spent much of his time in the Mexican League, "[p]layers on the teams in the Mexican league live just like big leagues. We have everything first class.... I mean that we are heroes here, and not just ball players.... I came back to Mexico ... because I've found freedom and democracy here.... Here in Mexico, I am a man."[10] For players like Wells, life in Mexico, Cuba, and other Latin American countries provided immense relief from living by the rules of Jim Crow.

Despite the opportunity for black players to find a better contract with another team, the economics of the Negro Leagues dictated that even the superstars of black baseball earned less than their white counterparts. Complicating matters, many players were unwilling to leave their families and their home country on a permanent basis to enjoy the less restrictive racial atmosphere of Latin America or the Caribbean. Thus, the challenging circumstances of black ball players' tenure in professional baseball meant that they, more than white players, played in spite of hardships. Faced with two unpleasant options, either to toil in the American Negro Leagues and deal with segregation or to leave behind their country of origin and work elsewhere, black baseball players often found a middle road of temporary stints south of the border with the majority of their playing time spent in the Negro Leagues. The black sport fan's awareness of the vulnerability of their favorite players and the problems faced by black baseball players due to Jim Crow contributed to a greater sense of attachment and identification.

The trickster tales that focused on attempts to pass racially in the major leagues had their equivalent in Negro Leagues naming choices. Much like the trickster did with narratives of racial subterfuge, the nicknames of both teams and individual players called into question racial categorization in general. The color line has always been a shifting one that historical actors have had a difficult time pinning down. It is within this context of racial dynamicism, and the longer history of naming, that one can seen the significance of team and individual nicknames for players, owners, and fans in the Negro Leagues.

Team nickname choices reflected collective racial interests, history, and desires. During the Jim Crow era, many black and Latino teams chose to use the name "Giants." The "Giants" had special meaning for the African American community for multiple reasons. First, the New York Giants were one of the more successful major league teams in the first decades of the twentieth century. By claiming the name of such a prominent major league club, the team owners and players were asserting their own athletic prowess, publicly claiming all of the connotations of what it meant to be a baseball "Giant" for themselves and for their race. Second, John McGraw, manager of the Giants, publicly praised the abilities of African American players on many occasions and in at least one instance attempted to sign and play an African American player in a major league game. Because of his attempt to use an African American player and his well-known admiration for the athletic promise of other African American players, the name "Giants" also came to stand for the possibility of integrated major league baseball. As a result, "Giants" signified the past hypocrisy and discrimination of the major leagues and a defiant optimism for the future.

Most notably, the use of the name "Giants" had great historical meaning for African Americans that predated the interest in the white major leagues. One of the earliest African American baseball teams was the Cuban Giants. The Cuban Giants, who "dominated black baseball in its infancy," were primarily composed of waiters working at a Long Island resort named the Argyle Hotel.[11] Historians have been unclear about the reason for the names, which preceded both McGraw's interaction with black baseball and the acceptance of light-skinned Cuban players in the white major leagues. Michael Lomax has suggested that the name "Cuban" was intended to reflect the skin tone of most of the players and their higher class status.

> There were two characteristics that linked them to the mulatto elite—occupational status and skin color. Both Frank Thompson (headwaiter) and Bud Fowler (barber) worked in occupations commonly associated with the black middle-class.... In terms of skin color, virtually every player, not to mention

those who played in Organized Baseball, were light skinned blacks. Thus the name "Cuban" was for their light skin.[12]

Lomax also suggests that the name Giants resulted from the fact that the team was a consolidation of smaller hotel-based teams.

Regardless of the origin of the name "Cuban Giants," the vast success of the team resulted in immense popularity of the name. A contemporary team went so far as to christen his club the "Cuban × Giants," leading to a lawsuit by the original Cuban Giants over copyright infringement.[13] By 1915, the majority of teams in the Chicago area had names containing some variation on the "Cuban Giants." In his autobiography, Buck O'Neil compiles an even longer list of baseball "Giants," listing 23 teams using the name. O'Neil notes that he was a Giant three different times in his career.[14] Consequently, teams using the terms "Cuban" or "Giants" called up not only connotations of the New York Giants and Cuban major leaguers, but also a long legacy of success for black baseball. By referencing that cultural history, African Americans were able to connect with a legacy of independent achievement.

As campaigns to encourage African Americans to "buy black" increased with the growing number of African Americans in the North during the Great Migration, a connection to such a legacy had significance for much of the black population. As Rube Foster took control of the Negro National League and emphasized black ownership of black teams, the self-reliance of these teams, in a long line of successful ventures, signified the wisdom of such policies.

After the first prominent all-black "Cuban Giants" gained widespread notice among African American baseball fans, they were quickly followed by a number of other black baseball teams eager to trade on the now-marketable name. Varied "Giants" and "X Giants" teams emerged in the aftermath of the original Cuban Giants' success. There is yet another significant explanation for the prevalence of teams using either "Cubans" or "Giants" for their nicknames. The prevalence of these names cannot be overstated. A perusal of the *Chicago Defender* reveals the pervasiveness of these names. In the July 1915 sports page in the *Defender*, the newspaper listed the baseball games to be played that weekend by black baseball teams in Chicago as well as results from the previous week's games. Among the teams mentioned were the *Cubans*, the *Cuban* Stars, the American *Giants*, the Chicago *Giants*, the Union *Giants*, the Lincoln *Giants*, the New York *Giants*, the Keystone *Giants*, and the Long Branch *Cubans*.[15] Similarly, a 1932 edition of the *Norfolk Journal and Guide* featured an advertisement for a championship game between Conner's New Bacharach Giants and Pettus' Richmond Giants. Rube Foster, founder of the Negro National League, would become the star pitcher for the "Leland Giants" and eventually own and manage his "Chicago American Giants." With the continued replication of the Giants team name, black baseball team owners were able to profit off of the immediate name recognition. Given the large number of Giants clubs, it was not uncommon to see a Giants vs. Giants match, especially in the years prior to the formation of the NNL and in semi-pro matches around the country. From the late nineteenth century through the 1930s, the name "Giants" functioned as a shorthand and in effect a brand name for black baseball.

Using "Giants" had another benefit: by trading on the long tradition of black baseball "Giants," teams could take advantage of a commodity that was often in short supply in black baseball—nostalgia and history. Without access to the white major leagues, African American baseball fans lacked the nostalgic and historic aspects of baseball that are so prized by aficionados. Record books did not record the feats of their favorite players or teams. But by rooting for a "Giants" team, African Americans could connect with a storied and valued past, even if it was one unacknowledged by broader society.

"Giants" was not the only signifier that came out of the success of the early Cuban Giants. Unpacking the team name further, one finds that the "Cuban" name had substantial meaning for African American communities in the late nineteenth and early twentieth centuries. Numerous teams, few of them actually Cuban at the beginning, seized on the name "Cuban" as their geographical name. This claiming of "Cuba" as a home space of sorts has been interpreted in multiple ways.[16] Generally, historians have viewed this action as both a code that would alert the public to the fact that an advertisement referred to a Negro Leagues club as well as an outward sign of the hope for better race relations. Coded signals were common in the Jim Crow era. A number of them were direct, such as "race" or "sepia" to alert consumers and readers that the people involved were black. Others used national symbols like "Ethiopian" to signal blackness. "Cuban" also functioned as a catch-all term for non-whiteness, encompassing people of many backgrounds who only had skin color in common.

Many African Americans viewed Cuba and other Latin American countries as racially tolerant in comparison to the United States.[17] At the time of the emergence of the very first "Cuban Giants" in the 1880s, the team was likely capitalizing on the strong positive association regarding Cuba held by African Americans. As early as the nineteenth century, many in African American communities viewed Cuba as a sort of "racial paradise," one that was geographically close but still unreachable. According to scholar Lisa Brock, "No country in the nineteenth century, other than Haiti, so stirred the African-American imagination as Cuba did."[18] This identification with Cuba as part of a pan–African and racial consciousness was long-lasting, and winter ball seasons spent in the island nation only reinforced the image of Cuba as a haven for African Americans. *Half-Century Magazine* lauded Cuba as a site of relative racial harmony in a

1919 article. "In Cuba no color line is drawn. Colored players from the United States often go there to play and have yet to encounter any discrimination on account of their color."[19] Although historians and scholars have pointed out that Cuba's racial climate fell short of a colorblind utopia at the time, for African Americans who traveled to Cuba the difference was striking.[20]

In interviews and news accounts, black ballplayers recalled both Cuba, specifically, and Latin American generally, as more comfortable places to live. Max Manning boasted that he loved playing in Cuba because he had unlimited access within the country: "[w]hen I was in Cuba, I lived in the best part of Cuba."[21] In contrast, segregation policies in the United States prevented even wealthy African Americans from living in elite areas. Despite American mythologies of rags to riches success, one could only abandon the rags and gain the power of riches if he had white skin. Manning added that the athletic facilities in Cuba were superior to those utilized by the Negro Leagues in the States, reflecting both the Cuban passion for baseball as a sport and the unprecedented access to topline facilities granted to all professional baseball players in Cuba, regardless of race. The combination of an inclusive national baseball fever and lack of baseball color line stood in stark contrast to the American situation. Similarly, Art Pennington described Mexico as "freedom," explaining that it was a country where the people did not "think about no [sic] color." Pennington also noted that conditions drastically changed as he and his (white) wife traveled by train from Mexico to the United States. After the Penningtons crossed the border, other passengers and rail workers harassed the interracial couple on their trip from Laredo, Texas, to Little Rock, Arkansas.[22] The degradation in treatment was a stark and unwelcome contrast to what the Penningtons had experienced in Mexico.

For Manning and others, competing in Latin America was the fulfillment of a dream to play in a country where they could be free to live, work, and play as they wished. Sug Cornelius, another Negro Leagues player, noted that Mexico was largely devoid of racial problems until 1939, at which point Cornelius argued that the increasing presence of American tourists made Mexico a less pleasant destination for Negro Leaguers. Cornelius attributed the turn in racial attitudes among Mexicans to the desire by the Mexican tourist industry to cater to white Americans.[23] The situation was similar in Cuba; in concert with the 1940s and 1950s increase in white American tourism, African American travelers "had to navigate the racially exclusionary practices of the U.S. dominated tourist sector on the island." With the import of white tourists came strict segregation, and "African Americans were often refused accommodations at hotels and were almost always prevented from entering Cuba's beaches."[24] Even if Cuba and Latin America did not always live up the expectation and hope of black visitors in the later years of Jim Crow, their historical connotation with racial equality was not easily erased. Utilizing the name "Cuban," African American ballplayers, owners, and managers could invoke thoughts of a more tolerant nation and a world free from segregation.

Negro Leagues players also participated in barnstorming through Canada. Although these players were generally treated well by locals, they [black teams] also had to emphasize racial difference. Thus, Canada was not viewed as the utopia that Cuba and Mexico were. "In order to attract fans, they often had to cultivate an image of 'otherness' that played upon white racial theories about the different characteristics of the races."[25] In other words, black ball players had to market their blackness in ways that could be commodified and sold to Canadian spectators.

In 1940, as the *Courier* and other publications focused on the integration of major leagues, sportswriter Chester Washington lamented the flow of black baseball talent to Latin and South America. Washington and his contemporaries were no longer content merely to applaud other nations' more progressive racial climates in the hope of inspiring domestic change. Instead, they underscored the hypocrisy of the color line and the unfair realities of life for African Americans under Jim Crow. Washington mused:

> The thought which struck the writer most forcefully Saturday was that in this so-called land of Opportunity how tragic it was that the greatest home run hitter in the game today—Josh Gibson—had to leave his native America to make a lucrative living in far-away Venezuela just because the Negro League can't afford to pay him the salary he's worth and the major leagues bar him because he is black."[26]

Anxious to accelerate the small incremental progress being made toward integration, sportswriters like Washington were growing impatient with the status quo and were becoming more vocal in their condemnation of the societal obstacles that prevented the flourishing of black athletes in the United States.

The argument that the choice to use the name "Cuban" was to trade upon the positive associations with the island in the African American imagination is compelling and probable, but there was another possible concurrent meaning for the moniker. Assuming the name "Cuban" challenged the notion that one could easily attach racial labels to a diverse population.[27] In particular, highlighting the Cuban situation allowed African Americans to challenge the arbitrary nature of one-drop laws that labeled one as black based on any black ancestry. Cubans and Mexicans, in contrast, were classified "white" or "black" merely on a visual determination. A Cuban with light skin was white, while one with dark skin was black. Of course, color determination was selective; Baltimore Elite Giants official Dick Powell recalled the Boston Braves expressing interest in a Cuban shortstop before deciding that "he was just a *little* too dark."[28] By giving nicknames that mocked the strict racial line of segregated baseball, Negro Leagues players made an implicit argument that race was too ambiguous to be an obstacle for inclusion in the "national game."

Despite the fact that major league baseball admitted light-skinned Cubans, Cuban players in the major leagues faced discrimination and harsh treatment. According to a contemporary magazine, "Some of the Cubans have doubtless felt the sting of being a human being in the United States with distinct Negro features."[29] Even more distressing for advocates of baseball integration, a *Pittsburgh Courier* writer noted that the dismal treatment of Cuban players indicated that black ball players would not be accepted into the white major leagues.

> So the question of the dark-skinned brother in the big leagues is answered by the comment on the Cubans of various abilities that have been on the Washington club roster for the past two seasons. And any question as to the "possibilities" of Negroes in the big leagues has its answer in the statements attributed to the manager who came from Pennsylvania's coal mines and was given an opportunity as a second baseman in Washington.[30]

Observing the travails of Cuban players in the white major leagues, black sportswriters concluded that the racism of white players, managers, and owners would not be an easy obstacle for black players to overcome.

Team naming using "Cuban" and "Giants" reflected the ways in which African Americans used rhetorical power to challenge racism, segregation, and discrimination during the black ball era. The chosen names provided an implicit critique of racial classification and American inequality. In addition, repeating the use of the names "Cuban" and "Giants" reinforced collective memories and established the visibility of black baseball in a country where the majority of the population ignored its existence.

In the 1930s, other team nicknames also reflected a more pan-national and African diasporic perspective on the part of many African Americans. During this time, the Miami Clowns changed their name to the Ethiopian Clowns. This alteration coincided with the Italian invasion of Ethiopia. Historians of Negro Leagues baseball have interpreted this name change in two different ways, either as an attempt to play up African heritage to white audiences in a minstrel show manner or as a strategy to capitalize on the publicity surrounding the invasion of Ethiopia to gain more attention for their team.[31] Undoubtedly, the owners of the Ethiopian Clowns envisioned financial improvement as a result of their name change. The name also reflected the growing dissatisfaction among African Americans with colonialism and an increasing interest in pan–African causes. African Americans found frequent mention of the Ethiopian situation in the morning paper. The black press devoted a great deal of column space to the invasion of Ethiopia, highlighting the invasion as an important issue for all African Americans. The Ethiopian coverage was second only to the black press's coverage of heavyweight champion Joe Louis during the period from 1933 to 1938. According to sociologists St. Clair Drake and Horace R. Cayton's study of black newspapers in Chicago, Joe Louis had an "incidence ranking" of 80 in regards to front page headlines and pictures during the time period. Haile Selassie, deposed leader of Ethiopia, was second with a ranking of 24. Drake and Cayton gave both Louis and Selassie the title of "Race Hero," noting that Selassie was the "leader of a nation to which Negroes felt kinship, during attack by a white nation, Italy."[32]

For African Americans struggling under Jim Crow and aghast at American miscarriages of justice in the Scottsboro Boys case, it was easy to find common cause with another group of African-descended people who found their freedom attacked by a more powerful white nation. The "Ethiopian" name thus signified a renewed political consciousness and a political protest against racist policies at home and abroad. Beneath the clowning antics of the Ethiopian Clowns was the claiming of a transnational identity, one of oppressed people desperate to gain liberty for themselves and their families.

Racially significant naming practices were not limited to teams alone. Individuals also took advantage of the power of self-naming or naming teammates to make pointed critiques of Jim Crow. In the 1920s, a number of black baseball players acquired individual nicknames that also referenced the ambiguity of racial classification. Throughout the first three decades of the twentieth century, adherents of eugenics and other racial hierarchy systems spent considerable time and effort trying to compose racial systems that could somehow quantify race. The ultimate goal was to establish "objective" and "scientific" measures by which one (or more importantly the state) could judge race. The most successful of these efforts resulted in racial purity or "one drop" laws that restricted the privilege of whiteness to those who could document the lack of non-white blood in their ancestry. This effort to codify racial categories into law was born of white supremacist anxiety around non-whites passing as "white" and therefore gaining power within society. In states like Virginia, white supremacist bureaucrats used these laws to legally punish women who allegedly misrepresented the race of their infants, midwives who attended such births, and interracial couples who dared to marry despite anti-miscegenation laws.[33]

The ambiguity of racial categories coupled with the strong desire by authorities to police those categories in spite of the inherent difficulties placed increasing burdens on African Americans in particular. As it became more and more difficult to define one's race through intelligence tests, phrenology, skull size, visual identification, ancestry, or athletic abilities, Americans began to accept a more dichotomous racial system, one in which the line between black and white was the most significant division.[34] Under these strictures, racial categorization was divided into those who were white and those who were non-white. No room remained for those who admitted to diverse racial ancestry.

Baseball was one of the earliest institutions (outside the South) to abide by this dual racial system, allowing men of all races to participate except for African Americans. A 1923 *Sporting News* editorial described the situation:

> In Organized Baseball there has been no distinction raised except tacit understanding that a player of Ethiopian descent is ineligible—the wisdom of which we will not discuss except to say that by such a rule some of the greatest players the game has ever known have been denied their opportunity. No player of any other "race" has been banned. We have had Indians, Chinese and Japanese playing ball and if a Malay should appear who could field and hit he would probably be welcomed.[35]

Negro Leagues players were acutely aware of the fact that the major leagues welcomed those of other races and ethnicities and excluded only African Americans and dark-skinned Cubans and Mexicans. In 1936, the *Chicago Defender* observed that the major leagues would include on their rosters "all nationalities save members of the Race. There, knowingly, will be no black boys."[36] This turn of phrase by the *Defender* had dual meaning itself—acknowledging the hardness of the color line in terms of the treatment of African Americans while winking to its readers by hinting at the possibility that "black boys" had successfully passed their way into the major leagues.

Cognizant of the oddities and contradictions of the major league color line, Negro Leagues players often played with racial categories in the development of nicknames for their lighter skinned teammates. Two of the more common nicknames for those African American players were "Red" or "Chief." By referencing the possibility of American Indian ancestry on the part of these lighter skinned teammates, black ball players could point out the inconsistency of a binary color line and perhaps call back to the near-passing story of Charlie Grant. Players also were given Spanish nicknames, indicating that they could potentially pass for Latino rather than black or indicating that they were Latino, but of too dark a complexion to be allowed to participate in the major leagues.[37] Once again, in this way, African Americans were able to shine a light on the ways in which visual racial identifiers could trump one's actual nationality.

At least one Negro Leagues player obtained a nickname similar to the name of an Indian major league ball player. Harold "Yellowhorse" Morris, a player for the black Detroit Stars and other Negro Leagues teams, was known as "Yellowhorse" in reference to Mose Yellowhorse. The original "Yellowhorse" was a Pawnee native and pitcher who had two successful years with the Pittsburgh

Pirates in the early 1920s. Although Mose Yellowhorse's biographer, Marshall Todd Fuller, does not provide any concrete evidence that Morris took the name "Yellowhorse" to cite the Pawnee baseball major leaguer, the timing of the two players' careers indicates a likely connection. Morris started in the Negro Leagues in 1927, one year after the original Yellowhorse's last professional game.[38] Through the employment of these ethnically and racially suggestive nicknames, black baseball players referred to the hypocrisy of racial binarism in major league baseball. Thus, they signified to their African American fans, communicating their knowledge of the subjective and problematic definitions of race.

For African Americans, the use of racially ambiguous nicknames had greater symbolism due to the open secret that black players had passed the white color line.[39] W. Rollo Wilson, sportswriter for the *Pittsburgh Courier*, noted in a 1924 column that contemporary athletes were passing as white and others had successfully done so in the past.[40] According to Wilson, African American fans and the black press had been clamoring for an accomplished track and field star, Charles Brookins, to admit that he was black. Wilson, unlike his colleagues, felt that Brookins should be allowed to "be what he wants to be." Continuing, Wilson claimed "we have known more than one big league ball player to 'get away with it.' One of the shining lights of the game today is whispered to have had a 'dark' past. And 'Indian' has been a disguise for several of our boys."[41] Thus, although Wilson approved of Brookins "passing," Wilson's readers and colleagues felt that Brookins needed to identify himself as African American to help advance the status of black athletes and African Americans in general. In an age that prized the loyal "race" man who would put the needs of his race and community above his own personal ambitions, Brookins' reluctance to reclaim his blackness after achieving success was viewed as problematic. Likewise, many black fans held out hope that Wilson's "star with a dark past" or "Indian" would unmask himself and demonstrate the degree to which the color line was an ineffective fraud. Wilson also reinforced the idea that an Indian racial identification could be a handy racial mask for African American athletes who wished to pass into the major leagues.

The unnamed subjects of Wilson's article were not the only major league ball players who faced rumors that they were passing as white. Quite notably, a number of Babe Ruth's contemporaries claimed that he was a black man passing as white.[42] According to Ruth biographer Robert Creamer,

> Ruth was called nigger so often that many people assumed he was indeed partly black and that at some point in time he, or an immediate ancestor, had managed to cross the color line. Even players in the Negro baseball leagues that flourished then believed this and generally wished the Babe, whom they considered a secret brother, well in his conquest of white baseball.[43]

Undoubtedly, these rumors partially stemmed from Ruth's mythic ascent from troubled reform school boy (a school that housed a large number of orphans) to baseball superstar.[44]

Almost two decades later, a 1942 *Chicago Defender* article noted that African Americans had played in the big leagues, passing as white on the basis of their light skin. According to the article, a contemporary rumor alleged that "the Chicago Cubs had an infielder once recently who wasn't exactly a Caucasian."[45] The language in the article is telling and again is a direct challenge to the racial binarism and purity that held up the color line. The infielder in question "wasn't exactly a Caucasian." The author here is both coyly alluding to a potential passing and also mocking the idea that one either was or was not Caucasian by referencing the fluidity of race and racial identification.

Other nicknames signified the athletic triumphs of black baseball in an attempt to celebrate black achievement during a time that prevented their ascension to major league stardom. As an added bonus, these nicknames often helped to dismantle the inferiority argument that some white baseball officials used to maintain baseball segregation. One of the best, and earliest, examples of this trend was Andrew "Rube" Foster. During the first three decades of the twentieth century, "Rube" was a common nickname among white baseball players and was a pejorative term for someone from a rural background. "Rube" implied both ignorance and backwardness. Considering the dual American mythologies of baseball pastoralism and the yeoman farmer, one might assume that to be a "rube" would be a benefit in the white major leagues. However, major league baseball teams operated in large urban centers. In the early twentieth century, the urbanization of the United States, flood of new immigrants, and the Great Northern Migration of African Americans meant that the population of those cities was racially, ethnically, and religiously diverse. Most significantly, these residents had often fled rural farming homes for the promise of industrial and manufacturing work in the city and did not romanticize the "rube." White major league players assigned the name "Rube" to teammates who came from rural backgrounds to reflect their displacement and difficult transition to the unfamiliar urban life.

Andrew "Rube" Foster, an ambitious and imposing man, did not fit the profile of an early twentieth century baseball "rube," yet he carried this nicknames with him throughout his career as a player, owner, and Negro Leagues official. Foster, unlike other "rubes," claimed his nickname was not due to his lack of sophistication but by virtue of his athletic talent. In 1902, Foster beat "Rube" Waddell, one of the preeminent white pitchers of the day and a future Hall of Famer, in a pitching duel.[46] As a reward of sorts for his victory, Foster's teammates dubbed him "Rube," and the nickname stuck. Thus, Foster signified or troped upon the accepted meaning of the name "rube," adding his own meaning. By employing the name "Rube," Foster could continually invoke a claim to athletic superiority over one of the major leagues' best players. Foster and his teammates were repeatedly able to lay claim to the type of athletic success that was not supposed to be achievable for African Americans. "Rube" Foster kept the name as a rhetorical trophy from a battle won. Therefore, the public use of the name "Rube" for Foster was an attempt to point out the cracks in segregated baseball and the white supremacist theories that maintained that segregation. As "Rube" Foster had shown in his triumph, black baseball players could not only compete against the very best of the white major leaguers, they could win against them. How then could the white major leagues defend the color line as a line of ability rather than race?

Foster's complete acceptance of the name "Rube" ensured that he would always be remembered for his defeat of Waddell. According to an article in *Half-Century Magazine*, Foster preferred to be identified as Rube: "'Rube' (for such I will unconsciously be calling him—for it is such that the baseball world knows him and it is his wish that that name pass on down in the athletic world)."[47] Clearly, Foster actively chose to claim and keep the name of "Rube" and hoped that the legacy of his achievement would become part of baseball folklore. By 1922, as chairman of the National Association of Professional Baseball Clubs, Inc., Foster billed himself on the letterhead as "A. Rube Foster" and signed his correspondence the same way.[48] In fact, Foster commissioned his tombstone to read "A.R. Foster," thus permanently inscribing Rube as a part of his name.[49] Foster's use of his nickname reflected how he had become "Rube." In other words, Foster carried with him and later left behind proof of his innate ability and a counterargument to the major leagues' racist policies as part of his identity and legacy.

Foster's impact on the game meant that not only did he help to ensure through his letterhead and tombstone that the name of "Rube" would carry on, but also that others in honoring his contributions to black baseball would help spread his name far and wide. In 1943, a group of black army soldiers at Fort Huachuca, Arizona, arranged for their 11,000-seat baseball stadium to be named "Andrew Rube Foster Memorial Field."[50] Sportswriter Fay Young, writing in the *Defender*, celebrated the occasion, noting "one can not be identified with the game today without always being reminded of Rube."[51] By extension, one could not identify with Rube and not help carry on the message of his chosen name—a message of black pride and success despite Jim Crow.

In the 1930s and 1940s, black sportswriters referred to some of the most well-known black baseball players with nicknames that drew attention to the arbitrary nature of the color line and highlighted the athletic prowess of those players. Just as they published articles that proclaimed the superior talent of black baseball players, these writers also utilized nicknames that directly (and favorably) compared black ballplayers to famous white players. Writers crowned Josh Gibson as "the Black Babe Ruth," while Buck Leonard was "the Black Lou Gehrig." By appropriating the names of the most accomplished (and popular) white major leaguers, the black sports media called attention to the abilities of Negro Leaguers. These nicknames inherently argued that black players were equally as skilled as the best white players, thus providing an argument for the integration of major league baseball. They also signaled the existence of a thriving black baseball world, one that could be easily compared to the best of the white major leagues.

In at least one instance, a member of the white press used a similar nickname and comparison while covering the 1934 East-West All-Star Game. Marvin McCarthy of the *Chicago Times* composed a largely complementary article about the black all-star game under the headline "The Black Matty." In this article, McCarthy argued that Satchel Paige's skills rivaled those of legendary white pitcher Christy Mathewson. Although some of McCarthy's imagery treaded the line between colorful commentary and racial stereotyping, his acknowledgment of Paige's talent was clear.[52] Any reader of McCarthy's article clearly understood that Paige was an athlete for the ages and that a black man could equal one of the great white pitchers. By employing the nickname "the Black Matty," McCarthy (whether he realized it or not) provided another bit of fodder for those clamoring for major league integration. These nicknames underscored the quality of baseball performed in the Negro Leagues, thus elevating the status of the league and its players. For white baseball aficionados, these nicknames made it easier to see the potentiality of black ball players and made the black baseball world more visible within the national conversation about race and baseball.

Looking more broadly at the language of black baseball itself, one again finds evidence of racial signifying. Throughout the first half of the twentieth century, the very terms used as shorthand descriptions for white and black baseball reflected the stereotypes of the time and the obstacles encountered by black ballplayers. Commonly, sportswriters referred to white baseball as "organized baseball." Sporting periodicals like *The Sporting News* as well as white newspapers used the phrase "organized baseball" to differentiate the white major leagues from the professional black leagues and semi-pro baseball. The term "organized" has a variety of implications, particularly as a term meant to highlight contrast between white and black baseball. Michael S. Kimmel has argued that Progressive reformers praised "organized sport" as activity that "would instill important moral values." Here also, one can see the laudatory effect for segregationists in labeling white baseball as "organized."[53] With this terminology, white baseball was not only more professional and structured, it also was doing the important moral work helping to shape generations of good American (white) men.

Negro Leagues star Buck Leonard and other black baseball players objected to the use of "organized" as a descriptor for white baseball. In particular, Leonard chafed at the implicit notion that if white baseball was organized, black baseball must be somehow inferior. Leonard noted that the Negro Leagues "were not disorganized, just unrecognized."[54] For Negro Leagues players anxious for acknowledgment of their teams and leagues, the designation of white baseball as "organized" merely reinforced the most derogatory assumptions about black baseball. Leonard's turn of phrase flipped the script and placed the blame for any potential shortcomings on an American society that was unwilling to acknowledge the talent and success of black baseball.

In 1940, *Saturday Evening Post* writer Ted Shane explicitly erased the history of the organized Negro Leagues. Discussing Satchel Paige's career, life, and reputation as a "clown," Shane noted that although African Americans had been playing baseball "since 1884 ... there had never been any attempts at organization."[55] Shane's article was full of inaccuracies and exaggeration, yet its widespread dissemination as part of a well-read magazine would have further perpetuated the myth of unorganized black baseball. This complete dismissal of black baseball's then–56 years of home runs, championship games, leagues, and no-hitters was incredibly shortsighted and clearly a product of baseball rhetoric that debased the importance of the Negro Leagues.

Black ballplayers also strenuously objected to the term "sandlotters" used to describe black baseball for many of the same reasons that they lobbied against the term "organized" for white baseball. These terms set up a false and publicly damaging dichotomy between black and white baseball, defining the color line as one of ability rather than merely of skin color. Those who referred to white baseball as "organized" provided ammunition for critics who objected to the inclusion of black ball players in the major leagues on the basis that Negro Leagues players were insufficiently professional. Moreover, the idea that the Negro Leagues were disorganized further fanned the flames of black sportswriters who were quick to criticize black fan behavior at games. This all-too-common designation of major league baseball as "organized" slowed progress toward integration, adding weight to the unwritten "gentlemen's agreement" that prevented blacks from participating in major league baseball.

With black baseball designated as merely a sandlot game and its players sandlotters, Negro Leagues players were denied the respect that they had earned as successful professional athletes. In many ways, it was the rhetorical equivalent of using "boy" to refer to African American men of all ages. The "sandlot" wording implied not only amateurism but also a lack of manhood. Within a society that continually denied the privileges of manhood to African Americans, the dismissive language referring to black baseball was yet another indignity among many.

Robert K. Fitts has traced how this denial of the Negro Leagues' organization, and by extension black baseball's professionalism and athletic talent, continued after integration through the minimization of African American players' Negro Leagues backgrounds on baseball cards. Fitts argues that this intentional slight was part of a larger attempt to erase the history of segregated baseball, a history that was inconsistent with the ideals of democracy and meritocracy assumed to be integral to the national game.[56]

Overall, just like with the radical folklore and trickster storytelling of black baseball, African Americans used language and challenged others' use of language in order to push against the tyranny of racial discrimination during the Jim Crow era. By reclaiming and signifying on names, both those of teams and individuals, African Americans worked to dismantle Jim Crow segregation in baseball and to connect with a political consciousness that found common cause with other oppressed people of color throughout the world. Each small act of linguistic rebellion was another hole in the armor of segregation. The historical actors who created and transmitted these names and stories performed admirably their role as set-up men—the pitches they (rhetorically) threw allowed their team to move into position and laid the groundwork for the closer. Their individual actions were part of a larger, and eventually successful, campaign to break the major league color line.

SIX

Send in the Clowns
Clowning Teams and Trickster Resistance

On July 17, 1943, Chicago held its second annual "Satchel Paige Day," honoring the larger-than-life pitcher with gifts, a ceremony, and, appropriately, a doubleheader. Although the true attendance numbers are hard to discern as two separate articles in the July 24, 1943, *Chicago Defender* gave different counts, by all accounts a substantial number of baseball fans made their way to Wrigley Field to honor the hurler. Paige did his part. Before a crowd of 22,000–25,000 "howling fans," Paige took the mound for the Memphis Red Sox and led them to victory over the Cuban Stars.[1] The second part of the doubleheader was a game between the Birmingham Barons and the Cincinnati Clowns.[2]

This 1943 mingling of black baseball's ultimate trickster, Paige, and the popular clowning team, the Clowns, and their owner, Syd Pollock, was not the first or last time that the two would intersect. In a day of game article in the *Defender* promoting the doubleheader, the writer singles out a few players to watch on the Clowns. "Fred Wilson, the team's new playing manager and star pitcher and outfielder, is leading the league in home runs. 'Goose' Tatum is spectacular both at bat and at first base and with the humorous 'King Tut' forms a comedy combination that is hard to beat."[3] This description highlights the two sides of the Clowns in the early 1940s, their athletic ability as well as their comedy performance.

Clowning teams occupied a unique niche within black baseball during Jim Crow and after its demise. They embodied the contradictions of Negro Leagues baseball and played to and with the racial stereotypes that were prevalent at the time. Emphasizing entertainment, especially comedy, the clowning teams drew fans and alienated black sportswriters in equal measure. Owned and operated, with a brief exception, by white men, the clowning teams challenged the goals of organized black baseball, particularly those of the Negro National and American Leagues.

The clowns included men who functioned as athletes or as comedians, and those who performed both roles. By examining the meaning of their naming choices, the visual images they employed, and their routines, one can see echoes and distortions of the trickster, the rebel, and the racially conscious protester. While the players, writers, fans, and officials of black baseball used cultural space and artifacts to debunk white supremacy and hasten the lifting of major league baseball's color line, many contemporary race men publicly denounced the clowns as counter-productive and damaging to the race. At the same time, the clown team officials and players argued that they were doing the same work as their critics, just in a different guise. Certainly, the clowning teams were able to outlive their Negro Leagues counterparts, continuing to tour and play into the 1980s.

Just as in their tenure, the clowning teams in this chapter exist in, around, and beyond the organized Negro Leagues. At times, they place themselves within the larger narrative of black baseball, inserting themselves by joining the Negro American League briefly. In other instances, they loom just beyond the main story, hiring players who would go on to compete in the major leagues, drawing thousands of fans, and embodying a version of public blackness that could be compelling or repellant depending on one's perspective. In spite of and because of their grass skirts, costumes, and warpaint, black baseball advocates strove to make them invisible and inconsequential, lest their transgressions negate the progress already made.

As a lens to the black experience and the different versions of black resistance, the clowns are irresistible. After their careers ended, the clowning players and performers themselves argued that they had been tricksters in the same way that Satchel Paige was and insisted on reframing clowning as a radical act. Interrogating those claims through an analysis of visual images and naming practices, one finds a slightly twisted version of the cultural resistance discussed in the previous chapters.

As discussed in Chapter Three, black newspapers frequently sought to feature visual images of black baseball and African Americans in general in ways that flipped the script of white racism. Yet, as publications tasked with reporting the news, black papers had little choice but to cover the clowning teams. Similarly, by the 1930s and 1940s, black baseball leagues themselves had to confront the relative success of the clowning teams.

One of the main points of contention for both the black press and the Negro Leagues was the ways in which the clowning teams seemingly embraced racial stereotypes. These teams were always a minority in the black game. But thanks to the popular novel and movie, *The Bingo Long Traveling All-Star and Motor Kings*, it is their image that comes to mind for many when the Negro Leagues are discussed.[4]

The publicity methods of so-called "clowning" teams were controversial. A number of sportswriters, black baseball players, and Negro Leagues officials argued that the majority of these teams put forth images, through both their advertisements and their public appearances in costumes, that were detrimental to the ultimate goals of establishing a profitable, black-owned baseball league and the desegregation of major league baseball. There were of course some exceptions. In 1925, the *Pittsburgh Courier* did applaud early teams such as the "Bellevue Clowns" for "play[ing] straight up-to-the-minute ball" and for providing both "comedy and class" during their games.[5] In the 1930s and 1940s, however, as the black press amped up the push for integration and black leaders began to push integration over black enterprise, clowning teams lost the goodwill of the black press. Even without the blessing of the black press, these teams drew large, enthusiastic crowds during barnstorming tours. Moreover, as traditional Negro Leagues teams struggled to maintain viability in a difficult economic environment, their relative profitability made them valuable commodities for black baseball.[6] Their financial success granted them power over the objections and reservations of Negro Leagues owners, players, and sportswriters.[7]

Many of the clown teams played on racial and national stereotypes related to Africans. The Zulu Cannibal Giants, for instance, competed in grass skirts and donned war paint prior to games.[8] The Cannibal Giants also featured players chanting and performing dances during lulls in the baseball action. Advertisements for upcoming Cannibal Giants games used images that strongly focused on the supposed African-ness of the players rather than highlighting their baseball prowess. The broadside poster's central image was that of the team logo (a globe centering on Africa) and four painted Giants in long grass skirts. Another advertisement for the team played on the same themes. This latter ad showed the players in full makeup, costume, and barefoot. Proclaiming that the team was the "Oddest Novelty in Baseball," the ad was an appeal not to potential paying fans but to baseball owners who might be willing to book a game against the Cannibal Giants. Team officials sought to market themselves by highlighting the ways in which the Cannibal Giants provided unique entertainment and emphasizing the "novelty" aspect of the performance rather than the sport of baseball itself. The Cannibal Giants management was aware of their potential draw for fans and wanted to capitalize on it in their dealings with opposing teams.

The choice to use African imagery in naming and promoting the Zulu Cannibal Giants and another 1930s clowning team, the Ethiopian Clowns, was not accidental. Instead, it capitalized on two prominent aspects of contemporary African American popular culture. The first was the increasing attention to the crisis in Ethiopia over sovereignty. Italy's twentieth-century threats to Ethiopian self-rule began in 1930 and culminated in an Italian invasion of the country in 1935. Coupled with the growing pan–Africanism among black civil rights advocates of the time, these international developments ensured a degree of name recognition and potentially a positive association within the black community for their namesake baseball teams.

Politically, in the twentieth century, diverse African American leaders such as Marcus Garvey and W.E.B. Du Bois advocated a pan–Africanist worldview that supposed common cause throughout the African diaspora, uniting those who had been the victims of colonialism, slavery, and oppression. While Garvey and Du Bois disagreed upon the degree to which African nations should gain autonomy and the importance of black American repatriation, they both publicly advocated the idea that African Americans should promote African self-rule.[9] These early calls for pan–Africanism, particularly Garvey's popular movement, laid the groundwork for a further expansion of political pan–Africanism. In the 1930s, Mussolini's takeover of Ethiopia energized black members of the Communist party who (thanks in part to Garvey's "Back to Africa" campaign) saw Ethiopia as a symbolic homeland for African Americans.[10] Stymied by an uncooperative U.S. government and therefore unable to join the fighting, a number of black Communists (more than 80) formed the Lincoln Brigade—a group that battled fascists in the Spanish Civil War.[11] On the home front, African American reformers, activists, journalists, and Communists protested the Italian invasion and watched eagerly for updates from Africa.

Culturally, New Negro intellectual Alain Locke promoted the adoption of an African aesthetic for Harlem Renaissance-era artists starting in the 1920s.[12] Locke argued that true artistic genius and achievement could be accomplished by African American artists who embraced both their African-ness and their particular experience as black Americans. According to Locke,

> So, if, as seems already apparent, the sophisticated race sense of the Negro should lead back over the trail of the group tradition to an interest in things African, the natural affinities of the material and the art will complete the circuit and they will most electrically combine. Especially with its inherent color and emotionalism, its freedom from body-hampering dress, its odd and tragic and mysterious overtones, African life and themes, apart from any sentimental attachment, offer a wonderfully new field and province for dramatic treatment.... More and more the art of the Negro actor will seek its materials in the rich native soil of Negro life, and not in the threadbare tradition of the Caucasian stage. In the discipline of art playing upon his own material, the Negro has much to gain. Art must serve Negro life as well as Negro talent serve art.[13]

In this persuasive essay on the nature of art and race, Locke elevates the standing of African American culture by identifying the beauty, genius, and singularity of the black experience for the dramatic arts in particular.

Other African American artists, writers, and musicians embraced his call and integrated African styles and history into their work. By promoting a common, ancestral African past, these cultural leaders were able to highlight a racial pride that had roots in a history that preceded the horrors of American slavery. This history had great kings and warriors and could counter the common contemporary trope that underlined white supremacy: namely, that white American Anglo-Saxon society was the apex of civilization.

Similarly, black newspapers like the *Chicago Defender* published articles to educate their readers on the true nature of Africa.[14] A 1932 article summed up the main point of such articles in its title: "Africa Is Not a Country of Cannibalism and Savagery: Education, Industry, Commerce Are Features of Its Daily Life."[15] Debunking myths about the "savagery" of Africa was an important component of this campaign to encourage a pan–African racial consciousness. When combined with the focus on African history, these accounts of contemporary African life helped to reshape African American notions of Africa. In light of these political and cultural movements, African names such as "Zulu" and "Ethiopian" both served as easy shorthand for fans looking for black baseball and also resonated with larger ideals of black pride for many African Americans.

As mentioned previously, the name "Giants" itself had a positive connotation among African American baseball fans. "Giants" was an incredibly popular team name for African American teams during the black ball era. The "Giants" name invoked memories of other successful African American and Latino baseball teams of the recent past. For baseball fans who longed to connect to a longer tradition of black baseball (in a way that was often less accessible to African American fans, whose teams came and went somewhat frequently), the Giants were a draw.

In addition, the Zulu Cannibal Giants were part of a larger trend of late 1930s media imagery and advertising that reasserted and propagated derogatory racial imagery that depicted blacks as cannibals and animal-like while highlighting the African origins of American blacks.[16] The 1933 World's Fair in Chicago likewise marketed attractions that claimed to present traditional Africans performing native acts. In reality, much like the Zulus, the performers were local, urban blacks hired to pose as native Africans.[17] Thus, the Zulu Cannibal Giants communicated contradictory messages to attract two diverse audiences. By playing on the popular advertising imagery of the late 1930s, the Zulu Cannibal Giants drew white crowds by reinforcing the contemporary racial stereotypes. Meanwhile, the Giants appealed to black fans through their association with an African heritage and their allusion to the great Negro Leagues "Giants" teams.

The Cannibal Giants were not alone in black baseball clowning, or in drawing connections to stereotyped African imagery. Within the world of sport, historians have noted the ways in which football teams like the Brown Bombers and basketball teams like the Harlem Globetrotters, not to mention individual athletes like Eddie Tolan and Jesse Owens, participated in vaudeville and minstrel-style performances designed to embrace and critique common racial stereotypes of the time.[18] Much like the clowning baseball teams, these athletes straddled the line between comedy and athleticism and often invited criticism from the black press in regards to their seeming conformity to negative stereotypes. Outside of the black sporting world, other African American entertainers capitalized on similarly stereotyped African imagery to win audiences. Notably, Josephine Baker performed exotic, African-themed shows to large, appreciative audiences in Paris.[19]

In all of these cases, the audiences for these performances were drawn in by a wide variety of motivators. For some it was the sheer entertainment or comedy; for others it was the demonstration of a particular type of black talent that fit with already formed assumptions regarding African Americans; for still others, it was the fetishization of the exotic, the proverbial "other" that delighted them and brought them back time and time again. And for some African American fans, it was the skillfulness and the playfulness with which the athletes performed both their sporting feats and their critique of white supremacy.

For black journalists, scholars, and writers, these performances were incredibly troubling because of the ways in which they could be received and interpreted by their audiences. For Alain Locke, these popular performances both required and masked the vast genius of the performers. Locke highlights Baker, "Bojangles" Robinson, and Bert Williams, arguing:

> But the real mine of Negro dramatic art and talent is in the sub-soil of the vaudeville stage, gleaming through its slag and dross in the unmistakably great dramatic gifts of a Bert Williams, a Florence Mills or a Bill Robinson. Give Bojangles Robinson or George Stamper, pantomimic dancers of genius, a Bakst or the expressionist setting; give Josephine Baker, Eddie Rector, Abbie Mitchell or Ethel Waters a dignified medium, and they would be more than a sensation, they would be artistic revelations. Pantomime, that most essential and elemental of the dramatic arts, is a natural *forte* of the Negro actor, and the use of the body and voice and facile control of posture and rhythm are almost as noteworthy in the average as in the exceptional artist. When it comes to pure registration of the emotions, I question whether any body of actors, unless it be the Russians, can so completely be fear or joy or nonchalance or grief.[20]

Locke, thus, posits that the artistic clowning of vaudeville is only possible with great skill and ability. Popular black vaudeville performers are caught in a difficult trap. To perform properly requires immense talents; the medium for that talent (vaudeville) trades upon stereotypes; therefore performers within that field do not receive artistic respect or recognition, they are dismissed as "comic." Worst of all, the most popular performances reinforced ugly racial stereotypes for a sizable percentage of their audience. Successful baseball "clowns" found themselves in the same untenable situation.

The Clowns, the most prominent clowning team in the immediate Jim Crow and post-segregation era, barnstormed throughout the country as at times a traveling clown team but in other years as a slightly more traditional black baseball team that was part of the Negro Leagues. The Clowns were known as the "Ethiopian Clowns" during the 1930s, the height of pan–African concern over the European imperialism in Africa. Negro National and American League officials and owners objected to the use of "Ethiopian," arguing that it was demeaning and problematic. These objections were eventually overshadowed by black baseball's desire for better attendance and profits. In 1943, the Clowns and the Negro Leagues came to an agreement. The Clowns would become the Cincinnati (later Indianapolis) Clowns, leaving out the Ethiopian signifier and dropping the "warpaint." In exchange, the Clowns would be invited into the Negro American League.[21] During their stint in the Negro Leagues, the Clowns operated more traditionally, limiting the amount of clowning that was employed as part of their games, while retaining their name and the pre- and post-game entertainment.[22] The Clowns were financially successful in their 1940s turn with the Negro American League, consistently recording strong attendance numbers, though they generally finished in the middle or lower half of the league standings.[23]

As such, the team known as the "Clowns" was one of the most prominent, long-running, and successful clowning teams during and after the blackball era. Team owner Syd Pollock and promoter Abe Saperstein were well known, and in some cases despised, within the world of black baseball.[24] Abe Saperstein was a strong presence in Negro Leagues baseball. A white businessman, Saperstein arranged many of the bookings for black baseball teams and, at times, held a monopoly on the bookings for sought-after sites. By the 1930s, he was a continual thorn in the side of the Negro National and Negro American League, as he often operated at cross purposes with the organized leagues. Saperstein profited from booking black, novelty, and semi-pro teams; however, league games were run by the leagues and therefore outside of his purview, control, and pocketbook. In 1940, Frank A. Young of the *Chicago Defender* accused Saperstein of poaching players from existing Negro Leagues teams in an attempt to force the Negro American League to dissolve. Saperstein, Young contended, was the worst sort of opportunist, "making his money off of Negro activities" but only concerned with the "present" and "what he can get out of it."[25] This lack of investment in the future of the race ran contrary to the mission of the black press and made Saperstein a target for much criticism from black sportswriters.

Sydney Pollock had a similarly combative relationship with black sportswriters, players, owners, and fans during his long career in black baseball. Negro Leagues owners loudly objected to his comedy teams' use of African stereotypes and minstrel characters in their games.[26] Just as the black press objected to what they viewed as Saperstein's profiteering off of racial discrimination, they also cried foul at Pollock's Clowns teams. In the view of black sportswriters in the 1940s and '50s, these teams publicly displayed and seemingly celebrated negative racial images of African Americans to the detriment of the race as a whole.[27]

Saperstein was also responsible for creating the Harlem Globetrotters, the clowning black basketball team.[28] He used his connections to cross-promote with his athletes and teams. Goose Tatum played for both the Indianapolis Clowns and the Harlem Globetrotters, while Satchel Paige made promotional appearances for the Globetrotters.[29] The Clowns appropriated characters from the then-defunct Zulu Cannibal Giants, popular minstrel shows, and the circus as part of their marketing schemes. Traveling the country for barnstorming and league games (depending on the year), the Clowns assembled a cast of comic characters in addition to their regular roster of players. Fans flocked to the ballpark to see their favorite comedy performers and acts in addition to a game of baseball.

An advertising poster from 1957 shows the wide variety of characters included on the Clowns. The poster names "King Tut" as one of its featured players. King Tut was actually a man named Richard King, who provided much of the pre- and post-game entertainment as well as skits and acts between innings and plays. Tut's tenure with the Clowns was long and noteworthy—he performed for the team from 1936 until 1958.[30] According to Pollock's son, Alan, Tut often would make his entrance in unforgettable style, emerging from a "smoking dugout ... clothed in prisoner's black and white striped suit and hat, and shackled by ball and chain." Alan Pollock claimed that Tut's entrance was a racial allegory of sorts, a message of transcendent freedom that could obliterate the chains of racism.[31]

Tut's teammates and fellow performers embodied other stereotypes that were common for the time. One of the larger images shows a man dressed as a tribal member, complete with grass skirt. Not only was James "Natureboy" Williams costumed as a stereotypical "other," he also played with gendered expectations. In addition to the skirt (which was an ethnic/racial signifier), Williams donned a padded bra and "was billed as "Clowns Firstbase Ma'am."[32] Although in his account of his father's team, Alan Pollock insisted that Wiliams did not effectively cross-dress, he certainly transgressed gender norms by wearing a bra and being referred to as "ma'am." Within the context of black manhood during Jim Crow, the dual diminutions of Williams's masculinity, through the use of "boy" and "ma'am" in his names and his costuming, further complicated his public image. By associating Williams with female gender characteristics, he became more comic and less threatening for audiences of the time. Other performance identities were more in line with traditional vaudeville and minstrelry acts. The broadside also features a ballplayer made up to look like a circus clown, while at the top of the poster, yet another ballplayer is depicted as the stereotypical dandy minstrel character. The clown is straightforward and expected within this tableau, and the dandy character had a long history within American history. White Americans had tried to police African American attire since the early days of slavery, going so far as to legislate black clothing after the seventeenth century Stono Rebellion, and the dandy had become a symbol of African American over-reaching and attempts to act "white" or above the low status enforced by Jim Crow.[33]

One character not pictured in the promotional flyer was Spec BeBop. BeBop was a dwarf who served as a performing partner for King Tut. Their completely opposite body types allowed for physical comedy that delighted audiences.[34] At games, the players would perform various comedic sketches to entertain the crowd, again using the stock characters to amuse fans. The Clowns were, in fact, part of a long Negro Leagues tradition that combined minstrelry and baseball. In the 1910s and 1920s, black ball teams would tour with a minstrel show company, and both groups would provide entertainment during their stops.[35]

The Clowns would outlast the integration of major league baseball, continuing to barnstorm for decades to come, performing a Harlem Globetrotters–like show in front of integrated audiences.[36] In fact, they outlasted the dissolution of the Negro American League. Other Negro Leagues teams were not so fortunate. With the exception of the Clowns, the other remaining Negro Leagues teams functioned as a minor league for the majors during the 1950s.

Although they never fully abandoned the comedy routines that marked their founding and the other similar clown teams, the Clowns were responsible for temporarily employing one of the great African American baseball talents of the post–Jackie Robinson Era. During their 1940s foray into developing Negro Leagues legitimacy, their baseball squad featured strong, talented players. Most notably, future major league baseball home run king Hank Aaron spent a portion of a season touring with the Clowns. Hank Aaron competed with the Clowns in 1952, during which Pollock sold Aaron's option to the Boston (soon to be Milwaukee) Braves.[37] In his autobiography, Aaron explained the balancing act that the Clowns tried to strike in the early 1950s. The entire team would take part in pre-game comedy routines like shadowball (in which the players would run through fielding practice without a ball). Once the game began, the comic performers like King Tut and Spec BeBop would employ sketches between innings or plays to entertain the crowds.[38]

That same year, the Clowns made history by adding a female player, Toni Stone, to their team.[39] Stone was later traded to the Kansas City Monarchs and retired in 1954.[40] The Clowns, however, continued to employ female players on the teams for a few years. Connie Morgan and Mamie Johnson also competed with the Clowns in the mid–1950s. In part due to their many publicity stunts and in part due to their actual athletic prowess, the Clowns were the last of the Negro Leagues teams.

By the mid–1950s, the Clowns had adopted a model quite similar to that of the Harlem Globetrotters. Instead of playing local teams or arranging games with competitive semi-professional teams, the Clowns traveled with their own competition—their version of the Washington Generals, the Globetrotters' patsies. At the time of the broadside announcing their 1957 showdown in Mississippi, their constant opponents were a team that called itself the Black Yankees. The Clowns survived until the 1980s trading on their status as a novelty act to attract crowds as they traveled the country.[41]

The presence and popularity of the black clowning team reflects the racial atmosphere of the time, particularly in terms of popular culture and entertainment. For many African Americans in the entertainment business, racial expectations of the time shaped the way they could craft their public images. African American performers navigated the fine line between making strides in traditional white arenas through their presence and avoiding the racial stereotypes and caricatures that undergirded their inclusion in white entertainment. Much like the black actors who only found opportunities portraying "mammies" or "sambos," black baseball players often found their most lucrative employment and acceptance by whites as members of clowning teams that played upon the tropes of minstrelry. The clowning players faced the difficult task of maintaining their own values and integrity while pursuing a profitable living. Many players who became involved with such teams came to terms with the contradictions between their private beliefs and their public act by arguing that they were only benefiting from the narrow-mindedness of white Americans, a narrow-mindedness that was unlikely to change in Jim Crow America.

In oral interviews, years after their playing days, a number of players expressed their belief that as performers in clowning performances, they in fact had the upper hand over their white audiences.[42] Similarly, Alan Pollock and his father interpreted the clowning performances of King Tut in more racially empowering terms, arguing that Tut and other "clowns" were confronting racism and sending a message of black pride.[43] Under this reasoning, the clowning players were able to justify their participation in the often embarrassing actions that were part of barnstorming as black baseball clowns. These players felt that they were playing the role of trickster. As such, they were the ones who were actually in control, and they were taking advantage of their white audiences, who played the role of the easily duped fools. The black trickster player was thus financially benefiting from the racial prejudice and stupidity of the white fans, earning a degree of power over the very people who usually held financial control within society. For these players, the joke was on their white audience, rather than on themselves. Even if they had to play a racial caricature, they ultimately profited from it as their white audience walked away from the performance with lighter pockets. Moreover, the trickster players performed what was merely a farce: they were able to protect themselves in a certain sense, by refusing to reveal too much to the whites who came to watch them play.[44]

Although some African American ballplayers were able to come to terms with their participation on clowning teams and see themselves as the ultimate benefactors of an unfair racial system, other Negro Leagues players and owners objected to the clown teams and their antics. Additionally, many of the more prominent black sportswriters found clown baseball to be antithetical to the goal of integrating major league baseball. In response to particular skits performed by the Ethiopian Clowns, for example, Negro Leagues officials banned league teams from playing against the Clowns in 1942. Both of the skits that were considered objectionable involved scatological humor, and Negro Leagues officials were unwilling to be associated with what they considered unseemly humor.[45]

The ban was short-lived and difficult to enforce. The Negro Leagues, dealing with internal jockeying for power, the limitations of wartime travel and the wartime service of players, and their quest to push for integration of the major leagues, were anxious to continue the ticket sale increases of the 1940s and could not manage to evade the ever-popular clowning teams. Like good set-up men, they focused on the ultimate goals, a victory for their team, and tried to neutralize the threat at the plate—even when that threat wore war paint and played shadowball.

Epilogue

Having spent extensive time discussing how black baseball tricksters, be they players, fans, writers, artists, or clowns, flipped the proverbial script by challenging all aspects of white supremacy during Jim Crow, I am going to try to do the same. In the final analysis, the door opened too late for *white* major league baseball. The majority of white baseball fans never witnessed the speed of Cool Papa Bell or the power of Josh Gibson. The 1927 Yankees did not further transcend baseball excellence by adding Smoky Joe Williams to their rotation. Babe Ruth, Lou Gehrig, Lefty Grove, and Jimmie Foxx led the league without challenge from Josh Gibson, Buck Leonard, and Satchel Paige. These match-ups are left to the imagination of baseball fans who argue over stats, aptitude, and legacies. For those who value the skill and accomplishments of the Negro Leagues stars, the official record books of the white major league era will always be incomplete, marked with an invisible asterisk that encompasses what could (and should) have been.

Outside of the white major leagues, so much happened for African Americans during the approximately 60 years of black baseball over the color line. African Americans, denied a chance at the pinnacle of American baseball and, thus, equal access to the national pastime, created their own leagues, teams, style of play, records, and folklore. As the nation moved into the twentieth century, through two World Wars and a Great Depression, black baseball was constantly changing and shifting, but it was also a constant presence. African American fans could not go to a major league game to see a race man play, but they could go to a major league park and take in a doubleheader with major league–caliber players. Concurrently, African Americans created a whole culture of black baseball—melding African American history, experience, politics, and race consciousness with sport in folktales, nicknames, cartoons, posters, and comedy. Within that culture, they found a safer space for their critiques and protests of segregation. Each of these cultural creations dismantled a small part of Jim Crow and reinforced black commitment to ending segregation. In 1947, with Jackie Robinson's Brooklyn Dodgers debut, that project had its most visible success.

Tragically, though, for the many people employed by the Negro Leagues, the integration of baseball spelled the demise of organized black baseball as an institution. The Negro Leagues held on for more than a decade, but never regained the status and importance it held during the golden years of black baseball. Yet, the consequences exceeded that of the dissolution of a sports league. For African Americans, the loss of the Negro Leagues was significant socially, culturally, politically, and economically.

Black fans lost not only the Negro Leagues, but also the leisure space they had established in their local baseball fields. The death of the league was the end of a black business enterprise, one that contributed economically to African American communities. The major leagues were willing to profit from the addition of African American players but unwilling to filter those profits back into African American communities. Major league owners refused, with few exceptions, even to compensate Negro Leagues owners for the loss of their players. Instead, they dismissed Negro Leagues contracts as insufficient and non-binding. Taking advantage of the well-established view in the white baseball world that the Negro Leagues were unprofessional and unorganized, major league owners were able to raid the black leagues of their talent, without paying anywhere near full value for the players.

Negro Leagues owners were caught in an impossible situation. To stand in the way of integration would put them at odds with the African American community, but they needed financial resources to continue. Black sportswriters were more than happy to publicly highlight and shame those who stood in the way of integration efforts, no matter what the situation. In the 1940s, Ed Gottlieb, the white owner of the Philadelphia Stars baseball club, attracted the ire of prominent *Courier* sportswriter Wendell Smith. Smith argued that Gottlieb unfairly discriminated against African Americans in establishing his basketball team. Despite owning a black baseball team, Gottlieb refused to support integration for professional basketball, and Smith used his column to alert African American readers to his hypocrisy.[1]

Aware of the potential financial dangers of alienating her fan base as well as the problem of losing her most valuable players, Effa Manley led a one-woman public campaign to shame major league owners into recognizing the legitimacy of Negro Leagues contracts. Unable to object to integration itself, for fear of losing fans, Manley instead sought monetary compensation for the loss of key players.[2] Manley also vehemently responded to slights on the Negro Leagues, including an *Ebony* article with Jackie Robinson, in which he painted an unflattering portrait of life in the Negro Leagues [Jackie Robinson, "What's Wrong with Negro Baseball?" *Ebony*, June 1948]. In addition to accusing Robinson of being "ungrateful and more likely stupid," Manley also argued that Branch

Rickey was a less than scrupulous businessman, having failed to provide compensation to the Kansas City Monarchs when signing Robinson.[3] Manley's outspokenness did not win her fans or stem the tide of black star players who made their way to the major leagues in the late 1940s and early 1950s. Scouts, brokers, and Negro Leagues power players maneuvered to secure positions as talent brokers and liaisons between the white and black leagues. Alex Pompez, former owner of the Cuban Stars, worked as a hybrid scout and supervisor for Latino and African American players with the San Francisco Giants.[4]

Overall, the integration of baseball was in part a token gesture. While it had been a major issue among those campaigning for racial equality and was a victory for the nascent civil rights movement, it did not eliminate racism in professional baseball. A number of major league teams instituted an unstated quota, limiting the number of roster spots for African Americans. The Boston Red Sox refused to integrate until 1959, twelve years after Jackie Robinson's debut. Phillip M. Hoose, in a study of sport and racism, has argued that white coaches and managers refused to give African Americans positions such as catcher and pitcher that were central to on-the-field decision making while numerous sportswriters and commentators have highlighted the lack of opportunities for African American baseball players who wish to enter into management or front office positions.[5] These are just the most obvious examples of the persistence of racism in major league after integration. The death threats targeting Hank Aaron, the implicit racism of sports commentators who employ racial signifiers that reinforce stereotypes, and the continually decreasing number of African American major leaguers reveal that racial prejudice has continued to plague the game long after the end of segregation.

Sports Illustrated ran an illuminating article in 1960 that explored the baseball experience for the "Negro player."[6] The author, Robert Boyle, described the exclusive society of black players after integration. Noting that there were 57 "Negro" players in the major leagues, Boyle argued that black players were "race men who prefer to keep away from the whites."[7] According to Boyle, American "Negro" players differentiated themselves from "Latin Negros," and the two groups did not associate with each other.

One of the most fascinating aspects of Boyle's article is his discussion of the "secret language" and "informal code of behavior" of black ball players after integration.[8] Boyle revealed that each black player had a nickname; some players' names were available for both black and white players to use while others were "so racial (probably) in origin that the players keep them absolutely to themselves."[9] Boyle did not explain what kind of name would be "so racial" that it must be held as a secret or what the implications of the wide dissemination of a racial name might be. Many of the rhetorical strategies Boyle identified—nicknaming, juggling the hidden and public transcript with language, and boasting—have their roots in the Negro Leagues experience.

During major league baseball's Jim Crow, those strategies helped foster community and protest, and after integration, the slow pace of progress meant that the same strategies were necessary for community, protest, and survival. A number of the issues faced by these players were unchanged. Just as Jack Johnson, Satchel Paige, and Joe Louis were warned about interracial relationships and black baseball players were cautioned to marry young and avoid women, so too did the first generation of black players in the major leagues worry about the possibility of professional ruin due to romantic entanglement.

> There are other factors which keep the Negro from intimate association with the white. One is women. "We're playing with fire with that," said a Negro player, "and we all know it." Players who have played with fire have been sent down.[10]

At the time of the article, it would still be seven years before the Supreme Court's *Loving vs. Virginia* ruling, which would invalidate anti-miscegenation laws and grant Americans the right to marry an opposite gender person of a different race than their own. With so many states barring interracial relationships, black baseball players justly feared the consequences of such liaisons.

Black ball players also were not able to speak freely about their political beliefs. In the quote below, Boyle tries to capture the racial situation for black players in larger society. The player is happy to talk and outline the most pressing issues, but he is unwilling to go on the record and be identified by name.

> Tension is another factor. "You don't realize the problems we have," a Negro player said. "You can go anywhere, do anything, but we have terrific tensions. We feel good among our own people. What bothers me is when I, well, pay taxes for something like a school, and I can't go there." The player quoted here said frankly that he had "a chip on my shoulder this wide"—he held his hands about a foot apart—about the race problem. "What annoys me most is to see a Negro woman with a white man," he said.[11]

African Americans in the major leagues still struggled with segregation during spring training, limited bonuses, and racial discrimination.[12] Speaking out about those issues could be devastating for their careers, however, so they initially continued the strategies of Jim Crow. With their more secure financial situation, black players also used money to contribute anonymously to the cause.

> The Negro players do accept responsibility as race men," Mal Goode says. "Fifteen of them are buying or already have bought life memberships in the NAACP. That's $500. Also many of them have made special contributions to the NAACP. When the NAACP was fighting in the Supreme Court, the NAACP would send telegrams asking players for money. I've only heard one [Negro] ballplayer make a derogatory remark.[13]

During the two decades after integration, African American players remained a decided minority in baseball. Two of the most storied franchises in the major leagues, the Boston Red Sox and the New York Yankees, resisted integration. New York established an anti-discrimination law that some credited with forcing the Brooklyn Dodgers to sign Jackie Robinson and integrate. Despite the existence of New York's anti-discrimination law and a similar measure in Massachusetts, the Yankees did not integrate until 1956 and the Red Sox held out until 1955. The Red Sox refused to integrate until twelve years after Robinson's major league debut.[14] The Cleveland Indians and Brooklyn Dodgers, clubs considered to be racially progressive and pioneering, maintained semi-official quotas, passing over more qualified African American players in order not to increase the number of black players on their rosters.[15] Baseball historian Steve Treder has also traced how race influenced personnel decisions on the New York (and later San Francisco) Giants under Horace Stoneham. According to the 1960 *Sports Illustrated* article, black players felt "that they [had] to be 'better' than the white players to stay. 'If two players are the same, and one is white and one is colored, and one has to go, nine out of 10 times the colored guy will be the guy.' Comparative statistics for hitters bear this out. In 1958 the average Negro major leaguer drove in 46 runs, hit 11 homers and batted .282."[16]

Once again, even in the major leagues, African American players had to prove themselves better qualified for the same job. Instead of hitting home runs across the state of Pennsylvania, players needed to put up the best measurable statistics in order to get and keep their chance to compete. Even overwhelming baseball success was not a guarantee of acceptance. As late as the 1970s, Hank Aaron received racially motivated hate mail and death threats as he approached and passed Babe Ruth's lifetime home run record.[17]

As a result of the poor treatment of black baseball players and the increased urbanization of African American populations, baseball's popularity has precipitously declined among black sports fans since integration.[18] Today, African American athletes and fans are much more likely to spend their leisure time on sports like basketball and football, rather than baseball. African American neighborhoods rarely contain sandlot baseball fields or sponsor local baseball clubs. Concrete basketball courts with metal rims have replaced grass baseball fields; young African American men practice lay-ups instead of taking batting practice.

In this book, I have tried to illuminate the history of the Negro Leagues in order to recover a relationship between African Americans and baseball that has since been lost. To that end, I have explored the intersections between black baseball, segregation, black enterprise, and racial identity during Jim Crow. Because black baseball was immensely popular among African Americans and represented a public display of segregated leisure, the ways in which black baseball players, fans, writers, and owners performed baseball was significant. Traveling to and from games, African American fans and players navigated the physical terrain of black baseball, in familiar and unfamiliar locations. In the best-case scenarios, fans occupied ballparks unmarked by the color line and were free to enjoy grandstand seats, and players had unfettered access to clubhouse showers. In many other instances, players and fans were forced to observe separate but unequal accommodations, relegated to the bleachers and refused service at restaurants and hotels. Within such a context, the black press highlighted the triumphs of the black baseball enterprise: black-owned parks, private Pullman cars, patronage by celebrities and the elite. On their frequent barnstorming tours, black players alternately accepted and challenged the color line—in some instances avoiding restaurants known to be hostile to African Americans and at other times transgressing racial boundaries by sending light-skinned teammates to obtain food and goods.

Similarly, the very conception of black manhood was the subject of debate and negotiation within the context of segregated baseball. Black sportswriters and owners hoped to advance the dual (and sometimes dueling) causes of integration and black enterprise by marketing black baseball players as gentleman and by showcasing the respectable nature of Negro Leagues fans. African American baseball players, on the other hand, were unwilling to capitulate fully to the standards of conduct endorsed by their owners and writers. Instead, they sought a more modern conception of manhood, one that allowed for individuality and fun. While black baseball players continued to enjoy leisure in ways contrary to that of the "respectable," the black press constructed unimpeachable public images for Negro Leagues players in an attempt to secure greater civil rights for African Americans.

The New Negro manhood ideal of the interwar period manifested itself in other ways. African Americans used visual images in the black press, trickster tales, and nicknames to critique segregation and white supremacy. On the pages of the *Chicago Defender*, *Pittsburgh Courier*, and other black periodicals, photographs and editorial art challenged everything from the supposed moral and athletic superiority of the white major leaguers to gross racial stereotypes. Likewise, trickster tales and nicknames spoke to the injustices of racially-biased law enforcement, the ambiguities of the black/white racial binarism of the time, and the remarkable achievements of black athletes. Through these critiques, African Americans displayed their dissatisfaction with American racism and their desire to effect change.

In this study, I have attempted to fill some of the holes in our understanding of black baseball and its role in black communities. In essence, I have argued that the African American performance of baseball, physically, discursively, and visually, revealed a counter-narrative that challenged the underpinnings of segregated society. The creators of this counter-narrative functioned as metaphorical set-up men ... the less known, unsung heroes whose statistics are not part of the official records but who had an immense impact on the national pastime.

Of course, there is still considerable work to be done. In particular, we know too little about the experiences of African American fans, especially working-class fans. Their voices are difficult to uncover, yet extraordinarily significant for a more complete picture of black baseball. I have attempted, wherever possible, to highlight the experience of African American fans as communicated through editorial letters and press descriptions of black baseball crowds. However, the extant evidence limits the degree to which one can extrapolate about the experience of African American fans. Similarly, very little scholarly attention has been paid to the men who created the incredible pieces of editorial art for the black newspapers. These astute critics of early twentieth-century race relations are important historical subjects in their own right and deserve to be the subject of study and historical investigation.

Baseball, the national pastime, has a challenging track record when it comes to race. African Americans, Latinos, and Japanese Americans understood the symbolic value of baseball in American society. Denied the right to participate fully, these oppressed groups sought to claim baseball for themselves and by extension to claim their American citizenship, privilege, and birth right. Striving for racial equality on ball fields and refusing simply to concede to white supremacy and scientific racism, African Americans fought back with the tools they had—their stories, their names, their space, their art, their journalism, and their comedy. Their slow dismantling of the brick wall of segregation opened up small holes that eventually made the whole thing crumble and fall.

Chapter Notes

Preface

1. Paul Votano, *Late and Close: A History of Relief Pitching* (Jefferson, NC: McFarland, 2002), 42.

2. "MLB Miscellany: Rules, regulations and statistics," *MLB Official Info*, http://mlb.mlb.com/mlb/official_info/about_mlb/rules_regulations.jsp, Accessed 7/19/2013.

Introduction

1. On the rise of baseball as an American sport, see John R. Betts, "The Technological Revolution and The Rise of Sport, 1850–1900," *The Mississippi Valley Historical Review* (September 1953), 232; George B. Kirsch, *Baseball in Blue and Gray: The National Pastime during the Civil War* (Princeton: Princeton University Press, 2003), 113–129; Benjamin C. Rader, *Baseball: A History of America's Game* (Urbana: University of Illinois Press, 2d ed, 2002), 2, 5–30; Mark Ribowsky, *A Complete History of the Negro Leagues, 1884–1955* (Secaucus, NJ: Citadel, 1995), 13; William J. Ryczek, *When Johnny Came Sliding Home: The Post-Civil War Baseball Boom, 1865–1870* (Jefferson, NC: McFarland, 1998), 72–74.

2. Ribowsky, *A Complete History*, 16–17.

3. David W. Zang, *Fleet Walker's Divided Heart: The Life of Baseball's First Black Major Leaguer* (Lincoln: University of Nebraska Press, 1995), 37–40, 61; Jules Tygiel, *Extra Bases: Reflections on Jackie Robinson, Race, and Baseball History* (Lincoln: University of Nebraska Press, 2002), 53–55.

4. Ribowsky, *A Complete History*, 31–32.

5. Tygiel, *Extra Bases*, 55.

6. Tygiel, *Baseball's Great Experiment: Jackie Robinson and His Legacy* (New York: Vintage, 1984), 14–15.

7. Ribowsky, *A Complete History*, 12–15; Christopher Threston, *The Integration of Baseball in Philadelphia* (Jefferson, NC: McFar-

land, 2003), 8–10. On Catto, see Daniel R. Biddle and Murray Dubin, *Tasting Freedom: Octavius Catto and the Battle for Equality in Civil War America* (Philadelphia: Temple University Press, 2010).

8. Michael E. Lomax, *Black Baseball Entrepreneurs, 1860–1901: Operating By Any Means Necessary* (Syracuse: Syracuse University Press, 2003), 50–53.

9. Ribowsky, *A Complete History*, 20–21.

10. For more information on early league attempts, see Lomax, *Black Baseball Entrepreneurs,* 61–149.

11. On the intricacies of black baseball maneuvers during the first two decades of the twentieth century, see Ribowsky, *A Complete History*, 40–104.

12. W.E.B. Du Bois, "Returning Soldiers," *The Crisis* XVIII (May 1919) 13. Du Bois's initial stance on African American involvement in World War I was complicated and problematic. See Mark Ellis, "'Closing Ranks' and 'Seeking Honors': W.E.B. Du Bois in World War I" *Journal of American History* 79 (June 1992): 96–124; William Jordan, "'The Damnable Dilemma': African American Accommodation and Protest During World War I," *Journal of American History* 81 (March 1995): 1562–1583; Ellis, "W.E.B. Du Bois and the Formation of Black Political Thought in World War I: A Commentary on 'The Damnable Dilemma,'" *Journal of American History* 81 (March 1995): 1584–1590.

13. For an examination of Foster's earlier forays into organized black baseball in Chicago, see Michael E. Lomax, " Black Entrepreneurship in the National Pastime: The Rise of Semiprofessional Baseball in Black Chicago," in Patrick B. Miller and David K. Wiggins, eds., *Sport and Color Line: Black Athletes and Race Relations in the Twentieth Century* (New York: Routledge, 2004), 25–44.

14. Robert C. Cottrell, *Blackball, the Black*

Sox, and the Babe: Baseball's Crucial 1920 Season (Jefferson, NC: McFarland, 2002), 142–153.

15. A counterpart to Foster's Chicago-based Negro National League soon developed. In 1922, Hilldale (Philadelphia) owner Ed Bolden established the Eastern Colored League to provide a home league for Eastern black clubs. Neil Lanctot, Negro League Baseball: The Rise and Ruin of a Black Institution (Philadelphia: University of Pennsylvania Press, 2004), 5; Threston, The Integration of Baseball in Philadelphia, 31–32.

16. Ribowsky, A Complete History, 72–73; Lanctot, Negro League Baseball, 9.

17. Lanctot, Negro League Baseball, 9; Ira F. Lewis, "'New' League Not Needed," The Competitor (May 1921), 39, 41.

18. Taylor, "The Future of Colored Baseball," The Competitor (February 1920), 76–79, quote 76.

19. Allan H. Spear, Black Chicago: The Making of a Negro Ghetto 1890–1920 (Chicago: University of Chicago Press, 1967), 117.

20. On the tensions between integrationist and segregationist camps in Chicago's African American community, see Spear, Black Chicago, 51–55.

21. On Garvey, see E. David Cronon, ed., Marcus Garvey (Englewood Cliffs, NJ: Prentice Hall, 1973); Tony Martin, Race First: The Ideological and Organizational Struggle of Marcus Garvey and the Universal Negro Improvement Association (Westport, CT: Greenwood, 1976); Judith Stein, The World of Marcus Garvey: Race and Class in Modern Society (Baton Rouge: Louisiana State University Press, 1986).

22. Lanctot, Negro League Baseball, 9.

23. Lanctot, Negro League Baseball, 9, 16–18.

24. Ribowsky, A Complete History, 177.

25. Lanctot, Negro League Baseball, 84, 95.

26. See Susan E. Johnson, When Women Played Hardball (Seattle: Seal Press, 1994); Patricia Vignola, ""The Patriotic Pinch Hitter: The AAGBL and How American Woman Earned a Permanent Spot on the Roster," Nine 12 (February 2004): 102–113.

27. Lanctot covers this tension in detail. Negro League Baseball, 96–100,

28. On Jackie Robinson, see Jules Tygiel, Baseball's Great Experiment: Jackie Robinson and His Legacy (New York: Vintage, 1984).

29. Spear, Black Chicago, 51–54.

30. Ribowsky, A Complete History, 314.

31. Robert Peterson, Only the Ball Was White: A History of Legendary Black Players and All-Black Professional Teams (New York: McGraw Hill, 1984); Donn Rogosin, Invisible Men: Life in Baseball's Negro Leagues (New York: Kodansha International, 1983, 1995).

32. William Brashler, Josh Gibson: A Life in the Negro Leagues (New York: Harper and Row, 1978); Monte Irvin with James A. Riley, Monte Irvin: Nice Guys Finish First (New York: Carroll and Graf, 1996); Wilmer Fields, My Life in the Negro Leagues (Westport, CT: Meckler, 1992); Buck Leonard with James A. Riley, Buck Leonard The Black Lou Gehrig: The Hall of Famer's Story in His Own Words (New York: Carroll and Graf, 1995); Effa Manley and Leon Herbert Hartwick, Negro Baseball ... Before Integration (Chicago: Adams Press, 1976); Kyle P. McNary, Ted "Double Duty" Radcliffe: 36 Years of Pitching and Catching in Baseball's Negro Leagues (Minneapolis: McNary, 1994); Buck O'Neil with Steve Wulf and David Conrads, I Was Right on Time: My Journey from the Negro Leagues to the Majors (New York: Fireside, 1997); James Overmyer, Queen of the Negro Leagues: Effa Manley and the Newark Eagles (Methuchen, NJ: Scarecrow, 1993); LeRoy (Satchel) Paige as told to David Lipman, Maybe I'll Pitch Forever: A Great Baseball Player tells the Hilarious Story Behind the Legend (Lincoln: University of Nebraska Press, 1962, 1993); Ellen Rendle, Judy Johnson: Delaware's Invisible Hero (Wilmington, DE: Cedar Tree, 1994); Mark Ribowsky, Don't Look Back: Satchel Paige in the Shadows of Baseball (New York: Simon and Schuster, 1994); Ribowsky, The Power and the Darkness: The Life of Josh Gibson in the Shadows of the Game (New York: Simon and Schuster, 1996); Frazier "Slow" Robinson and Paul Bauer, Catching Dreams: My Life in the Negro Baseball League (Syracuse: Syracuse University Press, 1999); Quincy Trouppe, 20 Years Too Soon: Prelude to Major league Integrated Baseball (St. Louis: Missouri Historical Society, 1995, 1977).

33. Stephen Banker, Black Diamonds: An Oral History of Negro Baseball, Cassette Tapes. (Washington: Tapes for Readers, 1978, 1992); John Holway, Voices from the Great Black Baseball Leagues; Holway, Blackball Stars: Negro League Pioneers (Westport, CT: Meckler, 1988); Brent Kelley, Voices from the Negro Leagues: Conversations with 52 Baseball Standouts of the Period 1924–1960 (Jefferson, NC: McFarland, 1998).

34. "Seventeen from Negro Leagues, pre–Negro Leagues Eras Elected to the Hall of

Fame by Special Committee," http://www.baseballhalloffame.org/news/2006/060227.htm, viewed June 13, 2006; George Vecsey, "Sports of the Time: Taking a Seat with the Guys Again," *New York Times*, 28 February 2006, D1.

35. Janet Bruce, *Kansas City Monarchs: Champions of Black Baseball* (Lawrence: University of Kansas Press, 1985); Lanctot, *Fair Dealing and Clean Playing: The Hilldale Club and the Development of Black Professional Baseball* (Jefferson, NC: McFarland, 1994); Rob Ruck, *Sandlot Seasons: Sport in Black Pittsburgh.* (Urbana: University of Illinois Press, 1987).

36. Leslie A. Heaphy, *The Negro Leagues, 1869–1960* (Jefferson, NC: McFarland, 2003); Lanctot, *Negro League Baseball*; Lomax, *Black Baseball Entrepreneurs, 1860–1901*; Ribowsky, *A Complete History.*

37. Larry Tye, *Satchel: The Life and Times of an American Legend* (New York: Random House, 2009).

38. Donald Spivey, *"If You Were Only White": The Life and Times of Leroy "Satchel" Paige* (Columbia: University of Missouri Press, 2012).

39. *Satchel Paige and Company: Essays on the Kansas City Monarchs, Their Greatest Star and the Negro Leagues*, ed by Leslie A. Heaphy (Jefferson, NC: McFarland, 2007).

40. In particular, I refer to the literature on the Great Migration, the 1920s, and the Great Depression. See for example, Peter Gottlieb, *Making Their Own Way: Southern Blacks' Migration to Pittsburgh, 1916–1930* (Urbana: University of Illinois Press, 1987); James R. Grossman, *Land of Hope: Chicago, Black Southerners, and the Great Migration* (Chicago: University of Chicago Press, 1989); Kenneth L. Kusmer, *Black Cleveland: A Ghetto Takes Shape, 1870–1930* (Urbana: University of Illinois Press, 1978); Gilbert Osofsky, *Harlem: The Making of a Ghetto, 1890–1930* (New York: Harper & Row, 1963); Kimberly L. Phillips, *Alabama-North: African American Migrants, Community, and Working-Class Activism in Cleveland, 1915–1945* (Urbana: University of Illinois Press, 1999); Joe William Trotter, *Black Milwaukee: The Making of an Industrial Proletariat, 1915–1945* (Urbana: University of Illinois Press, 1988); Joe William Trotter, Jr., ed. *The Great Migration in Historical Perspective: New Dimensions of Race, Class, and Gender* (Bloomington: Indiana University Press, 1991). John B. Kirby, *Black Americans in the Roosevelt Era* (Knoxville: University of Tennessee Press, 1980); Raymond Wolters, *Negroes and the*

Great Depression: The Problem of Economic Recovery (Westport CT: Greenwood, 1970). The majority of the above works deal with northern communities during Jim Crow. For a critical examination of Southern communities, see Tera W. Hunter, *To Joy My Freedom: Southern Black Women's Lives and Labors after the Civil War* (Cambridge: Harvard University Press, 1997); *Southern Discomfort: Women's Activism in Tampa, Florida, 1880s–1920s* (Urbana: University of Illinois Press, 2001); Robin D.G. Kelley, *Hammer and Hoe: Alabama Communists During the Great Depression* (Chapel Hill: University of North Carolina Press, 1990).

41. Key works include: Robin D.G. Kelley, *Race Rebels: Culture, Politics, and the Black Working Class* (New York: Free Press, 1994); Gena Dagel Caponi, ed., *Signifyin(g), Sanctifyin,' and Slam Dunking: A Reader in African American Expressive Culture* (Amherst: University of Massachusetts Press, 1999); David Krasner, "Parody and Double Consciousness in the Language of Early Black Musical Theatre," *African American Review* 29 (Summer 1995): 317–323; Patricia A. Turner, *I Heard it Through the Grapevine: Rumor in African American Culture* (Berkeley: University of California Press, 1993); Graham White and Shane White. *Stylin': Black Expressive Culture from its Beginnings to the Zoot Suit* (Ithaca: Cornell University Press, 1998).

42. Ribowsky, *A Complete History*, 57.

43. Ibid., 57.

44. James C. Scott, *Domination and the Arts of Resistance: Hidden Transcripts* (New Haven: Yale University Press, 1990); Henry Louis Gates, Jr., *The Signifying Monkey: A Theory of African American Literary Criticism* (New York: Oxford University Press, 1988).

Chapter One

1. Chester Washington, "Thrills, Frills and Spills Galore Feature Yankee Stadium Classic," *Pittsburgh Courier*, 12 July 1930; "Holiday Weekend Games: At Yankee Stadium 20,000 See Brotherhood Benefit Games," *New York Age*, 12 July 1930. The *New York Times* reported an attendance of just 15,000. "Lincoln Giants Split with Baltimore Team," *New York Times*, 6 July 1930.

2. "Rivals in Yankee Stadium Baseball Classic," *Pittsburgh Courier*, 5 July 1930, 4, second section; John Holway, *Voices From the Great Black Baseball Leagues*, 2d ed (New York: Da Capo, 1975, 1992), 18; "35,000 to see

Black Sox- Lincoln Giants," *New York Age*, 5 July 1930; "Bojangles Wins, But Phil Edwards Is Beaten in Half-Mile Handicap at Yankee Stadium Porters' Benefit," *New York Age*, 12 July 1930; "Holiday Weekend Games: At Yankee Stadium 20,000 See Brotherhood Benefit Games," *New York Age*, 12 July 1930, "Black Sox, Stars of Cuba, Fall Before Lincoln Giants," *Chicago Defender*, 12 July 1930; "Phil Edwards is Defeated in 880 at Yank Stadium," *Chicago Defender*, 12 July 1930; Bill Gibson, "Hear me Talkin' To Ya," *Baltimore Afro-American*, 28 July 1930; Gibson, "Hear Me Talkin' to Ya," *Baltimore Afro-American*, 12 July 1930; Chester Washington, "Thrills, Frills and Spills Galore Feature Yankee Stadium Classic," *Pittsburgh Courier*, 12 July 1930. The *New York Times* also published an account of the game, "Lincoln Giants Split with Baltimore Team," *New York Times*, 6 July 1930.

3. Chester Washington, "Thrills, Frills and Spills Galore Feature Yankee Stadium Classic," *Pittsburgh Courier*, 12 July 1930.

4. "Rivals in Yankee Stadium Baseball Classic," *Pittsburgh Courier*, 5 July 1930.

5. Washington, "Thrills, Frills and Spills." Robinson owned his own black baseball team, Bill Robinson's Harlem Stars, in 1931. "Changes Name of NY Stars," *Norfolk Journal and Guide*, 23 May 1931. Robinson was widely known to be a baseball fan and became an unofficial "mascot" for the New York Yankees. "Nuts About Baseball," *Saturday Evening Post*, March 2, 1930, 24, 56.

6. William A. Sundstrom, "Last Hired, First Fired? Unemployment and Urban Black Workers in the Great Depression," *The Journal of Economic History* 52, no. 2 (June 1992): 415–418.

7. Roi Ottley and William J. Weatherby, "The Depression in Harlem," reprinted in Bernard Sternsher, ed., *Hitting Home: The Great Depression in Town and Country* (Chicago: Quadrangle Books, 1970), 105–106. Also on African Americans and the Great Depression, see St. Clair Drake and Horace R. Cayton, *Black Metropolis: A Study of Negro Life in a Northern City* (New York: Harcourt, Brace, 1945), 77–98, 287–341; Stephanie J. Shaw, "Using the WPA Ex-Slave Narratives to Study the Impact of the Great Depression," *Journal of Southern History* 69 (August 2003): 623–658; Raymond Wolters, *Negroes and the Great Depression: The Problem of Economic Recovery* (Westport CT: Greenwood, 1970).

8. Sundstrom, "Last Hired, First Fired?," 417.

9. James Weldon Johnson, "The Making of Harlem," *Survey Graphic*, March 1925, 636–637; Charles S. Johnson, "Black Workers and the City," *Survey Graphic*, March 1925, 641: W.A. Domingo, "The Tropics in New York," *Survey Graphic*, March 1925, 648–650.

10. Washington, "Thrills, Frills and Spills," *Pittsburgh Courier*, 12 July 1930.

11. On the significance of dress for African Americans see Robin D.G. Kelley, "'We Are Not What We Seem': Rethinking Black Working-Class Opposition in the Jim Crow South," *Journal of American History* 80 (June 1993): 86 and Graham White and Shane White, *Stylin': African American Expressive Culture from its Beginnings to the Zoot Suit* (Ithaca: Cornell University Press, 1998).

12. "Rivals in Yankee Stadium Baseball Classic," *Pittsburgh Courier*, 5 July 1930, 4, second section.

13. Washington, "Thrills, Frills, and Spills Galore."

14. On Babe Ruth's significance, see Robert C. Cottrell, *Blackball, the Black Sox, and the Babe: Baseball's Crucial 1920 Season* (Jefferson, NC: McFarland, 2002); Robert W. Creamer, *Babe: The Legend Comes to Life* (New York: Fireside, 1974, 1992); Jim Reisler, *Babe Ruth: Launching the Legend* (New York: McGraw Hill, 2004); Ken Sobol, *Babe Ruth and the American Dream* (New York: Random House, 1974).

15. "Let's Fill the Yankees Stadium," Advertisement, *New York Age*, 5 July 1940.

16. On the significance of baseball parks, see Philip J. Lowry, *Green Cathedrals: The Ultimate Celebrations of All 273 Major league and Negro League Ballparks Past and Present* (Reading, MA: Addison-Wesley, 1992); Rich Westcott, *Philadelphia's Old Ball Parks* (Philadelphia: Temple University Press, 1996).

17. Bernadette Pruitt, "For the Advancement of the Race: The Great Migrations to Houston, Texas, 1914–1941," *Journal of Urban History* 31 (2005): 437–438.

18. Many migrants followed a "chain migration" north. Ronald L. Lewis, "From Peasant to Proletarian: The Migration of Southern Blacks to the Central Appalachian Coalfields," *Journal of Southern History* 55 (February 1989): 77–102. For a detailed case study of black migration to a southern city, see Pruitt, "For the Advancement of the Race," 435–478. Earl Lewis has provided a detailed examination of black life in Norfolk, Virginia, including the impact of the Great Migration. See Lewis, *In*

Their Own Interests: Race, Class, and Power in Twentieth Century Norfolk (Berkeley: University of California Press, 1991).

19. Eric Arnesen provides a detailed account of how white railroad unions fought not only to exclude African American railroad workers from their unions but also to prevent them from assuming advanced positions within railway companies. Arnesen, "'Like Banquo's Ghost, It Will Not Down': The Race Question and the American Railroad Brotherhoods, 1880–1920," *American Historical Review* (December 1994): 1601–1633. African American workers would encounter similar union exclusions and "job ceilings" in the North; see Epstein, *The Negro Migrant*, 32–34, 38–44; Johnson, "Black Workers and the City," 642–643.

20. The scholarship on the Great Migration is voluminous. For a sampling of the secondary works, see Peter Gottlieb, *Making Their Own Way: Southern Blacks' Migration to Pittsburgh, 1916–1930* (Urbana: University of Illinois Press, 1987); James R. Grossman, *Land of Hope: Chicago, Black Southerners, and the Great Migration* (Chicago: University of Chicago Press, 1989); Kenneth L. Kusmer, *Black Cleveland: A Ghetto Takes Shape, 1870–1930* (Urbana: University of Illinois Press, 1978); Gilbert Osofsky, *Harlem: The Making of a Ghetto, 1890–1930* (New York: Harper & Row, 1963); Kimberley L. Phillips, *AlabamaNorth: African American Migrants, Community, and Working-Class Activism in Cleveland, 1915–1945* (Urbana: University of Illinois Press, 1999); Joe William Trotter, *Black Milwaukee: The Making of an Industrial Proletariat, 1915–1945* (Urbana: University of Illinois Press, 1988); Joe William Trotter, Jr., ed. *The Great Migration in Historical Perspective: New Dimensions of Race, Class, and Gender* (Bloomington: Indiana University Press, 1991). For a statistical examination of black migration within the larger context of general internal migration in the United States, see Patricia Kelly Hall and Steven Ruggles, "'Restless in the Midst of Their Prosperity': New Evidence on the Internal Migration of Americans, 1850–2000," *Journal of American History* 90 (December 2004): 829–846.

21. Abraham Epstein, *The Negro Migrant in Pittsburgh*, reprint edition (New York: Arno Press and The New York Times, 1918, 1969), 7, 10, 18.

22. See Holway, *Voices from the Great Black Baseball Leagues*, 41–45, 62–64, 112–113, 145, 173, 181, 209–212, 221, 239, 252, 284, 302, 330.

23. Drake and Cayton, *Black Metropolis*, 110; Allan H. Spear, *Black Chicago: The Making of a Negro Ghetto 1890–1920* (Chicago: University of Chicago Press, 1967), 203. On leisure and public amusements generally, see David Nasaw, *Going Out: The Rise and Fall of Public Amusements* (New York: Basic Books, 1993). On working-class women and leisure, see Kathy Peiss, *Cheap Amusements: Working Women and Leisure in Turn-of-the-Century New York* (Philadelphia: Temple University Press, 1986). For working-class (especially immigrant) women, popular culture, and dime novels, see Nan Enstad, *Ladies of Labor, Girls of Adventure: Working Women, Popular Culture, and Labor Politics at the Turn of the Twentieth Century* (New York: Columbia University Press, 1999). Roy Rosenzweig has examined industrial immigrant workers and their attempt to carve out leisure time and space for visits to saloons and holiday celebrations in *Eight Hours for What We Will: Workers and Leisure in an Industrial City 1870–1920* (Cambridge: Cambridge University Press, 1983).

24. Drake and Cayton, *Black Metropolis*, 106.

25. Gerald R. Gems has explored issues of leisure and ethnic identities in *Windy City Wars: Labor, Leisure, and Sport in the Making of Chicago* (Landham, MD: Scarecrow, 1997). See also, Lizabeth Cohen, *Making a New Deal: Industrial Workers in Chicago, 1919–1939* (New York: Cambridge University Press, 1990).

26. Fred R. Moore, " Organizing Local Business Leagues," (1904) reprinted in *Black Nationalism in America*, ed. John H. Bracey, Jr., August Meier, and Elliott Rudwick (Indianapolis and New York: Bobbs-Merrill, 1970), 238–241; "Report of the Fourteenth Annual Convention of the National Negro Business League" (1913), reprinted in Bracey, et al, eds., *Black Nationalism*, 241–243; editorial, "Value of Negro Business Leagues," reprinted in Bracey, et al, eds. *Black Nationalism*, 243–245; W.E.B. Du Bois "Resolutions of the Atlanta University Conference on the Negro in Business," (1899) reprinted in Bracey, et al, eds., *Black Nationalism*, 262–263; Du Bois, *The Crisis* 19 (December 1919): 48, 50; George W. Blount, "The Virginia State Negro Business League," *The Competitor* (March 1920): 26.

27. See R.E. Treman to Walter White, Ithaca, NY, April 18, 1938; White to Treman, New York, April 19, 1938; White to Treman, New York, October 4, 1938, all of the letters are found in the Papers of the NAACP, Part 2,

Correspondence of select officials, Walter White, reels 17–18.

28. On the "Double Duty Dollar," see Drake and Cayton, *Black Metropolis*, 430–432.

29. Claude McKay, excerpt from *Harlem: Negro Metropolis*, reprinted in Francis L. Broderick and August Meier, eds., *Negro Protest Thought in the Twentieth Century* (Indianapolis and New York: Bobbs-Merrill, 1965), 109–118, quotes 115, 116, 118. On the Harlem boycott and other contemporary boycotts in Richmond and Washington D.C., see Du Bois, "Segregation in the North," *The Crisis* 41 (April 1934): 115–117. Hamid allegedly held extreme anti–Semitic feelings that most likely contributed to his disavowal by the Citizen's League. On Hamid as the "Black Hitler," see "Harlem's Hitler Brought to Court," *New York Times*, 9 October 1934; "'Black Hitler' Defended On," *New York Times*, 11 October 1934; "Free in Anti-Semitic Case," *New York Times*, 12 October 1934; "Harlem's 'Hitler' Jailed to Await Trial," *New York Times*, 20 January 1935. In the 1935 case, members of the Citizen's League testified against Hamid. It is unclear whether Hamid's views were exaggerated to make him a target or if they represented his true beliefs. Hamid was distributing a pamphlet advising African Americans to reject white supremacy prior to the January 1935 arrest. His second trial seemed to focus on the possibility that his boycott campaigns could incite race riots. "Harlem's 'Hitler' Jailed for Remarks," *New York Times*, 20 January 1935; "Injunction Halts 'Black Hitlerites,'" *New York Times,* 6 July 1935; "Plane Crash Fatal to Harlem Hitler," *New York Times*, 1 August 1938.

30. Herbert Aptheker, ed., *The Correspondence of W.E.B. Du Bois: Volume I Selections, 1877–1934* (Boston: University of Massachusetts Press, 1973), 272.

31. "Coast Newspapers Work To Get Race in Majors," *Chicago Defender*, 10 August 1935; "Major Leagues Jim Crowed," *Chicago Defender*, 30 May 1936; "Sox and Cubs," *Chicago Defender*, 16 January 1936; "Daily Scribe Speaks of Jim Crow in the Majors," *Chicago Defender*, 13 July 1935; "30,000 Jam Shows We're Game's Asset," *Chicago Defender*, 29 August 1936.

32. See Henderson, "The Participation of Negro Youth in Community and Educational Programs," *The Journal of Negro Education* 9 (July 1940): 417–418, 424.

33. Tygiel, *Baseball's Great Experiment*, 43.

34. For scholarly examinations of the end of the Negro Leagues, see Patricia Vignola, "The Enemies at the Gate: An Economic Debate about the Denouement of Negro League Baseball," *Nine* 13 (February 2005): 71–81.

35. On the first black baseball team, see Ribowsky, *A Complete History*, 16–17.

36. "Special to Courier," *Pittsburgh Courier,* 5 August 1911; "Thousands Celebrate Big Emancipation Day," *Cleveland Advocate,* 11 August 1917, 1; Richard White, "Civil Rights Agitation: Emancipation Days in Central New York in the 1880s," *The Journal of Negro History* 78 (Winter 1993): 16, 21; William H. Wiggins, Jr., *O Freedom! Afro-American Emancipation Celebrations* (Knoxville: University of Tennessee Press, 1987), 40–43, 96, 101. Booker T. Washington provided a detailed account of an Arizona Emancipation Day celebration in a 1911 article. Washington, "The Race Problem in Arizona," *The Independent* 71, October 26, 1911: 909–914.

37. Ralph Ellison, *Shadow and Act* (New York: Quality Paperback Book Club, 1964, 1994) 19; Gottlieb, *Making Their Own Way,* 21–22.

38. Ira F. Lewis, "National Baseball League Formed," *The Competitor* (March 1920), 67; Dick Powell, interview by Kelley, *Negro Leagues Revisited*, 86.

39. Dick Powell, interview by Kelley, *Negro Leagues Revisited*, 86.

40. Bruce Chadwick, *When the Game Was Black and White: The Illustrated History of the Negro Leagues* (New York: Abbeville, 1992), 106.

41. Michael L. Mullan, "Ethnicity and Sport: The Wapato Nippons and Pre-World War II Japanese American Baseball," *Journal of Sport History* 26 (Spring 1999): 103.

42. "Rivals in Yankee Stadium Baseball Classic," *Pittsburgh Courier*, 5 July 1930; *Baltimore Afro-American*, 16 July 1938.

43. "Personals," *Chicago Defender,* 28 May 1910; "K.C. Monarchs Leave to Start Drills in South," *Chicago Defender*, 21 April 1934.

44. "Grays-Crawfords Meet Decoration Day," *Pittsburgh Courier*, 28 May 1932; "Craws win 3, Grays 2; Beverly and Britt Pitch Classics; 10,000 Attend," *Pittsburgh Courier*, 4 June 1932. Easter Monday and Flag Day also were profitable holidays for black baseball. "Baseball Easter Monday," "Base Ball Easter Monday Classic," "Baseball Classic," *Norfolk Journal and Guide*, 18 April 1931; "Flag Day at Auburn Park," *Chicago Defender*, 14 May 1910.

45. Buck O'Neil, Steve Wulf, and David Conrads, *I Was Right on Time: My Journey from the Negro Leagues to the Majors* (New York: Fireside, 1997), 53.

46. Steven A. Riess, "Professional Baseball and Social Mobility," *Journal of Interdisciplinary History* 11 (Autumn 1980): 235.

47. C.I. Taylor, "The Future of Colored Baseball," *The Competitor*, February 1920, 76, emphasis original.

48. Lewis, "National Baseball League Formed," March 1920, 66.

49. Ira F. Lewis, "Who'll be the Next?" *The Competitor*, October–November 1920, 221–225, "The Good Old Days" *The Competitor*, October-November 1920, 225, 227; Ira F. Lewis, "Our Colleges and Athletics" *The Competitor*, December 1920, 290–292; *Chicago Defender*, 19 October 1921.

50. Michael E. Lomax, "The African American Experience in Professional Football," *Journal of Social History* 33 (1999): 163–165.

51. A.H. Wyman, "Recreation in Industrial Communities," *The Competitor*, July 1920, 13–14; Henderson, "The Participation of Negro Youth," 417–418, 424; See also Patrick B. Miller, "To 'Bring the Race Along Rapidly': Sport, Student Culture, and Educational Mission at Historically Black Colleges during the Interwar Years," *History of Education Quarterly* 35 (Summer 1995); Jeffrey J. Pilz, " The Beginnings of Organized Play for Black America: E.T. Attwell and The PRAA," *The Journal of Negro History* 70 (1985): 59–72. On less respectable leisure pursuits, race, and law enforcement in Harlem, see Marcy S. Sack, "'To Show Who Was in Charge': Police Repression of New York City's Black Population at the Turn of the Twentieth Century," *Journal of Urban History* 31 (September 2005): 799–819.

52. Kelley, "We Are Not What We Seem," 84.

53. "Douglass Track Team Denied," *Norfolk Journal and Guide*, 30 May 1931.

54. "Concerning Parks," *The Crisis* 1 (March 1911): 28; "Parks Again," *The Crisis* 2 (June 1911): 76–77.

55. "Atlanta Opens Swimming Pool for its Colored Citizens," *Norfolk Journal and Guide*, 16 September 1932.

56. Andrew M. Kaye, *The Pussycat of Prizefighting: Tiger Flowers and the Politics of Black Celebrity* (Athens: University of Georgia Press, 2004), 96–99.

57. "A New Orleans Baseball Park," *The Crisis* 23 (November 1921): 19–20. New Orleans had hosted interracial baseball games until 1890. Dale A. Somers, "Black and White in New Orleans: A Study in Urban Race Relations, 1865–1900," *Journal of Southern History* 40 (February 1974), 39–40.

58. Frank U. Quillan, *The Color Line in Ohio: A History of Race Prejudice in a Typical Northern State* (Ann Arbor, MI: George Wahr, 1913), 128.

59. For an extensive look at the playground movement, see Dominick Cavallo, *Muscles and Morals: Organized Playground and Urban Reform, 1880–1920* (Philadelphia: University of Pennsylvania Press, 1981); Gems, *Windy City Wars: Labor, Leisure, and Sport in the Making of Chicago*. (Landham, MD: Scarecrow, 1997); Gary Goodman, *Choosing Sides: Playground and Street Life on the Lower East Side* (New York: Schocken, 1979); Stephen Hardy, *How Boston Played* (Boston: Northeastern University Press, 1982); Mark A. Kadzielski, "As a Flower Needs Sunshine: The Origins of Organized Children's Recreation in Philadelphia, 1886–1911," *Journal of Sport History* 4 (Summer 1977): 169–188. Robert Pruter has discussed violence and rough behavior among Chicago youth baseball players in the era preceding organized recreation reform. Pruter, "Youth Baseball in Chicago, 1868–1890: Not Always Sandlot Ball," *Journal of Sports History* 26 (Spring 1999): 1–28.

60. Spear, *Black Chicago*, 174; A.H. Wyman, "Recreation in Industrial Communities," *The Competitor*, July 1920, 13–14; "Editorials" *Survey Graphic*, March 1925, 699; Henderson, "The Participation of Negro Youth," 417–418, 424. See also Epstein, *The Negro Migrant*, 70; Patrick B. Miller, "To 'Bring the Race Along Rapidly': Sport, Student Culture, and Educational Mission at Historically Black Colleges during the Interwar Years," *History of Education Quarterly* 35 (Summer 1995); Jeffrey J. Pilz, "The Beginnings of Organized Play for Black America: E.T. Attwell and The PRAA," *The Journal of Negro History* 70 (1985): 59–72. On less respectable leisure pursuits, race, and law enforcement in Harlem, see Marcy S. Sack, "'To Show Who Was in Charge': Police Repression of New York City's Black Population at the Turn of the Twentieth Century," *Journal of Urban History* 31 (September 2005): 799–819.

61. For representative examples of local coverage, see "Chicago Base Ball League," *Chicago Defender*, 25 June 1910, 4; "YMCA notes," *Pittsburgh Courier*, 5 August 1911;

"Standing of Clubs in Industrial and Community League," *Pittsburgh Courier*, 29 January 1927. The *Pittsburgh Courier* lauded the local YMCA for its commitment to "higher ideals, better men mentally, physically and morally." "Pay Your Subscriptions," *Pittsburgh Courier*, 10 June 1911.

62. Pilz, "The Beginnings of Organized Play for Black America," 59–72.

63. Spear, *Black Chicago*, 206, Drake and Clayton, *Black Metropolis*, 105–110.

64. On the related development of black-owned resorts, see Mark S. Foster, "In the Face of 'Jim Crow': Prosperous Blacks and Vacations, Travel and Outdoor Leisure, 1890–1945," *Journal of Negro History* 84 (Spring 1999): 130–149.

65. Spear, *Black Chicago*, 206. See also, Drake and Cayton, *Black Metropolis*, 110.

66. Quillan, *The Color Line*, 126; "Would Deny Bathing Privileges," *Norfolk Journal and Guide*, 17 June 1932; "At Buckeye Lake," *The Crisis* 17, 92; "Public Bathing in Pittsburgh," *The Crisis* 39 (February 1932): 57.

67. Turner, *I Heard it Through the Grapevine: Rumor in African American Culture* (Berkeley: University of California Press, 1993), 50; William M. Tuttle, *Race Riot: Chicago in the Red Summer of 1919* (Urbana: University of Illinois Press, 1996).

68. "At Buckeye Lake," *The Crisis* 17, 92, "Public Bathing in Pittsburgh," *The Crisis*, 57; Pilz, " The Beginnings of Organized Play for Black America," 64.

69. "New York Puts Ban on 'African Dodger,'" *Chicago Defender*, 24 April 1915; "300,000 at Coney, 3,000 Sport in Surf," *New York Times*, 22 May 1922; "In September The County Fair Blooms," *New York Times*, 11 September 1927.

70. E.S. Martin, *Life*, December 2, 1926, 24.

71. Philip McGowan, *American Vaudeville: Seeing and Reading American Culture* (Westport, CT: Greenwood, 2001), 67.

72. See "Revenue of Fair Put at $35,000,000," *New York Times*, 3 November 1933.

73. Roy Campanella, interview by Stephen Banker, in *Black Diamonds: An Oral History of Negro Baseball* (Washington: Tapes for Readers, 1978, 1992), *audiocassette*.

74. Cohen, *Making a New Deal*, 36–38, 148–149; Phillips, *AlabamaNorth*, 155–159, 164–165; Spear, *Black Chicago*, ix, 130, 167.

75. Ribowsky, *A Complete History*, 105–106. Ribowsky has argued that Foster touted the Negro National League as a race enterprise to engender good will and drive any competitors out of business, rather than out of an altruistic commitment to racial uplift. On another contemporary black institution, black insurance companies, see Robert E. Weems, Jr., *Black Business in a Black Metropolis: The Chicago Metropolitan Assurance Company, 1925–1985* (Bloomington: Indiana University Press, 1996). The founder of the CMAC, Robert Cole, purchased the Chicago American Giants in 1932. Al Monroe, "What Say," *Chicago Defender*, 9 July 1932; "There Will Be Baseball Here; Who'll Have Club," *Chicago Defender*, 27 January 1934; Al Monroe, "Sporting Around," *Chicago Defender*, 5 May 1934.

76. Ira F. Lewis, "National Baseball League Formed," *The Competitor*, March 1920, 67.

77. Ira F. Lewis, "'New' League Not Needed," *The Competitor*, May 1921, 39.

78. George W. Blount, "The Virginia State Negro Business League," *The Competitor*, March 1920, 26.

79. For a case study, see Vignola, "The Enemies at the Gate," 71–81.

80. Drake and Cayton, *Black Metropolis*, 445–449.

81. Ira F. Lewis, "'New' League Not Needed," *The Competitor*, May 1921, 39, 41; W. Rollo Wilson, "Eastern Snapshots," *Pittsburgh Courier*, 7 June 1924; Cum Posey, "The Sportive Realm," *Pittsburgh Courier*, 29 January 1927; W. Rollo Wilson, "Sports Shots," *Pittsburgh Courier*, 2 April 1927; "Negro Baseball," *The Brown American*, Fall-Winter 1942, 5, 19.

82. Judy Johnson, interview by Banker, *Black Diamonds*, Cassette #1, Side Two.

83. See Ribowsky, *A Complete History*, 85–86, 143–144. For players' recollections of Wilkinson, see Bill Drake, interview by Holway, *Voices from the Great Black Baseball Leagues*, 28, 31;

84. Ira F. Lewis, "'New' League Not Needed," *The Competitor*, May 1921, 39.

85. David Malarcher, interview by Holway, *Voices from the Great Black Baseball Leagues*, 45. The Cuban Stars used the Cincinnati Reds' park, Redland Field, during the 1921 season. Ira F. Lewis, "Baseball Men Hold Successful Meeting," *The Competitor*, January-February 1921, 52. On the New York All-Stars and Yankee Stadium, see "Colored Team to Open in Yankee Stadium," *Norfolk Journal and Guide*, 18 April 1931. On the other rental arrangements and the economic climate, see Charles C. Alexander, *Breaking the Slump: Baseball in*

the Depression Era (New York: Columbia University Press, 2002), 209.

86. Neval H. Thomas, "Protest is Sent to Griffith," *Pittsburgh Courier,* 12 September 1926.

87. For a pre-integration look at Griffith's career in the white major leagues, see Bob Considine and Shirely Povich, "The Old Fox Turns Magnate: Baseball's Red-Eyed Magnate and Arch-Conservative," *Saturday Evening Post,* April 20, 1940, 18–24.

88. Neval H. Thomas, "Protest is Sent to Griffith," *Pittsburgh Courier,* 12 September 1926.

89. Ribowsky, *A Complete History,* 251.

90. Paige, *Maybe I'll Pitch Forever,* 66; Paige, interview by Banker, in *Black Diamonds,* Cassette #1, Side One.

91. Kaye, *The Pussycat of Prizefighting,* 59–65.

92. Bill Drake, interview by Holway, in *Voices from the Great Black Baseball Leagues,* 30; Ribowsky, *A Complete History,* 123, emphasis original. See also Alton King, interview by Kelley, *Negro Leagues Revisited,* 107.

93. On Harlem nightclubs and segregation, see David Levering Lewis, *When Harlem Was in Vogue* (New York: Oxford University Press, 1989), 105–106, 209–210; Osofsky, *The Making of a Ghetto,* 185.

94. Hughes, "In Love With Harlem," (1963) reprinted in Milton Meltzer, ed., *In Their Own Words: A History of the American Negro 1916–1966* (New York: Thomas Y. Crowell, 1967), 47.

95. Bill Drake, interview by Holway, *Voices from the Great Black Baseball Leagues,* 30.

96. James "Cool Papa" Bell, interview by Arthur Shaffer and Charles Korr, University of Missouri–St. Louis Oral History Program. September 8, 1971. Transcript, in James "Cool Papa" Bell player file, Ashland Collection, National Baseball Hall of Fame and Museum, 28.

97. Chadwick, *When the Game Was Black and White,* 79; Wilmer Fields, *My Life in the Negro Leagues* (Westport, CT: Meckler, 1992), 68.

98. Nasaw, *Going Out: The Rise and Fall of Public Amusements* (New York: Basic Books, 1993), 100.

99. Fred Van Ness, "Distinguished Gathering Throngs Stadium for Heavyweight Battle," *New York Times,* 26 June 1935, 24, emphasis mine.

100. "Cuban Stars and Leland Giants," *Chicago Defender,* 31 July 1909, 1.

101. Ribowsky, *A Complete History,* 123, emphasis original.

102. Chadwick, *When the Game Was Black and White,* 68.

103. "Great Base Ball Attraction," *Norfolk Journal and Guide,* 2 September 1932; "Base Ball Extraordinary," *Norfolk Journal and Guide,* 2 September 1932; "Base Ball Championship Game," *Norfolk Journal and Guide,* 9 September 1932.

104. Robinson, *Catching Dreams,* 53.

105. "22,000 Fans Expected To Attend Kansas City Opener," *Pittsburgh Courier,* 23 May 1925, 13.

106. Bruce, *The Kansas City Monarchs,* 52.

107. Spear, *Black Chicago,* 211–213; Drake and Cayton, *Black Metropolis,* 91, 104–106.

108. On 1919 racial violence, calls for increased democracy at home, and the return of World War I black servicemen, see Lewis, *When Harlem Was In Vogue,* 15–24; Boyd, "Residential Segregation by Race and the Black Merchants of Northern Cities During the Early Twentieth Century," *Sociological Forum* 13 (December 1998): 595–609.

109. Best, *Passionately Human,* 47.

110. *Alexander's Magazine,* 15 May 1905, 42.

111. Walter S. Buchanan, "Race Progress and Race Adjustment," *The Competitor,* June 1921, 10–11. See also, Johnson, "The Making of Harlem," 637; George E. Haynes, "The Church and the Negro Spirit," *Survey Graphic,* March 1925, 695–697, 708.

112. James Weldon Johnson, "The Making of Harlem," *Survey Graphic,* March 1925, 638.

113. *Ibid.,* 638.

114. Kelly Miller, "The Harvest of Race Prejudice," *Survey Graphic,* March 1925, 711. Miller goes on to note that race patronage "awaits the time when the Negro shall have developed the business aptitude to compete with the white dealer, who is shrewd enough to hold prejudice in restraint for the sake of trade." 712.

115. Ribowsky, *A Complete History,* 74–77.

116. *Ibid.,* 74.

117. Bruce, *Kansas City Monarchs,* 11–12. Yet, in the case of Foster, most of the Chicago black press kept quiet about his ties to white business to support Foster's black enterprise. Ribowsky, *A Complete History,* 74–75.

118. Drake and Cayton, *Black Metropolis,* 431.

119. "A Monument to Racial Industry," *The Half-Century Magazine,* November-December 1922, 3, 15.

120. Howard A. Phelps, "Andrew 'Rube' Foster," *The Half-Century Magazine*, March 1919: 8.

121. *Ibid.*

122. Gale Williams "About Foster's Baseball Team," *The Half-Century Magazine* (April 1919): 17.

123. Drake and Cayton, *Black Metropolis*, 432, 445–453.

124. Frank Young, "More About Foster's Baseball Team," *The Half-Century Magazine*, June 1919: 8.

125. Ribowsky, *A Complete History*, 117.

126. Frank A. Young, "A Digest of the Sports World," *Chicago Defender*, 29 August 1931. Black press coverage in the 1930s constructed the myth of Foster as the sole founder of the Negro National League. As a result, the important role of Indianapolis A.B.C. owner C.I. Taylor was erased from the public memory. For contemporary accounts of Taylor's involvement in the founding of the NNL, see sports coverage in *The Competitor*, all of the 1920 issues. For more on Foster's public persona as an unimpeachable and indefatigable advocate for black baseball, see Ribowsky, *A Complete History*, 136–138.

127. Frank A. Young, "A Digest of the Sports World," *Pittsburgh Courier*, 29 August 1931. Michael Lomax argues that a lack of related business development in Chicago was significant in preventing the Giants from establishing themselves as a successful race enterprise. "Black Baseball, Black Community, Black Entrepreneurs: The History of the Negro National and Eastern Colored Leagues, 1880–1930" (PhD dissertation, Ohio State University, 1996), 503. Because of Foster's widespread involvement in other league teams, the impact of his death was felt beyond Chicago. Particularly in Detroit, Foster's death contributed to the demise of the Negro National League Detroit Stars. On Foster and the Stars, see Richard Bak, *Turkey Stearnes and the Detroit Stars: The Negro Leagues in Detroit, 1919–1933* (Detroit: Wayne State University Press, 1994), 178–179.

128. Drake, interview by Holway, *Voices from the Great Black Baseball Leagues*, 29.

129. W. Rollo Wilson, "Sports Shots," *Pittsburgh Courier*, 25 April 1931. See also, "Knoxville Fans Decide to Stay Away," *Chicago Defender*, 30 April 1932.

130. For a discussion of African American boycotts and their connection with the campaigns of Booker T. Washington and Marcus Garvey, see Lizabeth Cohen, *A Consumers' Re-*

public: *The Politics of Mass Consumption in Postwar America* (New York: Alfred A. Knopf, 2003), 41–43.

131. Wendell Smith, "A Strange Tribe," *The Pittsburgh Courier*, 14 May 1938, reprinted in David K. Wiggins and Patrick B. Miller, *The Unlevel Playing Field: A Documentary History of the African American Experience in Sport* (Urbana: University of Illinois Press, 2003), 136.

132. *The Crisis*, (June 1940): 180.

133. "Baseball Season Over: No Big League Tryouts," *Chicago Defender*, 10 October 1942.

134. Art Rust, Jr., *Get That Nigger Off the Field!: A Sparkling, Informal History of the Black Man in Baseball* (New York: Delacorte, 1976); Max Manning, interview by Kelley, *Voices from the Negro Leagues*, 67; Holloway, interview by Holway, *Voices from the Great Black Baseball Leagues*, 62; James Crutchfield, interview by Banker, *Black Diamonds*, Cassette #2, Side One; Mitchell, "This is Me! I'm Somebody!" 80.

135. Dan Parker, "Ebbets Field Goes High Yellow," *Daily Mirror*, 19 May 1935; Jimmy Powers "The Powerhouse," *Daily News*, 4 February 1935, in Effa Manley file, Ashland Collection, NBHFM; Ribowksy, *A Complete History*, 194. The 1938 Black Yankees used Yankee Stadium as a home field. "Twin Bill to Aid Charity," *New York Times*, 22 June 1938.

136. "Cleveland Promised Greatest Baseball Season in History," *Pittsburgh Courier*, 16 April 1932.

137. "Comments on Cleveland's E-W Ball Club," *Pittsburgh Courier*, 4 June 1932. This movement coincided with several similar boycott movements in Cleveland and foreshadowed the larger protests staged by the Future Outlook League in subsequent years. Phillips, *AlabamaNorth*, 198–199, 205–225. Cleveland was not the only major Ohio city that failed to maintain a viable Negro Leagues franchise. Residents of Columbus also tried and failed to establish a long-lasting Negro Leagues club. Sol White, "Sol White's Column of Baseball Dope," *Cleveland Advocate*, 19 April 1919; White, "Sol White's Column of Baseball Dope," *Cleveland Advocate*, 02 August 1919.

138. Alexander, *Breaking the Slump*, 213.

139. The Hill District was home to many new migrants in Pittsburgh. "Where They Live," *The Brown American* 4 (September 1930): 5, 38–39; Peter Gottlieb, *Making Their Own Way: Southern Blacks' Migration to Pittsburgh, 1916–1930* (Urbana: University of Illinois Press, 1987). For an interesting, contemporary study

that examined black life in Pittsburgh at the beginning of the Great Migration, see Epstein, *The Negro Migrant in Pittsburgh*. Writing in 1918, Epstein detailed the early stages of black migration to Pittsburgh.

140. "Crawfords to 'Carry On' in this Bus," *Pittsburgh Courier*, 27 February 1932; Chadwick, *When the Game Was Black and White*, 84. On Greenlee's rise and fall as a power broker in the Negro National League, see Lanctot, *Negro League Baseball*, 10–147.

141. On Greenlee's rise and fall as a power broker in the Negro National League, see Lanctot, *Negro League Baseball*, 10–147.

142. Ribowsky describes him as having "introduced it [the black game] into a higher level of the underworld." Ribowsky, *A Complete History*, 157. Black boxers also had a close relationship with the policy game. One of Joe Louis's backers was a numbers man, and Greenlee managed light heavyweight John Henry Lewis. "Joe Backed by Profits on 'Policy,'" *Chicago Defender*, 9 May 1936; "Experts Predict Joe Louis Will Be Denied Title Bout," *Chicago Defender*, 13 July 1935; "History is Being Made Here, Folks," *Chicago Defender*, 20 June 1936; "John Henry Lewis To Turn To Heavyweights, Gus Says," *Chicago Defender*, 16 July 1937. Major league baseball historically had been connected with gambling interests and corrupt political machines. Steven A. Reiss, "The Baseball Magnates and Urban Politics in the Progressive Era: 1895–1920," in idem., *The American Sporting Experience: A Historical Anthology of Sport in America* (Champaign, IL: Leisure Press, 1984): 271–290. The numbers racket also made its mark on professional football. Art Rooney was a numbers man in Pittsburgh before purchasing the Steelers. Ribowsky, *A Complete History*, 159. For an additional contemporary and white view of the policy racket, see J. Saunders Redding, "Playing the Numbers," *The North American Review* 238, December 1934, 533–542. On gambling and the NFL, see Michael E. Lomax, "'Detrimental to the League': Gambling and the Governance of Professional Football, 1946–1963," *Journal of Sport History* 29 (Summer 2002): 289–311.

143. Winthrop D. Lane authored an article on the popularity of the numbers game and other vice operations in Harlem during the 1920s. See Lane, "Ambushed in the City: The Grim Side of Harlem," *Survey Graphic*, March 1925, 692–694, 713. Numbers rackets advertised in the *Baltimore Afro-American* sports pages. For one example, see *Baltimore Afro-American*, 28 May 1932.

144. "Baptists to War on 'Numbers,'" *Baltimore Afro-American*, 28 June 1930.

145. Adrian Burgos, Jr., *Cuban Star: How One Negro-League Owner Changed the Face of Baseball* (New York: Hill and Wang, 2011), 81–82.

146. "To Reveal How Policy Barons Juggle Numbers," *Chicago Defender*, 24 July 1937; "Open Million Dollar Policy Racket Trial," *Chicago Defender*, 21 May 1938. See also Leonard, *Buck Leonard*, 79; Rogosin, *Invisible Men*, 17; Robert E. Weems, Jr., *Black Business in a Black Metropolis: The Chicago Metropolitan Assurance Company, 1925–1985* (Bloomington: Indiana University Press, 1996), 62.

147. J. Winston Harrington, "Policy ... What Do You Think About It?" *Chicago Defender*, 25 November 1939. See also, Drake and Cayton, *Black Metropolis*, 484, 492.

148. "'Stamp Out Numbers Racket'–Bishop Gregg," *Chicago Defender*, 1 October 1938; "Says Press, Clerics Won't Fight Policy," *Chicago Defender*, 4 March 1939.

149. "Policy," *Chicago Defender*, 25 November 1939.

150. "Suave and Debonair Racketeers Crashing Exclusive D.C. Society," *Norfolk Journal and Guide*, 9 May 1931.

151. Drake and Cayton, *Black Metropolis*, 470–494.

152. "Open Million Dollar Policy Racket Trial," *Chicago Defender*, 21 May 1938.

153. "Policy Barons Fear Racket on Way Out in Washington," *Chicago Defender*, 26 November 1938.

154. Sacks, "'To Show Who Was in Charge,'" 813; Hughes, "In Love with Harlem," 47. See also, Harrington, "Policy"; Drake and Cayton, *Black Metropolis*, 492–494.

155. Lawrence D. Hogan, *Shades of Glory: The Negro Leagues and the Story of African-American Baseball* (Washington, D.C.: National Geographic, 2006), 282–283.

156. Ribowsky discusses Greenlee's philosophy and feud with Posey in *A Complete History*, 162–168.

157. C.E. Pendleton, "Public's Non-Support Makes Crawford's Future Dubious," *Pittsburgh Courier*, 6 June 1931.

158. For a history of the Crawfords' early years and financial struggles, see Jim Bankes, *The Pittsburgh Crawfords* (Jefferson, NC: McFarland, 2001), 13–17.

159. "Westerners To Test Grays Strength

At Forbes Field Friday," *Pittsburgh Courier*, 19 July 1930.

160. Ribowsky, *A Complete History*, 163; Bruce, *Kansas City Monarchs,* 68–72; Michael Harkness-Roberto and Leslie A. Heaphy, "The Monarchs: A Brief History of the Franchise," *Satchel Paige and Company: Essays on the Kansas City Monarchs, Their Greatest Star and the Negro Leagues* ed. Leslie A. Heaphy (Jefferson, NC: McFarland, 2007), 103–104.

161. "Grays vs. Detroit" and "To 'Show Way' to Grays-Davids," *Pittsburgh Courier* 14 May 1932.

162. "Westerners to Test Grays Strength at Forbes Field Friday," *Pittsburgh Courier*, 19 July 1930. White baseball would not employ lights until 1935. Ribowsky, *A Complete History*, 146; and White, *Creating the National Pastime,* 176.

163. "Westerners To Test Grays Strength At Forbes Field Friday," *Pittsburgh Courier*, 19 July 1930; Ribowsky, *A Complete History*, 144–145; Bruce, *Kansas City Monarchs,* 71.

164. Irvin N. Rosee, "Brooklyn's Colored League Entry May Influence Dodgers to Play Night Baseball in 1936," *Brooklyn Times Union*, 16 January 1935; Bob Luke, *The Most Famous Woman In Baseball: Effa Manley and the Negro Leagues* (Washington D.C.: Potomac, 2011), 17–18. On the history of night baseball, see David Pietrusza, *Lights On! The Wild Century-Long Saga of Night Baseball* (Lanham, MD: Scarecrow, 1997).

165. Lonnie Harrington, *Pittsburgh Courier*, 14 May 1932; "Chocolate May Fight in New Greenlee Field," *Pittsburgh Courier*, 28 May 1932.

166. Chester L. Washington, "Sportively Speaking," *Pittsburgh Courier*, 7 May 1932.

167. "Expect Record Crowd At Park," *Pittsburgh Courier*, 30 April 1932.

168. Ribowsky, *A Complete History*, 163.

169. William C. Nunn, "Rowdyism in Baseball," *Pittsburgh Courier*, 14 May 1932.

170. "Greenlee Should Make Good President," *Pittsburgh Courier*, 4 March 1933.

171. Lawrence D. Hogan, *Shades of Glory,* 301–302; Mark Ribowsky, *Don't Look Back: Satchel Paige in the Shadows of Baseball* (New York: Simon and Schuster, 1994), 158, 162–163, 173–175; Lawrence Tye, *Satchel: The Life and Times of An American Legend* (New York: Random House, 2009), 108–116.

172. Ribowsky, *A Complete History*, 226. The *Courier* had previously praised Greenlee for his hiring of a black umpire at Greenlee Field. "Crawfords to Use At Least 1 Negro Umpire at New Uptown Park," *Pittsburgh Courier*, 6 February 1932.

173. Ribowsky, *Don't Look Back*, 174.

174. W. Rollo Wilson, "Sports Shots," *Pittsburgh Courier*, 6 February 1932; Leonard, *Buck Leonard*, 17.

175. William "Sug" Cornelius, interview by Holway, *Voices from the Great Black Baseball Leagues*, 237.

176. *Ibid.*, 237.

177. Bell, interview, 9.

178. John Edgar Wideman, "Michael Jordan Leaps the Great Divide," *Esquire* 1990, reprinted in Gena Dagel Caponi, ed., *Signifyin(g), Sanctifyin,' & Slam Dunking* (Amherst: University of Massachusetts Press, 1999), 396.

179. Jules Tygiel, *Baseball's Great Experiment: Jackie Robinson and His Legacy* (New York: Vintage, 1984), 216.

180. Myra B. Young Armistead, "Revisiting Hotels and Other Lodgings: American Tourist Spaces through the Lens of Black Pleasure-Travelers, 1880–1950," *The Journal of Decorative and Propaganda Arts* 25 (2005): 136–159; Cotton Seiler, "'So That We as a Race Might Have Something Authentic to Travel By': African American Automoblity and Cold-War Liberalism," *American Quarterly* 58 (December 2005): 1091–1117; Gilbert King, *Devil in the Grove: Thurgood Marshall, the Groveland Boys, and the Dawn of a New America* (New York: Harper Perennial, 2013), 126. Calvin Alexander Ramsey has written a play and children's book about the Green Book (published by Victor H. Green from 1936 to 1964). Ramsey, *Ruth and the Green Book* (Carolrhoda Books, 2010).

181. "The Chicago Giants Baseball Club," *Chicago Defender*, 22 January 1910, 1; "The Leland Chicago Giants," *Chicago Defender*, 16 April 1910, 1; John L. Clark, "I Believe You Should Know: Following the Crawfords," *Pittsburgh Courier*, 9 April 1932; "Houston to Oppose Local Team Next Week," *Pittsburgh Courier*, 2 April 1932; John L. Clark, "I Believe You Should Know," *Pittsburgh Courier*, 16 April 1932. See also Lanctot, *Negro League Baseball*, 157. Despite the long (and documented) history of black spring training, a *Saturday Evening Post* writer contended that black teams had more recently adopted the practice to "ape[d] their white peers." Ted Shane, "The Chocolate Rube Waddell," *Saturday Evening Post*, July 27, 1940, 20.

182. On travel of prosperous blacks during

this time period, see Foster, "In the Face of 'Jim Crow,'" 130–149. Sherrie Tucker examines the travel of all-black girl bands in *Swing Shift: "All-Girl" Bands of the 1940s* (Durham: Duke University Press, 2000), 135–226.

183. Angela Y. Davis, *Blues Legacies and Black Feminism* (New York: Random House, 1998; reprint, New York: Vintage, 1999), 67. Davis analyzes the importance of travel themes in black women's blues music in the 1920s. *Blues Legacies and Black Feminism*, 66–90. Similarly, Lawrence Levine documents an emphasis on mobility in his study of the blues and black culture. Levine, *Black Culture and Black Consciousness*, 261–267.

184. Rogosin, *Invisible Men*, 130–131.

185. Robinson, *Catching Dreams*, 9.

186. "The Chicago Giants Baseball Club," *Chicago Defender*, 22 January 1910, 1: "The Leland Chicago Giants," *Chicago Defender*, 16 April 1910, 1. In *Swing Shift*, Sherrie Tucker notes that protected transportation was crucial to the very existence of black all-girl bands traveling through the South. In one instance, a female musician claimed that the loss of "their private Pullman-type sleeper bus" contributed to the dissolution of the International Sweethearts of Rhythm. Tucker, *Swing Shift*, 67.

187. John L. Clark, "I Believe You Should Know," *Pittsburgh Courier*, 16 April 1932. For press coverage of spring training trips through the south, see also, "Rube Foster's Bunch Bound for Chicago," *Chicago Defender*, 9 April 1921; "Enjoying the Southern Sun," *Chicago Defender*, 2 April 1932; "Jim Brown Has Outfit in the Land of Dixie," *Chicago Defender*, 2 April 1932; "Cleveland Plans to Train in South," *Chicago Defender*, 7 April 1934; "Kansas City Monarchs Leave to Start Drills in South," *Chicago Defender*, 21 April 1934. All-girl bands also traveled by private buses in some instances. Tucker, *Swing Shift*, 138–139.

188. John L. Clark, "I Believe You Should Know," *Pittsburgh Courier*, 9 April 1932.

189. Rogosin, *Invisible Men*, 16.

190. O'Neil, *I Was Right on Time*, 47.

191. Chadwick, *When the Game Was Black and White*, 69.

192. O'Neil, *I Was Right on Time*, 83; Bruce, *Kansas City Monarchs*, 61, 78. During World War II, the black all-female swing band, the International Sweethearts of Rhythm, employed a similar bus "equipped with eating and sleeping facilities to temper the risks of traveling through Jim Crow territory." For bands like the International Sweethearts, which were often

covertly integrated, private transportation also ameliorated the stresses inherent in their attempt to protect "passing" band members. Tucker, *Swing Shift*, 67.

193. O'Neil, *I Was Right on Time*, 51.

194. Page, interview by Holway, *Voices from the Great Black Baseball Leagues*, 151–152; Leonard, interview by Holway, *Voices from the Great Black Baseball Leagues*, 255–256. William Brashler provides a fictionalized version of these very common Negro Leagues stories in *Bingo Long*.

195. O'Neil, *I Was Right on Time*, 55. Othello Renfroe "hoboed" to join a team in Chicago. Othello Renfroe, interview by Holway, *Voices from the Great Black Baseball Leagues*, 342.

196. Leonard, interview by Holway, *Voices from the Great Black Baseball Leagues*, 259.

197. Tye, *Satchel*, 153–154.

198. "Travels by Own Plane," *New York Times*, 9 July 1946.

199. Marshall, interview by Banker, *Black Diamonds*; Peterson, *Only the Ball Was White*, 154–155; Rogosin, *Invisible Men*, 126.

200. Leonard, interview by Holway, *Voices from the Great Black Baseball Leagues*, 259.

201. Ribowsky, *Complete History of the Negro Leagues*, 143–144; Earl Wilson, Sr., interview by Kelley, *Negro Leagues Revisited*, 29; Buster Haywood, interview by Kelley, 110–111.

202. Burnis "Wild Bill" Wright, interview by Kelley, *Voices From the Negro Leagues*, 37.

203. Ribowsky, *A Complete History*, 144.

204. Glenda E. Gill, *White Grease Paint on Black Performers: A Study of the Federal Theatre, 1935–1939* (New York: Peter Lang, 1988), 17.

205. Tucker, *Swing Shift*, 139, 135–162.

206. Cowan "Bubba" Hyde, interview by Kelley, *Voices from the Negro Leagues*, 10. See also, William "Bobby" Robinson, interview by Brent Kelley, *The Negro Leagues Revisited*, 5.

207. Robinson, *Catching Dreams*, 62; O'Neil, *I Was Right on Time*, 87; Chadwick, *When the Game Was Black and White*, 78.

208. Leonard, *Buck Leonard*, 127.

209. Tucker describes how Duke Pilgrim, manager of a black "all-girls" band in the 1940s, was similarly able to circumvent the color line. Pilgrim was light skinned and "had straight hair." As such, he would pass for white when necessary to avert "potential troubles on the road." Tucker, *Swing Shift*, 160–161.

210. Leonard, *Buck Leonard*, 127. This ambiguity of the American color line created difficulties for Latino players attempting to adjust

to life and racial policies in the United States. See Burgos, Jr., "Playing Ball in a Black and White Field of Dreams," 67–104. Such actions could be dangerous. If a business owner realized that a player was part of a black team, the owner could react violently, feeling he had been fooled. Rogosin, *Invisible Men*, 131.

211. Cornelius, interview by Holway, *Voices from the Great Black Baseball Leagues*, 244.

Chapter Two

1. Judy Johnson, interview by Stephen Banker, *Black Diamonds*, Cassette Tape #1, Side Two.

2. Langston Hughes, "The Negro Artist and the Racial Mountain," (*The Nation*, June 23 1926) *reprinted in Francis L. Broderick and August Meier*, Negro Protest Thought in the Twentieth Century *(Indianapolis and New York: Bobbs-Merrill, 1965)*, 92–97, quotes 93, 94, 96.

3. "Rumors and Facts," *Pittsburgh Courier*, 7 March 1925, 7.

4. Marlon B. Ross, *Manning the Race: Reforming Black Men in the Jim Crow Era* (New York: New York University Press, 2004), 98–99.

5. Gail Bederman, *Manliness and Civilization: A Cultural History of Gender and Race in the United States, 1880–1917* (Chicago: University of Chicago Press, 1995), 1–32.

6. Ross, *Manning the Race*, 90–144.

7. On race and respectability in sport, see Gwendolyn Captain, "Enter Ladies and Gentlemen of Color: Gender, Sport, and the Ideal of African American Manhood and Womanhood During the Late Nineteenth and Early Twentieth Century," *Journal of Sport History* 18 (Spring 1991): 81–102; Patrick B. Miller, "To 'Bring the Race Along Rapidly': Sport, Student Culture, and Educational Mission at Historically Black Colleges during the Interwar Years," *History of Education Quarterly* 35 (Summer 1995): 111–133. On respectability and gender in African American life, see Mia Bay, *To Tell the Truth Freely: The Life of Ida B. Wells* (New York: Hill and Wang, 2010); Glenda Elizabeth Gilmore, *Gender and Jim Crow: Women and the Politics of White Supremacy in North Carolina, 1896–1920* (Chapel Hill: University of North Carolina Press, 1996); Evelyn Brooks Higginbotham, *Righteous Discontent: The Women's Movement in the Black Baptist Church* (Cambridge: Harvard University Press, 1993), 20–21, 25–31; Deborah Gray White, *Too Heavy a Load: Black*

Women in Defense of Themselves, 1894–1994 (New York: W.W. Norton, 1999), 68–86.

8. See, for example, representative works on Joe Louis and Jesse Owens: Richard Bak, *Joe Louis, The Great Black Hope* (New York: Da Capo, 1996, 1998); William J. Baker, *Jesse Owens: An American Life* (New York: The Free Press, 1986); Donald McRae, *Heroes Without A Country: America's Betrayal of Joe Louis and Jesse Owens* (New York: HarperCollins, 2002); Chris Mead, *Champion-Joe Louis: Black Hero in White America* (New York: Charles Scribner's Sons, 1995). On the earlier period, see the following representative works: Bederman, *Manliness and Civilization*; Earnestine Jenkins and Darlene Clark Hine, eds., *A Question of Manhood: A Reader in U.S. Black Men's History and Masculinity*, Volume 2: *The 19th Century: From Emancipation to Jim Crow* (Bloomington: Indiana University Press, 2001).

9. On New Negro Manhood, see Ross, *Manning the Race*. Martin Summers has written an important analysis of black middle-class manhood, especially as performed within organizations like the freemasons and the United Negro Improvement Association (Garvey's UNIA). Summers, *Manliness and its Discontents: The Black Middle Class and the Transformation of Masculinity, 1900–1930* (Chapel Hill: University of North Carolina Press, 2004).

10. Jeff Nickel and Sarah Trembanis, "'What Moves Our People To-day': Voter Apathy and the Rise of Sport, 1880–1916," conference paper, presented at the Annual Meeting of the North American Society for Sport History (NASSH), Columbus, Ohio, May 2003.

11. On Muscular Christianity, see Clifford Putney, *Muscular Christianity: Manhood and Sports in Protestant America, 1880–1920* (Cambridge: Harvard University Press, 2003).

12. See Graham White and Shane White, *Stylin': Black Expressive Culture from its Beginnings to the Zoot Suit* (Ithaca: Cornell University Press, 1999), 192.

13. *The Half-Century Magazine*, July 1917, cover page. On Overton's career in the beauty industry, see Kathy Peiss, *Hope in a Jar: The Making of America's Beauty Culture* (Philadelphia: University of Pennsylvania Press, 2011). For a brief biography, see Russell L. Adams, *Great Negroes, Past and Present, Volume I* (Chicago: African American Images, 1984), 87 and his obituary, "Anthony Overton," *The Journal of Negro History* 32 (July 1947): 394–396.

14. On informal recreation and black migrants, see Robin D.G. Kelley, "'We Are Not

What We Seem': Rethinking Black Working-Class Opposition in the Jim Crow South," *Journal of American History* (June 1993): 84; Ronald L. Lewis, "From Peasant to Proletarian: The Migration of Southern Blacks to the Central Appalachian Coalfields," *Journal of Southern History* (February 1989): 77–102.

15. "Leland Giants in Double Header," *New York Times*, 17 September 1910, 7; "Donlin and Raymond Play Today," *New York Times*, 25 September 1910, C6; "Leland Giants to Play Ridgewood," *New York Times*, 30 September 1910, 9; "Leland Giants Against Ridgewood," *New York Times*, 1 October 1910, 11; "Sunday Baseball Games," *New York Times*, 27 August 1911, C6.

16. On informal recreation and black migrants, see Robin D.G. Kelley, " 'We Are Not What We Seem' ": Rethinking Black Working-Class Opposition in the Jim Crow South" *Journal of American History* (June 1993): 84; Ronald L. Lewis, "From Peasant to Proletarian: The Migration of Southern Blacks to the Central Appalachian Coalfields," *Journal of Southern History* (February 1989): 77–102.

17. Images of African American males that refuted racialist assumptions about "oversexed" and "brute Negroes" were particularly prevalent in the first decades of the twentieth century. On racial stereotypes regarding black manhood, see George M. Fredrickson, *The Black Image in the White Mind: The Debate on Afro-American Character and Destiny 1817–1914* (New York: Harper and Row, 1971), 276–283.

18. Howard A. Phelps, " Andrew 'Rube' Foster," *The Half-Century Magazine*, March 1919, 8.

19. *Ibid.*, 8.

20. *Ibid.*, 8.

21. *Ibid.*, 8

22. *Ibid.* See also, "The Leland Chicago Giants," *Chicago Defender*, 16 April 1910, 1.

23. Emmett J. Scott and Lyman Beacher Stowe, "Booker T. Washington: Builder of a Civilization" (originally published 1916), reprinted in Hugh Hawkins, ed., *Booker T. Washington and His Critics: Black Leadership in Crisis* (Lexington, MA: D.C. Heath, 1974, 1962), 42.

24. Scott and Stowe, "Booker T. Washington," 43.

25. In contrast, memoirist William Pickens "demand[ed] equal treatment for all deserving men," including access to a Pullman car. Ross, *Manning the Race*, 103.

26. Scott and Stowe, "Booker T. Washington," 43.

27. Lewis, "National Baseball League Formed," *The Competitor*, March 1920, 67.

28. Dave Wyatt, "National League of Colored Clubs Prepare for Season's Opening," *The Competitor*, April 1920, 73.

29. Wyatt, "National League of Colored Clubs," 74.

30. Webster MacDonald, interview by Holway, *Voices from the Great Black Baseball Leagues*, 78.

31. Buck O'Neil, *I Was Right on Time* (New York: Simon and Schuster, 1996, 1997), 92; Lawrence Tye, *Satchel*, 141.

32. O'Neil, *Right on Time*, 92; Bruce, *The Kansas City Monarchs*, 43.

33. Cum Posey, "The Sportive Realm," *Pittsburgh Courier*, 14 November 1925.

34. Webster McDonald, quoted in Holway, *Voices from the Great Black Baseball Leagues*, 39.

35. On Babe Ruth, see Robert C. Cottrell, *Blackball, the Black Sox, and the Babe: Baseball's Crucial 1920 Season* (Jefferson, NC: McFarland, 2002); Robert W. Creamer, *Babe: The Legend Comes to Life* (New York: Fireside, 1974, 1992).

36. Bak, *Turkey Stearnes and the Detroit Stars: The Negro Leagues in Detroit, 1919–1933* (Detroit: Wayne State University Press, 1994), 178.

37. "Jack Johnson Professor of Pugilists," *Pittsburgh Courier*, 8 January 1927; "Respress Drops Us A Line on Johnson," *Pittsburgh Courier*, 9 July 1921; "The Return of Jack Johnson," *The Competitor*, July 1920, 71; Howard A. Phelps, "Memories of Champions," *The Half-Century Magazine*, July 1919, 8. Historians of black sport have frequently grappled with Jack Johnson and his role in shaping an alternative manhood ideal for African Americans. On Johnson's life and times, see Al-Tony Gilmore, *Bad Nigger! The National Impact of Jack Johnson* (Port Washington, NY: 1975); Gilmore, "Jack Johnson and White Women: The National Impact," *Journal of Negro History* (January 1973): 18–38; Jack Johnson, *Jack Johnson is a Dandy, An Autobiography* (New York: Chelsea House, 1969); Geoffrey C. Ward, *Unforgivable Blackness: The Rise and Fall of Jack Johnson* (New York: Alfred A. Knopf, 2004). On Johnson as a "bad man" and subject of folk song and celebration, see Lawrence Levine, *Black Culture and Black Consciousness: Afro-American Folk Thought From Slavery to Freedom* (New York: Oxford

University Press, 1977, 1978), 419–420; Leon Litwack, *Trouble in Mind: Black Southerners in the Age of Jim Crow* (New York: Alfred A. Knopf, 1998), 441–444. For a sampling of the scholarship on Johnson's legacy for subsequent black athletes, see Richard Bak, *Joe Louis, The Great Black Hope* (New York: Da Capo, 1996, 1998), 43–76; Geoffrey C. Ward, *Unforgivable Blackness: The Rise and Fall of Jack Johnson* (New York: Alfred A. Knopf, 2004), 437–445; Howard Binham and Max Wallace, *Muhammad Ali's Greatest Fight: Cassius Clay vs. the United States of America* (New York: M. Evans, 2000), 29–49.

38. Cool Papa Bell, Ted Page, Willie Wells, and James "Joe" Greene, interviews by John Holway, *Voices from the Great Black Baseball Leagues* (New York: DaCapo, 1975, 1993), 127, 149, 224, 305.

39. On the rediscovery of Negro Leagues baseball, see Robert K. Fitts, "Baseball Cards and Race Relations," *Journal of American Culture* 17 (Fall 1994): 75–85; Daniel A. Nathan, "Bearing Witness to Blackball: Buck O'Neil, the Negro Leagues, and the Politics of the Past," *Journal of American Studies* 35 (2001): 453–469.

40. For a 1930s explanation of "race men," see Drake and Cayton, *Black Metropolis*, 394–395.

41. According to Driggs and Haddix, the Monarchs were an incredible source of pride for black Kansas City residents, bringing "the community prestige and respect." *Kansas City Jazz*, 28.

42. Pee Wee Butts, interview by Holway, *Voices from the Great Black Baseball Leagues*, 345.

43. Bruce, *Kansas City Monarchs*, 41–42; Leonard, *Buck Leonard*, 104–105; O'Neil, *Right on Time*, 97–99; Ribowsky, *Don't Look Back*, 76. On Kansas City's black jazz community, see Frank Driggs and Chuck Haddix, *Kansas City Jazz: From Ragtime to Bebop—A History* (New York: Oxford University Press, 2005).

44. *Kansas City Jazz*, 28.

45. Greene, interview by Holway, *Voices from the Great Black Baseball Leagues*, 305. For a fictional take on nightlife in the Negro Leagues, see William Brashler, *The Bingo Long Traveling All-Stars and Motor Kings* (New York: Signet, 1973).

46. Bruce, *The Kansas City Monarchs*, 43.

47. Kyle P. McNary, *Ted "Double Duty" Radclilffe: 36 Years of Pitching and Catching in Baseball's Negro Leagues* (Minneapolis: McNary Publishing, 1994), 22.

48. Ted Page, interview by Holway, *Voices From the Great Black Baseball Leagues*, 149.

49. Page, interview by Holway, *Voices From the Great Black Baseball Leagues*, 158.

50. Sherrie Tucker, *Swing Shift*, 137–141.

51. Susan Cahn, *Coming on Strong*, 150–152, 155.

52. Rogosin, *Invisible Men*, 162.

53. Gerald Early, *The Culture of Bruising: Essays on Prizefighting, Literature, and Modern American Culture* (Hopewell, New Jersey: Ecco, 1994), 6.

54. Gena Dagel Caponi, *Signifyin(g), Sanctifyin,' and Slam Dunking: A Reader in African American Expressive Culture* (Amherst: University of Massachusetts Press, 1999), 3.

55. Aaron Baker discusses how Hollywood films in the Jackie Robinson era downplayed the combination of "creative flair with competitive efficacy" that black athletes brought to professional sports. Baker, "From Second String to Solo Star," 47–48.

56. Paige, interview by Banker, *Black Diamonds*.

57. Trouppe, *20 Years Too Soon*, 56.

58. Larry Lester, David Marasco, and Patrick Rock, "The Historical Satchel Paige: True Stories and Tales Truly Told," in *Satchel Paige and Company*, 40–41.

59. Tye, *Satchel Paige*, 79.

60. Ribowsky, *Don't Look Back*, 114; Terrie Aamodt, "Cracking a Chink in Jim Crow: Satchel Paige and the Integration of Baseball," in *Satchel Paige and Company*, 71; Satchel Paige, *Maybe I'll Pitch Forever* (Lincoln, NE: Bison, 1993), 88.

61. *Ibid.*, 129.

62. Rogosin, *Invisible Men*, 135; John Holway, "Introduction," *Maybe I'll Pitch Forever*, vii.

63. O'Neil, *Right on Time*, 118–119.

64. In his 1962 autobiography, Paige claimed that a similar stunt established his reputation as a top pitcher in Alabama semi-pro baseball. Paige, *Maybe I'll Pitch Forever*, 34–35.

65. Frazier "Slow" Robinson and Paul Bauer, *Catching Dreams: My Life in the Negro Baseball Leagues* (Syracuse: Syracuse University Press, 1999), 32; Tom Gilbert, *Baseball and the Color Line* (New York: Franklin Watts, 1995), 125. Robinson caught for Satchel as part of the 1939 Satchel Paige's All-Stars.

66. Larry Lester, "Leroy 'Satchel' Paige: the Mystique and Milestones of da Man," in *Satchel Paige and Company*, 12; Larry Tye, *Satchel*, 262.

67. Brown, interview by Holway, *Voices from the Great Black Baseball Leagues,* 220.

68. Aaron Baker describes Hollywood's unwillingness to recognize these trickerations or stylized athletic performances in the construction of movie narratives, particularly *The Jackie Robinson Story,* "From Second String to Solo Star," *Classic Hollywood, Classic Whiteness,* 47–48.

69. Brown, interview by Holway, *Voices from the Great Black Baseball Leagues,* 220.

70. Ira F. Lewis, "The Passing Review," *Pittsburgh Courier,* 30 April 1932.

71. Gene Roberts and Hank Klibanoff, *The Race Beat: The Press, The Civil Rights Struggle, and the Awakening of a Nation* (New York: Vintage, 2007), 12–23.

72. "Great Base Ball Attraction," *Norfolk Journal and Guide,* 2 September 1932; "Base Ball Extraordinary," *Norfolk Journal and Guide,* 2 September 1932; "Base Ball Championship Game," *Norfolk Journal and Guide,* 9 September 1932.

73. Al Monroe, "It's News to Me," *Chicago Defender,* 25 September 1937.

74. See Satchel Paige, *Maybe I'll Pitch Forever;* Tye, *Satchel,* 103–104.

75. Wendell Smith, Paige 'Thumbs Nose' at His Public Here," *Pittsburgh Courier,* 26 June 1943.

76. Ibid.

77. Leonard, interview by Holway, *Voices from the Great Black Baseball Leagues,* 269.

78. "Those Foolish Contemporaries," *Life,* November 14, 1930, 24.

79. Al Monroe, "Speaking of Sports," *Chicago Defender,* 30 June 1934.

80. Jim Taylor, "Taylor Says Poor Umpiring, Bad Management Harmful," *Chicago Defender,* 22 February 1936.

81. Ibid.

82. Sam Lacy, "Players Indifferent About Entering Major leagues," *Baltimore Afro-American,* 5 August 1939; On the 1939–1941 Elite Giants, see Bob Luke, *The Baltimore Elite Giants: Sport and Society in the Age of Negro League Baseball* (Baltimore: Johns Hopkins University Press, 2009), 43.

83. "Globe Trotters Visit Night Spots—And Lose," *Chicago Defender,* 29 March 1941.

84. On "race heroes," see St. Clair Drake and Horace R. Cayton, *Black Metropolis: A Study of Negro Life in a Northern City* (New York: Harcourt, Brace, 1945), 390–397.

85. Robert Farris Thompson, "An Aesthetic of the Cool: West African Dance," in *Signifyin(g), Sanctifyin,' & Slam Dunking: A Reader in African American Expressive Culture,* Gena Dagel Caponi, ed. (Amherst: University of Massachusetts Press, 1999), 83–84.

86. Wendell Smith, quoted in Donn Rogosin, *Invisible Men: Life in Baseball's Negro Leagues* (New York: Kodansha International, 1995, 1983), 149.

87. "Sol Butler on All-American Track Team," *The Competitor* February 1920, 80. On everyday resistance during Jim Crow, see Kelley, *Race Rebels,* 55–76.

88. Roberts, *From Trickster to Badman,* 211–212.

89. Bingham and Wallace, *Muhammad Ali's Greatest Fight.*

90. Drake and Cayton, *Black Metropolis,* 295; Roberts, *From Trickster to Badman,* 213.

91. Al-Tony Gilmore. *Bad Nigger! The National Impact of Jack Johnson* (Port Washington, NY: 1975), 21.

92. Foster, "In the Face of 'Jim Crow': Prosperous Blacks and Vacations, Travel and Outdoor Leisure, 1890–1945," *Journal of Negro History* 84 (Spring 1999): 143.

93. Ibid., 143.

94. Rogosin, *Invisible Men,* 133.

95. Frank Duncan, Jr., interview by Kelley, *Voices from the Negro Leagues,* 100.

96. Douglas A. Blackmon, *Slavery by Another Name: The Re-Enslavement of Black Americans from the Civil War to World War II* (New York: Anchor, 2009).

97. Herbert J. Seligmann, "Why Negroes Leave the Farm: A Federal Investigation Must Come," *The Competitor* (June 1921): 6.

98. "Georgia and Peonage," *The Competitor* (May 1921): 3. See also, "The Colored Press on Georgia Peonage," *The Competitor* (May 1921): 8–12. On violence encountered by another group of performers, black all-girl bands, see Sherrie Tucker, *Swing Shift: "All-Girl" Bands of the 1940s* (Durham: Duke University Press, 2000), 137, 144–147.

99. Leon F. Litwack, *Trouble in Mind: Black Southerners in the Age of Jim Crow* (New York: Alfred A. Knopf, 1998), 140–141.

100. Blackmon, *Slavery by Another Name,* 1–2, 402.

101. Berry spent time in prison for a string of armed robberies committed when he was a teenager. Bruce Pegg, *Brown Eyed Handsome Man: The Life and Hard Times of Chuck Berry* (New York: Routledge, 2002), 14–15, 67.

102. Roberts, *From Trickster to Badman,* 197.

103. Litwack describes the fear and distrust many blacks in the South had for police officers. Litwack, *Trouble in Mind*, 15–16.

104. Greene interview by John Holway, *Voices from the Great Black Baseball Leagues*, 340. According to Bruce Chadwick, Paige earned $50,000 a year during the Depression. *When the Game Was Black and White: The Illustrated History of the Negro Leagues* (New York: Abbeville, 1992).

105. Troupe, "Pain and Glory: Some Thoughts on My Father" in Don Belton, ed., *Speak My Name: Black Men on Masculinity and the American Dream* (Boston: Beacon, 1995), 243.

106. Roberts, *From Trickster to Badman*, 197–198.

107. *Trouble in Mind*, 152–163.

108. Arthur Knight, "Star Dances: African American Constructions of Stardom, 1925–1960," *Classic Hollywood, Classic Whiteness*, Daniel Bernardi, ed. (Minneapolis: University of Minnesota Press, 2001), 406.

109. Mark Ribowsky, *Don't Look Back: Satchel Paige in the Shadows of Baseball.* (New York: Simon and Schuster, 1994), 62

110. Knight, "Star Dances," 405–406. For more information on black celebrity athletes, see Andrew M. Kaye, *The Pussycat of Prizefighting: Tiger Flowers and the Politics of Black Celebrity* (Athens: University of Georgia Press, 2004), 103–140.

111. Aaron Baker, "From Second String to Solo Star: Classic Hollywood and the Black Athlete," *Classic Hollywood, Classic Whiteness* edited by Daniel Benardi (Minneapolis: University of Minnesota Press, 2001): 31–51.

112. Penny M. von Eschen, *Satchmo Blows Up the World: Jazz Ambassadors Play the Cold War* (Cambridge: Harvard University Press, 2004). On Baker and Robeson, see Mary L. Dudziak, "Josephine Baker, Racial Protest, and the Cold War," *Journal of American History* 81 (1994): 543–570; on Robeson, the Black Left, and the Cold War, see Barbara J. Beeching, "Paul Robeson and the Black Press: the 1950 Passport Controversy," *The Journal of African American History* 87 (Summer 2002): 339–354; and Kimberley L. Phillips, *War! What Is It Good For? Black Freedom Struggles & the U.S. Military from World War II to Iraq* (Chapel Hill: University of North Carolina Press, 2012), 156–185.

113. Rogosin, *Invisible Men*, 133.

114. Trouppe, *20 Years Too Soon*, 102.

115. Roberts, *From Trickster to Badman*, 205.

116. Kelley, *Race Rebels*, 55–76.

117. *Ibid.*, 205–213.

Chapter Three

1. F.A. Conningham, *Currier & Ives* (Cleveland: World Publishing, 1950), 40–41: Michael D. Harris, *Colored Pictures: Race and Visual Representation* (Chapel Hill: University of North Carolina Press, 2006), 62–63.

2. On minstrel stereotypes and their dissemination, see Joseph Boskin, *Sambo: The Rise and Demise of an American Jester* (New York: Oxford University Press, 1986); John W. Roberts, *From Trickster to Badman: The Black Folk Hero in Slavery and Freedom* (Philadelphia: University of Pennsylvania Press, 1989). On stereotypes and archetypes in movies, see Donald Bogle, *Toms, Coons, Mulattoes, Mammies, and Bucks: An Interpretive History of Blacks in American Films* (New York: Viking, 1973); Daniel J. Leab, *From Sambo to Superspade: The Black Experience in Motion Pictures* (Boston: Houghton Mifflin, 1975).

3. Graham White and Shane White, *Stylin': African American Expressive Culture from Its Beginning to the Zoot Suit* (Ithaca: Cornell University Press, 1998), 140–141, 151–152. Studying a later time period, Robin D.G. Kelley has analyzed how wearing a zoot suit during World War II represented a political form of working-class, African American resistance. See Kelley, *Race Rebels: Culture Politics, and the Black Working Class* (New York: Free Press, 1996), 161–182.

4. Albert Spalding perpetuated the myth of white baseball as a pastoral and patriotic American invention to benefit his sporting goods business. Albert Spalding, *America's National Game* (New York: American Sports Publishing, 1911). On the mythology of American baseball, see David McGimpsey, *Imagining Baseball: America's Pastime and Popular Culture* (Bloomington: University of Indiana Press, 2000).

5. Allan H. Spear, *Black Chicago: The Making of a Negro Ghetto 1880–1920* (Chicago: University of Chicago, 1967), 44–46, 204–205.

6. *Chicago Daily News* negatives collection, Chicago Historical Society (CHS), 1903, SDN-001216 and SDN-001217.

7. *Chicago Daily News*, 1905, SDN-003080.

8. *Chicago Daily News*, 1909, SDN-0055384.

9. *Chicago Daily News,* 1909, SDN-003137 and SDN-003083.

10. *Chicago Daily News,* 1907, SDN-055358, SDN-055361, SDN-055355, and SDN-055360.

11. *Chicago Daily News,* 1907, SDN-055360.

12. William "Sug" Cornelius recalled that metropolitan white newspapers rarely reported on black baseball until Abe Saperstein, a white promoter, began petitioning the white media on behalf of the Negro Leagues. William "Sug" Cornelius interview by Holway, *Voices from the Great Black Baseball Leagues* (New York: DaCapo, 1975, 1993), 246. Small-town papers, however, would highlight black baseball when it came to the local area.

13. Lizabeth Cohen, *Making A New Deal: Industrial Workers in Chicago, 1919–1939* (New York: Cambridge University Press, 1990), 29, 34–36.

14. Spear, *Black Chicago,* 201.

15. Spear, *Black Chicago,* 206–208.

16. On the significance of black World War I soldiers, see Steven A. Reich, "Soldiers of Democracy: Black Texans and the Fight for Citizenship, 1917–1921," *Journal of American History* (March 1996): 1478–1504; Leon Litwack, *Trouble in Mind: Black Southerners in the Age of Jim Crow* (New York: Alfred A. Knopf, 1998), 331.

17. Ren Mulford Jr., "War Boss a Fan," *Sporting Life,* 22 October 1904.

18. Frederick Courtenay Barber, "The Knothole in the Fence," *Sporting Life,* 7 May 1910.

19. "Regarding Crooked Baseball," *Pittsburgh Courier,* 11 October 1924.

20. Daniel Okrent and Harris Lewine, editors, *The Ultimate Baseball Book* (New York: Eisenbery, McCall, and Okrent, 1979, reprint, Boston: Houghton Mifflin, 1991), 103–104; G. Edward White, *Creating the National Pastime: Baseball Transforms Itself, 1903–1953* (Princeton: Princeton University Press, 1996), 86–115. On the context for and impact of the Black Sox Scandal, see Eliot Asinof, *Eight Men Out: The Black Sox and the 1919 World Series* (New York: Holt, Rinehart and Winston, 1963); Robert C. Cottrell, *Blackball, the Black Sox, and the Babe: Baseball's Crucial 1920 Season* (Jefferson, NC: McFarland, 2002); Daniel A. Nathan, *Saying It's So: A Cultural History of the Black Sox Scandal* (Urbana: University of Illinois Press, 2003).

21. White, *Creating the National Pastime,* 89–91, 111–113.

22. Al Monroe, "What Say," *Chicago Defender,* 14 May 1932.

23. For a few examples of white press coverage of black and interracial baseball during the 1930s, see "Deans to Play at Dexter Park," *New York Times,* 10 October 1934; "Deans Play in Paterson," *New York Times,* 20 October 1934; "Twin Bill to Aid Charity," *New York Times,* 22 June 1938; "Crawfords Set Back Black Yankees," *New York Times,* 27 June 1938.

24. For a further discussion of racism in broadcasting in the last quarter of the twentieth century, see Phillip M. Hoose, *Necessities: Racial Barriers in American Sports* (New York: Random House, 1989); John M. Hoberman, *Darwin's Athlete: How Sports Has Damaged Black America and Preserved the Myth of Race* (Boston: Houghton Mifflin, 1997). For a discussion of "articulate" as a racial marker in the twenty-first century, see H. Samy Alim and Geneva Smitherman, *Articulate While Black: Barack Obama, Language, and Race in the U.S.* (New York: Oxford University Press, 2012); Lynette Clemetson, "The Racial Politics of Speaking Well," *New York Times,* 4 February 2007.

25. Bob Ray, "He's Just a Big Man from the South," Satchel Paige file, National Baseball Hall of Fame and Museum, undated.

26. *Ibid.*

27. *Ibid.*

28. Ribowsky, *A Complete History,* 188, 191–192.

29. Kyle P. McNary, *Ted "Double Duty" Radcliffe: 36 Years of Pitching and Catching in Baseball's Negro Leagues* (Minneapolis: McNary Publishing, 1994), 30. Black hockey players in Quebec faced similar restrictions. Although a number of hockey teams were integrated, "Black players were told to leave the province if they fraternized with women in the white community." William Humber, *Diamonds of the North: A Concise History of Baseball in Canada* (Toronto: Oxford University Press, 1995), 139. Very little work has been done on the experience of black athletes in the upper Midwest. Steven R. Hoffbeck has collected a series of short pieces on Minnesota and black baseball, but they are mainly descriptive pieces about individual players or events and provide little context or analysis. Hoffbeck, ed., *Swinging for the Fences: Black Baseball in Minnesota* (St. Paul: Minnesota Historical Society, 2005).

30. Colin Howell, *Northern Sandlots: A Social History of Maritime Baseball* (Toronto: University of Toronto Press, 1995), 173.

31. Ribowsky, *A Complete History,* 192.

32. Tye, *Satchel,* 103–104.

33. Ribowsky, *A Complete History,* 192–193, Ribowsky, *Don't Look Back,* 126–133.

34. "Joins K.C. Monarchs," *Bismarck Tribune*, 28 August 1935.

35. "National Negro League is alright: Our Baseball Players Rank as High as Others," *Pittsburgh Courier*, 29 March 1930; W. Rollo Wilson, "Eastern Snapshots," *Pittsburgh Courier*, 12 September 1925; Wilson, "Sports Shots," *Pittsburgh Courier*, 4 March 1933; Chester L. Washington, "Sez Ches," *Pittsburgh Courier*, 18 May 1940.

36. George Lee, "Sporting Around," *Chicago Defender*, 7 April 1934, 21 April 1934, 12 May 1934, 16 June 1934, 21 July 1934.

37. Foster, interview by Holway, *Voices from the Great Black Baseball Leagues*, 201.

38. Daniel J. Kevles, *In the Name of Eugenics: Genetics and the Use of Human Heredity* (Cambridge: Harvard University Press, 1985, 1995), 83.

39. Page, interview by Holway, *Voices from the Great Black Baseball Leagues*, 149.

40. On blacks in the comics and the most common stereotypes, see Fredrik Strömberg, *Black Images in the Comics: A Visual History* (Fantagraphics Books, 2003), 29–30.

41. Dan Parker, "Ebbets Field Goes High Yellow," *Brooklyn Times Union*, 19 May 1935; Jimmy Powers "The Powerhouse," *New York Daily News*, 4 February 1935.

42. "Pebbles," *The Independent* 87, 10 July 1916, 64.

43. Parker, "Ebbets."

44. *Ibid.*

45. *Ibid.*

46. Dan Parker, "Major Club Owners Who Welcome Negro Patrons Shouldn't Bar Players," *Pittsburgh Courier*, 25 March 1933.

47. *Ibid.*

48. "White Sports Writer, Backed by N.Y. Daily, Fights for Race Players In Major leagues!" *Chicago Defender*, 15 August 1936.

49. "Fight Films Cost Joe Louis Victory, Says Blackburn," *Baltimore Afro-American*, 11 July 1938; Bennie Butler, "Powers Tirade on Joe Louis Protested," *Baltimore Afro-American*, 15 July 1939.

50. Wendell Smith, "The Sports Beat," *Pittsburgh Courier* 10 August 1946.

51. Smith, "The Sports Beat: All Sportswriters Aren't Liberal or Fair," *Pittsburgh Courier*, 23 February 1946.

52. On comic depictions of Africans and African Americans, see Stromberg, *Black Images in the Comics*, particularly 48–55, 58–59, 64–67, 96–97.

53. For comparison, see Figures 3.1 and 3.2.

For a representative strip of Felix the Cat, see Stromberg, *Black Images in the Comics*, 58–59.

54. "Speed is His Middle Name," *Baltimore Afro-American*, 7 May 1932; "Signs—Storm Center—All Set," *Pittsburgh Courier* 6 February 1932; "May Start," *Pittsburgh Courier*, 25 April 1931; "Will They be in Hero Roles Again This Year?" *Pittsburgh Courier*, 19 September 1925; "New Addition to Rube Foster's Pitching Staff," *Chicago Defender*, 30 April 1921; "The Babe Ruth of the National League," *Chicago Defender*, 9 July 1921; "Ranks with the Best," *Chicago Defender*, 30 April 1932.

55. Richard Bak, *Joe Louis: The Great Black Hope* (New York: Da Capo, 1998), 132, 149.

56. Randy Roberts, *Joe Louis: Hard Times Man* (New Haven: Yale University Press, 2010), 140–141.

57. Jules Tygiel, *Extra Bases* (Lincoln: University of Nebraska Press, 2002), 88.

58. Rob Ruck, *Raceball: How the Major Leagues Colonized the Black and Latin Game* (Boston: Beacon, 2011), 55–69; Tye, *Satchel*, 109–111.

59. Tye, *Satchel*, 111–112.

60. Eric Paul Roorda, *The Dictator Next Door: The Good Neighbor Policy and the Trujillo Regime in the Dominican Republic, 1930–1945* (Durham: Duke University Press, 1998), 127–135; Tye, *Satchel*, 112–113.

61. Roorda, *Dictator Next Door*, 59.

62. Adrian Burgos, Jr., *Playing America's Game: Baseball, Latinos, and the Color Line* (Berkeley: University of California Press, 2007), 125–127.

63. Burgos, *Playing America's Game*, xiii–xv, 4–6.

64. "Flint Majors Drop Two to the Cubans," *Chicago Defender*, 28 May 1930.

65. David B. Welky, "Viking Girls, Mermaids, and Little Brown Men: U.S. Journalism and the 1932 Olympics," *Journal of Sport History* 24 (Spring 1997): 39–41.

66. Mark Dyreson, "Marketing National Identity: The Olympic Games of 1932 and American Culture," *Olympika: The International Journal of Olympic Studies* (1995): 37.

67. Burgos, *Playing America's Game*, 11.

68. Joe Louis with Edna and Art Rust, Jr. *Joe Louis: My Life* (New York: Harcourt Brace Jovanovich, 1978), 39.

69. William C. Rhoden, "A Rival for Owens, and a Question of What If?" *New York Times*, 6 May 2012; Roberts, *Joe Louis*, 141; Bert Randolph Sugar, *Boxing's Greatest Fighters* (Guilford, CT: The Lyons Press, 2006), 4–6; Gena

Caponi-Tabery, *Jump for Joy: Jazz, Basketball, and Black Culture in 1930s America* (Amherst: University of Massachusetts Press, 2008), 47; "Olympic Roll Call," *Painesville Telegraph,* 14 March 1936; "Albritton Enters Meet With Burke," *New York Times,* 28 January 1937; and "Marquette Track Prospects Good-With Reservations," *Milwaukee Journal,* 25 December 1938.

70. James B. Roberts and Alexander G. Skutt, *The Boxing Registry: International Boxing Hall of Fame Official Record Book* (Ithaca, NY: McBooks, 2006), 154–155 and Bert Randolph Sugar, *Boxing's Greatest Fighters,* 133–135.

71. Roberts and Skutt, *The Boxing Registry,* 155.

72. Welky, "Viking Girls, Mermaids, and Little Brown Men," 35–38.

73. "Eddie Tolan, '32 Olympic Winner In Two Dash Events, Dead at 57," *New York Times,* 1 February 1967.

74. Sugar, *Boxing's Greatest Fighters,* 5; Donald Spivey, "'End Jim Crow in Sports': The Protest at New York University Press, 1940–1941," *Journal of Sport History* 15 (Winter 1988): 284.

75. Tygiel, *Extra Bases,* 64.

76. "Olympic Roll Call," *Painesville Telegraph,* 14 March 1936; "Albritton Enters Meet 2ith Burke," *New York Times,* 28 January 1937; and "Marquette Track Prospects Good—With Reservations," *Milwaukee Journal,* 25 December 1938.

77. Ruck, *Raceball,* 42, 60.

78. Lewis Erenberg, *The Greatest Fight of our Generation: Louis vs. Schmeling* (New York: Oxford University Press, 2006).

79. Jaime Schultz, "'A Wager Concerning a Diplomatic Pig': A Crooked Reading of the Floyd of Rosedale Narrative," *Journal of Sport History* 32 (Spring 2005): 6–7.

80. *Ibid.,* 12–15 and Michael Oriard, *King Football,* 6, 302–307.

81. "He'll Toss them for Chicago's Provident Hospital Sunday," *Chicago Defender,* 30 August 1941, in Satchel Paige file, Ashland Collection, National Baseball Hall of Fame and Museum.

82. Neil Lanctot, *Negro League Baseball: The Rise and Ruin of a Black Institution* (Philadelphia: University of Pennsylvania Press, 2004), 90, 98.

83. William A. Brower, "Time for Baseball to Erase the Blackball," *Opportunity* 20 (June 1942): 165.

84. *Ibid.,* 165–167.

85. "Committee Report to Mayor, Asks Equal Rights for Negro in Baseball," *New York Times,* 19 November 1945.

86. "Committee Report to Mayor, Asks Equal Rights for Negro in Baseball," *New York Times,* 19 November 1945. "Black Yanks Break Even," *New York Times,* 12 May 1941; "Mayor To Open Negro Series," *New York Times,* 12 September 1942. See also Henry D. Fetter, "The Party Line and the Color Line: The American Communist Party, the Daily Worker, and the Jackie Robinson," *Journal of Sport History* 28 (Fall 2001): 383. Marlon B. Ross, *Manning the Race: Reforming Black Men in the Jim Crow Era* (New York: New York University Press, 2004), 180–181.

87. Kelley, *Race Rebels,* 51; Reich, "Soldiers of Democracy," 1485.

88. Patricia A. Turner, *I Heard it Through the Grapevine: Rumor in African American Culture* (Berkeley: University of California Press, 1993), 44–45.

89. Tygiel, *Baseball's Great Experiment,* 43; Fetter, "The Party Line and the Color Line," 382.

90. James Overmyer, *Queen of the Negro Leagues: Effa Manley and the Newark Eagles* (Landham, MA: Scarecrow, 1998); Effa Manley and Leon Herbert Hartwick, *Negro Baseball ... Before Integration* (Chicago: Adams, 1976); Larry Lester, *Black Baseball's National Showcase: The East-West All-Star Game 1933–1953* (Lincoln: University of Nebraska Press, 2001), 142.

91. "Hazel Scott Concert" letter, "Hire Negro Clerks," *New York Age,* 4 August 1934; Wendell Smith, "New Duties Indicate Moguls Have Finally Recognized Her Ability As An Executive," in "Smitty's Sports-Spurts" *Pittsburgh Courier,* 30 January 1943; "Provides Shows for Soldiers," in "New Jersey Afro Honor Roll," 12 February 1944, Effa Manley file, Ashland Collection, National Baseball Hall of Fame and Museum.

92. "Provides Shows for Soldiers," in "New Jersey Afro Honor Roll," 12 February 1944, Effa Manley file, Ashland Collection, National Baseball Hall of Fame and Museum.

93. Barry Singer, *Black and Blue: The Life and Lyrics of Andy Razaf* (New York: Schirmer, 1992), 62, 67, 217–220.

94. Singer, *Black and Blue,* xii, 49–51, 307–309, 313–314, 379.

95. Andy Razaf, Eubie Blake, and Chas L. Cooke, "We are Americans Too" (New York: Handy Brothers Music), Effa Manley file, Ashland Collection, National Baseball Hall of Fame and Museum.

96. Walter White, "It's Our Country, Too," *Saturday Evening Post,* 14 December 1940, 61.

97. *Ibid.,* 27.

98. *Ibid.,* 68.

99. Arnold Rampersad, ed., *The Collected Poems of Langston Hughes* (New York: Random House, 1995), 46.

100. Singer, *Black and Blue,* 379.

101. Bruce, *The Kansas City Monarchs,* 100–101.

102. Lester, *Black Baseball's National Showcase,* 197.

103. Randy Dixon, "The Sports Bulge: Revolt Almost Wrecked East-West Classic," *Pittsburgh Courier,* 5 September 1942.

104. Bruce, *The Kansas City Monarchs,* 103; Paige, *Maybe I'll Pitch Forever,* 159–160.

105. Bruce, *The Kansas City Monarchs,* 103; Paige, *Maybe I'll Pitch Forever,* 163–165; Ribowsky, *Don't Look Back,* 223–224: Lester, *Black Baseball's National Showcase,* 228–231.

106. "Satchell Says He's Satisfied to Be Outlaw," *Richmond Afro-American* in Satchel Paige file, Ashland Collection, National Baseball Hall of Fame and Museum.

107. Ric Roberts, "Negro Big League Baseball A Two-Million Dollar Business," *Negro Baseball Pictorial Yearbook,* 1944, 5. See also Donald Spivey, "The Black Athlete in Big-Time Intercollegiate Sports, 1941–1968," *Phylon* 44 (1983): 120–121.

108. Bruce, *The Kansas City Monarchs,* 100–101.

109. Leonard, *Buck Leonard,* 149–150, 162; Lanctot, *Negro League Baseball,* 128–136.

110. On black ball player service, see Art Carter, "Negro Baseball Players Star for Uncle Sam," *Negro Baseball Pictorial Yearbook,* 1944, 22–23, 27; Leonard, *Buck Leonard,* 162.

111. Kelley, *Race Rebels,* 171–172.

112. Howard Bingham and Max Wallace, *Muhammad Ali's Greatest Fight: Cassius Clay vs. the United States of America* (New York: M. Evans, 2000), 112–119.

113. Effa Manley file, National Baseball Hall of Fame and Museum.

114. Neil Lanctot, *Campy: The Two Lives of Roy Campanella* (New York: Simon and Schuster, 2011), 93.

115. *Ibid.,* 5. Ribowsky, *Don't Look Back,* 188–190.

116. Donald Spivey has attributed the integration of baseball and other professional sports to World War II. Spivey also notes that most major intercollegiate football teams had at least one black team member by the conclu-

sion of the war. Spivey, "The Black Athlete," 121.

Chapter Four

1. *There Was Always Sun Shining Someplace,* Producer Craig Davidson, Refocus Productions in Association with Southwest Texas Public Broadcasting Corporation, 1989.

2. Laura Browder, *Slippery Characters: Ethnic Impersonators and American Identities* (Chapel Hill: University of North Carolina Press, 2000), 111–131.

3. George Lipsitz, *Time Passages: Collective Memory and American Popular Culture* (Minneapolis: University of Minnesota Press, 1990), 4. On the theory of recovering these coded (or hidden) meanings, see James C. Scott, *Domination and the Arts of Resistance: Hidden Transcripts* (New Haven: Yale University Press, 1990), 3–41, 136–156.

4. Scott, *Domination and the Arts of Resistance,* 3–41, 136–156.

5. Henry Louis Gates, Jr., *The Signifying Monkey: A Theory of African American Literary Criticism* (New York: Oxford University Press, 1988).

6. *Ibid.,* xxiv.

7. Geneva Smitherman, *Talkin and Testifyin: The Language of Black America* (Detroit: Wayne State University Press, 1986), 59.

8. Laura C. Jarmon, *Wishbone: Reference and Interpretation in Black Folk Narrative* (Knoxville: University of Tennessee Press, 2003), 221.

9. John W. Roberts describes the process of hero creation in *From Trickster to Badman: The Black Folk Hero in Slavery and Freedom* (Philadelphia: University of Pennsylvania Press, 1989), 1–5. On Jack Johnson's significance to African Americans, see Geoffrey C. Ward, *Unforgivable Blackness: The Rise and Fall of Jack Johnson* (New York: Alfred A. Knopf, 2004), 131, 144–145, 219–220, 236–237.

10. Kyle P. McNary claims that "It was black baseball, after all, that first introduced base coaches, not only to help runners and give signs, but to entertain crowds with a constant line of chatter." McNary, *Ted "Double Duty" Radcliffe: 36 Years of Pitching and Catching in Baseball's Negro Leagues* (Minneapolis: McNary Publishing, 1994), 29. Writers and owners, at times, criticized players for talking during the games, especially when that talking led to disputes with umpires or fans. William Nunn, "Rowdyism in Baseball," *Pittsburgh Courier,* 14 May 1932.

11. Roberts, *From Trickster to Badman,* 5.

12. Ralph Ellison, *Going to the Territory* (New York: Vintage International, 1986), 216.

13. Mark Ribowsky, *Don't Look Back: Satchel Paige in the Shadows of Baseball* (New York: Da Capo, 2000), 51. Shane, "The Chocolate Rube Waddell," *Saturday Evening Post,* 27 July 1940, 80–81.

14. Robert Boyle, "The Private Life of the Negro Ballplayer," *Sports Illustrated,* 21 March 1960, http://sportsillustrated.cnn.com/vault/article/magazine/MAG1134572/index.htm, accessed August 19, 2013.

15. Shane, "The Chocolate Rube Waddell," *Saturday Evening Post,* 27 July 1940, 80–81.

16. Tom Gilbert, *Baseball and the Color Line* (New York: Franklin Watts, 1995), 104.

17. *Ibid.,* 104.

18. Letter from M/Sgt. Bertran T. Beagle, U.S. Army retired, "Bullet Joe Rogan" player file, Ashland Collection, National Baseball Hall of Fame and Museum, 3; Robinson, interview by Brent Kelley, *The Negro Leagues Revisited: Conversations with 66 More Baseball Heroes* (Jefferson, NC: McFarland, 2000), 8; Lindsay, interview by Kelley, *Negro Leagues Revisited,* 19; Powell, interview by Kelley, *Negro Leagues Revisited,* 87.

19. Charles Alexander, *John McGraw* (Lincoln: University of Nebraska Press, 1988), 75.

20. Larry Brown, interview by John Holway, *Voices from the Great Black Baseball Leagues* (New York: Da Capo, 1992), 207–209. Mark Ribowsky notes that Cobb "was outhit and overshadowed by [Negro League stars] John Henry Lloyd, Home Run Johnson, and Bruce Petway" during his 1910 trip to Cuba. Ribowsky, *A Complete History,* 68.

21. Janet Bruce, *The Kansas City Monarchs: Champions of Black Baseball* (Lawrence: University of Kansas Press, 1985), 9; Louis A. Perez, *On Becoming Cuban: Identity, Nationality, and Culture* (Chapel Hill: University of North Carolina Press, 1999), 266.

22. Brown, interview by Holway, *Voices from the Great Black Baseball Leagues,* 207–209; Sol White, "Sol White's Column of Baseball Dope," *Cleveland Advocate,* 10 May 1919; W. Rollo Wilson, "Sports Shots," *Pittsburgh Courier,* 25 April 1931.

23. Charles Klinetobe and Steve Bullock, "Complicated Shadows: Ty Cobb and The Public Imagination," *Nine: A Journal of Baseball History and Culture* 18 (Fall 2009): 22–23.

24. Sol White, "Sol White's Column of

Baseball Dope," *Cleveland Advocate,* 10 May 1919; W. Rollo Wilson, "Sports Shots," *Pittsburgh Courier,* 25 April 1931.

25. LeRoy (Satchel) Paige as told to David Lipman, *Maybe I'll Pitch Forever: A Great Baseball Player tells the Hilarious Story Behind the Legend* (Lincoln: University of Nebraska Press, 1962, 1993), 44.

26. Kathy Peiss, *Hope in a Jar: The Making of America's Beauty Culture* (New York: Metropolitan Books, 1998), 207–212, 226, 231–233.

27. For a discussion of advertising images of African Americans, see Marilyn Kern-Foxworth, *Aunt Jemima, Uncle Ben, and Rastus: Blacks in Advertising, Yesterday, Today, and Tomorrow* (Westport, CT: Greenwood, 1994).

28. Quincy Trouppe, *20 Years Too Soon: Prelude to Major league Integrated Baseball* (St. Louis: Missouri Historical Society, 1995, 1977), 26. Trouppe was born in 1912 and began his baseball career in the 1930s, placing this story's roots to the 1930–1940 time frame.

29. Arthur Rust, Jr., *Get That Nigger off the Field: An Oral History of Black Ballplayers from the Negro Leagues to the Present* (New York: Delacourt, 1976), 44.

30. Webster MacDonald, interview by Holway, *Voices from the Great Black Baseball Leagues,* 87.

31. Cool Papa Bell, interview by Holway, *Voices from the Great Black Baseball Leagues,* 125.

32. Lester, *Black Baseball's National Showcase,* 155.

33. Ollie Stewart, "A Line of Two," *Baltimore Afro-American,* 5 June 1937.

34. James "Cool Papa" Bell, interview by Arthur Shaffer and Charles Korr, University of Missouri–St. Louis Oral History Program. September 8, 1971. Transcript, in "Cool Papa" Bell player file, Ashland Collection, National Baseball Hall of Fame and Museum, 35.

35. Hilton Smith, interview by John Holway, Hilton Smith file, National Baseball Hall of Fame and Museum, 28. *New York Age,* 24 July 1943.

36. Cool Papa Bell, interview by Holway, *Voices from the Great Black Baseball Leagues,* 107.

37. O'Neil, *I Was Right on Time,* 148.

38. Muhammad Ali in *When We Were Kings* (directed by Leon Gast, 1996). Although *When We Were Kings* was not released until 1996, it was a documentary filmed in 1974.

39. "Baseball Oddities," *Pittsburgh Courier,*

11 February 1933; Ted Shane, "The Chocolate Rube Waddell," *Saturday Evening Post*, 27 July 1940, 81.

40. Robert Peterson, *Only the Ball Was White: A History of Legendary Black Players and All-Black Professional Teams* (New York: McGraw Hill, 1984), 158.

41. "Gibson Holds Griffith Stadium Record," *Negro League Baseball*, 27. See also, Ribowsky, *A Complete History*, 152.

42. Buck Leonard with James A. Riley, *Buck Leonard: The Black Lou Gehrig: The Hall of Famer's Story in His Own Words* (New York: Carroll and Graf, 1995), 188; W. Rollo Wilson, "They Could Make the Big Leagues," *The Crisis*, October 1934, 306; Chester L. Washington, "Sez Ches," *Pittsburgh Courier*, 18 May 1940. See also Ribowsky, *A Complete History*, 152.

43. See Howard A. Phelps, "Inter-Racial Baseball Should Come To Fruition," *The Half-Century Magazine*, April 1919, 8; Sol White, "Sol White's Column of Baseball Dope," *Cleveland Advocate*, 23 March 1919.

44. "Yanks Triumph Over Two White Teams, Sunday," *Pittsburgh Courier*, 28 May 1932; "Paige and Willis Do it Once More; Whip Big League Aces," *Chicago Defender*, 27 January 1934.

45. e, "Chocolate Rube Waddell," 81.

46. Peterson, *Only the Ball Was White*, 143.

47. "No Negroes Allowed," *Crisis* 39 (August 1932): 263.

48. "K.C. Monarchs Leave to Start Drills in South," *Chicago Defender*, 21 April 1934; Spivey, *If You Were Only White*, 109–110.

49. Heaphy, *The Negro Leagues, 1869–1960* (Jefferson, NC: McFarland, 2003), 71; Willie Wells, interview by John Holway, Willie Wells file, National Baseball Hall of Fame Museum, 6. Buck O'Neil relates the same story about Wells in his memoir, *I Was Right on Time*, 144–145.

50. Peterson, *Only the Ball Was White*, 173–181. For a discussion of the Communist campaign for baseball integration, see Kelly Elaine Rusinack, "Baseball on the Radical Agenda: the Daily and Sunday Worker on the Desegregation of Major league Baseball, 1933 to 1947" (M.A. Thesis: Clemson University, 1995); "Baseball Season Over: No Big League Tryouts," *Chicago Defender*, 10 October 1942; Buck Leonard, interview by Holway, *Voices from the Great Black Baseball Leagues*, 268–269. On the Communist Party's attempt to attract black workers in Chicago, see Lizabeth

Cohen, *Making a New Deal: Industrial Workers in Chicago, 1919–1939* (Cambridge: Cambridge University Press, 1990), 261–265.

51. See for example, W. Rollo Wilson, "Many Players Should Make It," *Pittsburgh Courier*, 4 March 1933; "Major Club Owners Who Welcome Negro Patrons Shouldn't Bar Players," *Pittsburgh Courier*, 25 March 1933; W. Rollo Wilson, "The Could Make the Big Leagues," *The Crisis* (October 1934): 305–306; "Negro Players in Major league Baseball," *The Crisis* (April 1937): 112; Edwin B. Henderson, "The Negro Athlete and Race Prejudice," *Opportunity* 14 (March 1936): 77–80; William A. Brower, "Time for Baseball to Erase the Blackball," *Opportunity* 20 (June 1942): 164–167.

Chapter Five

1. Peter Wood, *Black Majority: Negroes in Colonial South Carolina from 1670 through the Stono Rebellion* (New York: Norton, 1996).

2. James Skipper, *Baseball Nicknames* (Jefferson, NC: McFarland, 1992), xvii–xviii.

3. Lanctot, *Negro League Baseball*, 182–183.

4. Lester, *Black Baseball's National Showcase*, 153–154.

5. Spivey, *If You Were Only White*, 108.

6. Charles C. Alexander, *Breaking the Slump: Baseball in the Depression Era* (Oxford: Oxford University Press, 2002), 224. Alexander, *Breaking the Slump*, 225; Peterson, *Only the Ball Was White*, 136; University of Missouri–St. Louis, Oral History Program. Oral History Interview with James "Cool Papa" Bell, September 8, 1971, transcript, in "Cool Papa" Bell file, Ashland Collection, National Baseball Hall of Fame and Museum, 29.

7. "Majors' Baseball Bar Drove Paige to Cuba," *Chicago Defender*, 29 May 1937; "Wells Fails to Join Newark" *Chicago Defender*, 22 April 1944; "McKinnis, Pennington, Douglas Jump to Mexico," *Chicago Defender*, 27 April 1946. See Cum Posey, "Sportive Realm," *Pittsburgh Courier*, 29 January 1927; "Negro Leagues Adopt Constitution of Majors," *Chicago Defender*, 22 December 1945.

8. Leonard, *Buck Leonard*, 203.

9. Wilmer Fields, *My Life in the Negro Leagues* (Westport, CT: Meckler, 1992), 33.

10. Jim Reisler, *Black Writers/Black Baseball: An Anthology of Articles from Black Sportswriters who covered the Negro Leagues* (Jefferson, NC: McFarland, 1994), 45–46. See also,

Andrew "Pullman" Porter, interview by Kelley, *Negro Leagues Revisited*, 24; Buck O'Neil, interview by Kelley, *Negro Leagues Revisited*, 67; Art Pennington, interview by Kelley, *Voices from the Negro Leagues*, 79.

11. Peterson, *Only the Ball Was White*, 34–35.

12. Michael Lomax, "Black Baseball, Black Community, Black Entrepreneurs: The History of the Negro National and Eastern Colored Leagues, 1880–1930" (PhD dissertation, Ohio State University Press, 1996), 76.

13. Peterson, *Only the Ball Was White*, 35.

14. O'Neil, *I Was Right on Time*, 40–41.

15. *Chicago Defender*, 24 July 1915, 7, emphasis mine.

16. Brock and Bijan Byane, "Not Just Black: African Americans, Cubans, and Baseball," in *Between Race and Empire*, 169, 175–176.

17. Rogosin, *Invisible Men*, 61.

18. Lisa Brock, "Introduction: Between Race and Empire," in *Between Race and Empire: African Americans and Cubans Before the Cuban Revolution*, Lisa Brock and Digna Castañeda Fuertes, eds. (Philadelphia: Temple University Press, 1998), 9.

19. "The Cuban Stars Baseball Team," *The Half-Century Magazine*, October 1919, 8; Washington, "If Doors Were Open Men Like Gibson Wouldn't be in Venezuela," *Pittsburgh Courier* 18 May 1940.

20. Brock, *Between Race and Empire*, 9.

21. Pennington, interview by Kelley, *Voices from the Negro Leagues*, 71.

22. Kelley, *Voices From the Negro Leagues*, 77.

23. Holway, *Voices from the Great Negro Leagues*, 236.

24. Frank Andre Guridy, *Forging Diaspora: Afro-Cubans and African Americans in a World of Empire and Jim Crow* (Chapel Hill: University of North Carolina Press, 2010), 153.

25. Howell, *Sandlots*, 173.

26. Washington, "If Doors Were Open Men Like Gibson Wouldn't Be in Venezuela," *Pittsburgh Courier*, 18 May 1940.

27. For a discussion of baseball's influence on Cuban identity, see Perez, *Becoming Cuban*.

28. Powell, interview by Kelley, *Negro Leagues Revisited*, 87.

29. *The Half-Century Magazine*, October 1919, 8.

30. "Cuban Ball Players on Washington Senators Snubbed by Own Team Mates," *Pittsburgh Courier*, 8 June 1940.

31. Chadwick, *When the Game was Black*

and *White*, 94; and Colin Howell, *Sandlot—A Social History of Maritime Baseball* (Toronto: University of Toronto Press, 1995), 176.

32. Drake and Cayton, *Black Metropolis*, 403.

33. J. David Smith, *The Eugenic Assault on America: Scenes in Red, White, and Black* (Fairfax, VA: George Mason University, 1992).

34. On eugenics and racial classification, see Daniel J. Kevles, *In the Name of Eugenics: Genetics and the Uses of Human Heredity* (Cambridge: Harvard University Press, 1985, 1995); Edward J. Larson, *Sex, Race, and Science: Eugenics in the Deep South* (Baltimore: Johns Hopkins University Press, 1995); Richard B. Sherman "'The Last Stand'; The Fight for Racial Integrity in Virginia in the 1920s," *Journal of Southern History* 54 (February 1988): 69–92; David J. Smith, *The Eugenic Assault on America: Scenes in Red, White, and Black* (Fairfax, VA: George Mason University Press, 1993). On scientific racism and skull studies, see Ann Fabian, *The Skull Collectors: Race, Science, and America's Unburied Dead* (Chicago: University of Chicago Press, 2010).

35. Dean A. Sullivan, *Middle Innings: A Documentary History of Baseball, 1900–1948* (Lincoln: University of Nebraska Press, 2001), 120.

36. "Sox and Cubs," *Chicago Defender*, 16 January 1936. See also, "Negro Baseball," *The Brown American*, Fall-Winter 1942, 5, 13, 19–20.

37. Rogosin, *Invisible Men*, 61; and Perez, *Becoming Cuban*, 266.

38. Marshall Todd Fuller, "'60 Feet 6 Inches and Other Distances From Home: A Creative Biography About Mose YellowHorse, Baseball, Cartoons, and the Pawnee" (PhD dissertation, Oklahoma State University, 1999), 58.

39. Robert Boyle, "The Private Lifeof the Negro Ballplayer," *Sports Illustrated*, 21 March 1960, http://sportsillustrated.cnn.com/vault/article/magazine/MAG1134572/index.htm, accessed August 19, 2013.

40. W. Rollo Wilson, "Eastern Snapshots," *Pittsburgh Courier*, 28 June 1924; Robert W. Creamer, *Babe: The Legend Comes to Life* (New York: Fireside, 1974, 1992), 185. See also, Jim Reisler, *Babe Ruth: Launching the Legend* (New York: McGraw Hill, 2004), 23. On Ruth's childhood and enrollment at reform school, see Creamer, *Babe*, 28–32.

41. W. Rollo Wilson, "Eastern Snapshots," *Pittsburgh Courier*, 28 June 1924.

42. Robert Boyle, "The Private Life of the Negro Ballplayer," *Sports Illustrated*, 21 March

1960, http://sportsillustrated.cnn.com/vault/
article/magazine/MAG1134572/index.htm,
accessed August 19, 2013.
43. Robert W. Creamer, *Babe: The Legend
Comes to Life* (New York: Fireside, 1974, 1992),
185.
44. See also Jim Reisler, *Babe Ruth: Launching the Legend* (New York: McGraw Hill, 2004),
23. On Ruth's childhood and enrollment at reform school, see Creamer, *Babe*, 28–32.
45. "Baseball Season Over: No Big League
Tryouts," *Chicago Defender*, 10 October 1942.
46. Howard A. Phelps, "Sporting News,"
The Half Century Magazine, March 1919, 8;
Peterson, *Only the Ball Was White*, 107.
47. Howard A. Phelps, "Sporting News,"
The Half-Century Magazine March 1919, 8.
48. To W.T. Smith from A. Rube Foster,
November 15, 1922, Chicago, IL, in "Rube"
Foster file, National Baseball Hall of Fame and
Museum.
49. Peterson, *Only the Ball Was White*, 107.
50. Fay Young, "Through the Years: Past-
Present-Future," *Chicago Defender*, 17 July
1943; Steven D. Smith, "The African American Soldier at Fort Huachuca, 1892–1946" Report Prepared for U.S. Army Fort Huachuca,
Arizona, and the Center of Expertise for Preservation of Historic Structures& Buildings,
U.S. Army Corps of Engineer, Seattle District,
February 2001, http://artsandsciences.sc.edu/
sciaa/PDFdocs/military-research/AfricanAmericanSoldier-FortHuachuca.pdf, accessed 17
August 2013, 101.
51. Fay Young, "Through the Years: Past-
Present-Future," *Chicago Defender* 17 July 1943.
52. Ribowsky, *Don't Look Back*, 106.
53. Kimmel, "Baseball and the Reconstitution of American Masculinity, 1880–1920,"
*Sport, Men, and the Gender Order: Critical
Feminist Perspectives*, Michael A. Messner and
Donald F. Sabo, eds. (Champaign, IL: Human
Kinetics, 1990), 60.
54. Buck O'Neil, *I Was Right on Time*, 139.
55. Shane, "The Chocolate Rube Waddell,"
79.
56. Fitts, "Baseball Cards and Race Relations" *Journal of American Culture* 18 (Fall
1994): 75–85, especially 80–81.

Chapter Six

1. "25,000 See Paige Trim Cubans 1–0,"
Chicago Defender, 24 July 1943; "Divorce Summons Darkens Satchel's Brilliant Day," *Chicago
Defender*, 24 July 1943.
2. "Chicago Will Pay Homage to Mr.
Paieg [sic]," *Chicago Defender*, 17 July 1943;
"25,000 see Paige Trim Cubans 1–0," *Chicago
Defender*, 24 July 1943.
3. "Chicago Will Pay Homage to Mr.
Paieg [sic]," *Chicago Defender*, 17 July 1943.
4. See William J. Brashler, *Bingo Long
Traveling All-Stars & Motor Kings* (Champaign: University of Illinois Press, 1973, 1993).
For a more recent assessment of *Bingo Long*,
see Raymond Doswell, "'We Can't Never
Lose': The *Bingo Long Traveling All-Stars &
Motor Kings* 30 Years Later" in *Satchel Paige
and Company*, Heaphy, ed., 198–206.
5. "They'll Furnish Comedy and Class
Against Grays Saturday," *Pittsburgh Courier*,
29 August 1925.
6. Richard Ian Kimball, "Beyond the
Great Experiment: Integrated Baseball Comes
to Indianapolis," *Journal of Sport History* 26
(Spring 1999): 153–154.
7. Lanctot, *Negro League Baseball*, 138.
8. "Zulu Cannibals Still Have War Paint,"
Chicago Defender, 6 June 1936.
9. David Levering Lewis, *W.E.B. Du Bois:
The Fight for Equality and the American Century, 1919–1963* (New York: Henry Holt,
2000), 60–78, 114, 119–120.
10. Harry Haywood, *Black Bolshevik: Autobiography of an Afro-American Communist*
(Chicago: Liberator Press, 1978), 448–457.
11. Robin D.G. Kelley, *Race Rebels: Culture, Politics, and the Black Working Class* (New
York: The Free Press, 1994, 1996), 123–158.
12. Marlon B. Ross, *Manning the Race: Reforming Black Men in the Jim Crow Era* (New
York: New York University Press, 2004), 82–89.
13. Alain Locke, "The Negro and the
American Stage, "*Theatre Arts Monthly*" 10.2
(Feb. 1926): 119.
14. Max Yargan, "Africa is Not a Country
of Cannibalism and Savagery: Education, Industry, Commerce Are Features of Its Daily
Life," *Chicago Defender*, 12 November 1932:
Lucius C. Harper, "Dustin' Off the News:
Why Africa is the Great Prize in This War," 22
August 1942.
15. Max Yargan, "Africa is Not a Country
of Cannibalism and Savagery: Education, Industry, Commerce Are Features of Its Daily
Life," *Chicago Defender*, 12 November 1932.
16. Marilyn Kern-Foxworth, *Aunt Jemima,
Uncle Ben, and Rastus: Blacks in Advertising,
Yesterday, Today, and Tomorrow* (Westport,
CT: Greenwood, 1994), xix.
17. Philip McGowan, *American Carnival:*

Seeing and Reading American Culture (Westport, CT; Greenwood, 2001), 67.

18. Michael Oriard, *King Football: Sport & Spectacle in the Golden Age of Radio & Newsreels, Movies & Magazines, The Weekly & The Daily Press* (Chapel Hill: University of North Carolina Press, 2003), 321–325; Ben Green, *Spinning the Globe: The Rise, Fall, and Return to Greatness of the Harlem Globetrotters* (New York: HarperCollins, 2005); "Eddie Tolan, '32 Olympic Winner In Two Dash Events, Dead at 57," *New York Times*, 1 February 1967; Jeremy Schaap, *Triumph: The Untold Story of Jesse Owens and Hitler's Olympics* (New York: Houghton Mifflin, 2007), 234.

19. See Mary L. Dudziak, "Josephine Baker, Racial Protest, and the Cold War," *Journal of American History* 81 (1994): 545; Michel Fabre, "International Beacons of African American memory: Alexandre Dumas pere, "Henry O. Tanner, and Josephine Baker as Examples of Recognition," in Genevieve Fabre and Robert O'Meally, eds., *History and Memory in African American Culture* (New York: Oxford University Press, 1994), 127–129.

20. Locke, "The Negro and the American Stage," 114.

21. "Cincinnati Clowns to Start Practice April 16," *Chicago Defender*, 27 February 1943; Tygiel, *Extra Bases*, 64: Pollock, *Barnstorming to Heaven*, 113.

22. Martha Ackman, *Curveball: The Remarkable Story of Toni Stone, the First Woman to Play Professional Baseball in the Negro League* (Chicago: Lawrence Hill, 2010), 93–94.

23. Pollock, *Barnstorming to Heaven*, 153, 156–157.

24. Lanctot, *Negro League Baseball*, 108.

25. Frank A. Young, "Lefty Bowe Joins Clowns—East-West Game Meant No Money To Him," 10 August 1940.

26. Burgos, Jr., *Cuban Star*, 145, 201.

27. Alan J. Pollock, *Barnstorming to Heaven: Syd Pollock and His Great Black Teams*, James A. Riley, ed. (Tuscaloosa: University of Alabama Press, 2006), 95–97; Donald Spivey, *"If Only You Were White": The Life and Times of Leroy "Satchel" Paige* (Columbia: University of Missouri Press, 2012), 258–259.

28. Young, "Lefty Bowe Joins Clowns," 10 August 1940; David K. Wiggins, "'Great Speed But Little Stamina': The Historical Debate Over Black Athletic Superiority," *Journal of Sport History* 16 (Summer 1989): 165; Green, *Spinning the Globe*.

29. Othello Renfroe, interview by Holway,

Voices from the Great Black Baseball Leagues, 340–341; Donald Spivey, *"If Only You Were White,"* 258–259.

30. Alan J. Pollock, *Barnstorming to Heaven*, 8.

31. *Ibid.*, 9.

32. *Ibid.*, 34.

33. White and White, *Sylin.'*

34. *Ibid.*, 9.

35. Bruce, *Kansas City Monarchs*, 80; Buck Leonard with James A. Riley, *Buck Leonard: The Black Lou Gehrig: The Hall of Famer's Story in His Own Words* (New York: Carroll and Graf, 1995), 6.

36. Tygiel, *Baseball's Great Experiment*, 299–302.

37. Hank Aaron, *I Had a Hammer: The Hank Aaron Story* (New York: Harper Collins, 1991), 24–39; Burgos, Jr., *Cuban Star*, 200–202; Richard Ian Kimball, "Beyond the Great Experiment: Integrated Baseball Comes to Indianapolis," *Journal of Sport History* 26 (Spring 1999): 156.

38. Aaron, *I Had a Hammer*, 31–32.

39. Robert Peterson, *Only the Ball Was White: A History of Legendary Black Players and All-Black Professional Teams* (New York: Oxford University Press, 1970), 204; James A. Riley, *The Negro Leagues* (Philadelphia: Chelsea House, 1997), 90.

40. Martha Ackman, *Curveball: The Remarkable Story of Toni Stone, the First Woman to Play Professional Baseball in the Negro League* (Chicago: Lawrence Hill, 2010).

41. Richard Ian Kimball, "Beyond the Great Experiment," 156.

42. Satchel Paige and Judy Johnson, interviews by Stephen Banker, *Black Diamonds*; Bruce Chadwick, *When the Game was Black and White: The Illustrated History of the Negro Leagues* (New York: Abbeville, 1992), 96; Othello Renfroe, interview by Holway, *Voices from the Great Black Baseball Leagues*, 340–341.

43. Pollock, *Barnstorming to Heaven*, 8–9.

44. For an account of black musical performers and the double meaning of seemingly racist performances, see David Krasner, "Parody and Double Consciousness in the Language of Early Black Musical Theatre," *African American Review* 29 (Summer 1995): 317–323.

45. Leonard, *Buck Leonard*, 139.

Epilogue

1. Smith, "'Brother Eddie' Gottlieb Was There" *Pittsburgh Courier* (date unknown),

found in Wendell Smith Papers, National Base-ball Hall of Fame and Museum; Smith, "The Strange Case of 'Brother' Gottlieb," *Pittsburgh Courier*, 8 February 1947, Wendell Smith Papers, National Baseball Hall of Fame and Museum.

2. See "Negro Club Head Chides Robinson," 23 May 1948; "Jackie 'Ungrateful to Negro Ball,' Says Woman Club Owner," *The Sporting News*, 26 May 1948, in Effa Manley File, Ashland Collection, National Baseball Hall of Fame and Museum; Effa Manley, interview by John Holway, *Voices From the Great Black Baseball Leagues* (New York: De Capo, 1992), 324; Effa Manley and Leon Herbert Hardwick, *Negro Baseball ... Before Integration* (Chicago: Adams, 1976), 92; Tygiel, *Baseball's Great Experiment*, 213.

3. "Effa Manley Answers Robinson's Criticism of Negro Baseball," *The Telegram*, 23 May 1948, in Effa Manley File, National Baseball Hall of Fame and Museum.

4. Boyle, "The Personal Life" *Sports Illustrated*.

5. On this point, see Jules Tygiel, "Blackball: The Integrated Game" *Extra Bases: Reflections on Jackie Robinson, Race, & Baseball History* (Lincoln: University of Nebraska Press, 2002), 110–113. See *Necessities: Racial Barriers in American Sports* (New York: 1989).

6. Boyle, "The Personal Life" *Sports Illustrated*.

7. Boyle, "The Personal Life." *Sports Illustrated*.

8. *Ibid.*

9. *Ibid.*

10. *Ibid.*

11. *Ibid.*

12. *Ibid.*

13. Boyle, "The Personal Life," *Sports Illustrated*.

14. Henry D. Fetter, "The Party Line and The Color Line: The American Communist Party, the Daily Worker, and Jackie Robinson," *Journal of Sport History* 28 (Fall 2001): 383–384.

15. See Steve Treder, "The Persistent Color Line: Specific Instances of Racial Preference in Major League Player Evaluation Decisions After 1947," *Nine* 10 (Fall 2001): 1–30. See Treder, "A Legacy of What-If's: Horace Stoneham and the Integration of the Giants" *Nine* 10 (Spring 2002): 71–101.

16. Boyle, "The Personal Life," *Sports Illustrated*.

17. For a discussion of Aaron's pursuit of the home run record and the resultant racial unrest, see Sandy Tolan, *Me and Hank: A Boy and His Hero, Twenty-Five Years Later* (Free Press, 2000). On the difficulties encountered by African American baseball players after integration, see Arlene Howard and Ralph Wimbish, *Elston and Me: The Story of the First Black Yankee* (Columbia: University of Missouri Press, 2001), 19–52, 99–103; Larry Moffi and Jonathan Kronstadt, *Crossing the Line: Black Major Leaguers, 1947–1959* (Jefferson, NC: McFarland, 1994). On the *Daily Worker* after integration, see Fetter, "The Party Line and the Color Line," 389–390.

18. "Where Have You Gone, Jackie Robinson? In College Baseball the Diamonds Are Almost All White," *The Journal of Blacks in Higher Education* (Summer 2001): 50–52.

Bibliography

Newspapers and Magazine Articles (Primary Sources)

Abbott's Monthly
Alexander's Magazine
Baltimore Afro-American
The Black Man
The Brown American
Chicago Daily News
Chicago Defender
Cleveland Advocate
Cleveland Gazette
The Competitor
Crisis
The Half-Century Magazine
Negro Baseball 1944 Yearbook (Washington, D.C.: Sepia Sports Publications, 1944)
Negro Baseball 1946 Yearbook (Washington, D.C.: Sepia Sports Publications, 1946)
New York Age
New York Times
Norfolk Journal and Guide, 1931–1932.
Opportunity: Journal of Negro Life, Charles S. Johnson, ed., 1923
Pittsburgh Courier
The Saturday Evening Post, 1940.
Silhouettes : The official newsletter of the Negro Leagues Baseball Museum Vol 1, no 1, Spring 1992 (Kansas City).
Survey Graphic, March 1925.
Sporting Life
The Sporting News
Tuskegee Messenger 1929
Union

Paper Collections

Effa Manley and Newark Eagles Papers, Newark Public Library

National Baseball Hall of Fame and Museum: A Bartlett Giamatti Research Center:
Margaret and Franklin Steele Sheet Music Collection
Wendell Smith Papers
Photo File: Bell, James Thomas "Cool Papa"
Photo File: Charleston, Oscar McKinley
Photo File: Dandridge, Raymond Emmett
Photo File: Foster, Andrew "Rube"
Photo File: Foster, William Hendrick,
Photo File: Gibson, Joshua.
Photo File: Irvin, Montford Merrill "Monte"
Photo File: Johnson, William Julius "Judy"
Photo File: Leonard, Walter Fenner "Buck"
Photo File: Lloyd, John Henry
Photo File: Paige, Leroy Robert "Satchel"
Photo File: Rogan, Wilbur "Bullet Joe"
Photo File: Smith, Hilton.
Photo File: Stearnes, Norman Thomas "Turkey"
Photo File: Wells, Willie James
Photo File: Williams, Joe "Smokey"
Player File: Banks, Ernest
Player File: Bell, James Thomas
Player File: Campanella, Roy
Player File: Charleston, Oscar McKinley
Player File: Dandridge, Raymond Emmett
Player File: Day, Leon
Player File: Dihigo, Martín
Player File: Doby, Lawrence Eugene
Player File: Foster, Andrew
Player File: Foster, William Hendrick
Player File: Gibson, Joshua
Player File: Irvin, Montford Merrill
Player File: Johnson, William Julius
Player File: Leonard, Walter Fenner
Player File: Lloyd, John Henry

Player File: Paige, Leroy Robert
Player File: Rogan, Wilbur Joe
Player File: Smith, Hilton
Player File: Stearnes, Norman Thomas
Player File: Wells, Willie James
Player File: Williams, Joe

Books and Journal Articles

Aaron, Hank. *I Had a Hammer: The Hank Aaron Story*. New York: HarperCollins, 1991.

Abrahams, Roger D. *Deep Down in the Jungle: Negro Narrative Folklore from the Streets of Philadelphia*. Chicago: Aldine Publishing, 1963, 1970.

_____. *Positively Black*. Englewood Cliffs, NJ: Prentice Hall, 1970.

Ackman, Martha. *Curveball: The Remarkable Story of Toni Stone, the First Woman to Play Professional Baseball in the Negro League*. Chicago: Lawrence Hill, 2010.

Adelman, Melvin L. *A Sporting Time: New York City and the Rise of Modern Athletics*. Urbana: University of Illinois Press, 1986.

Adelson, Bruce. *Brushing Back Jim Crow: The Integration of Minor-League Baseball in the American South*. Charlottesville: University of Virginia Press, 1999.

Alexander, Charles C. *Breaking the Slump: Baseball in the Depression Era*. New York: Columbia University Press, 2002.

_____. *John McGraw*. Lincoln: University of Nebraska Press, 1995.

Alim, H. Samy, and Geneva Smitherman. *Articulate While Black: Barack Obama, Language, and Race in the U.S.* New York: Oxford University Press, 2012.

Alston, Lee J., and Kyle J. Kauffman. "Agricultural Chutes and Ladders: New Estimates of Sharecroppers and 'True Tenants' in the South, 1900–1920." *The Journal of Economic History* 57 (June 1997): 464–475.

Andreano, Ralph. *No Joy in Mudville: The Dilemma of Major League Baseball*. Cambridge, MA: Schenkman, 1965.

Aptheker, Herbert, ed. *The Correspondence of W.E.B. Du Bois: Volume I Selections, 1877–1934*. Boston: University of Massachusetts Press, 1973.

Ardell, Jean Hastings. "Baseball Annies, Jack Johnson, and Kenesaw Mountain Landis: How Groupies Influenced the Lengthy Ban on Blacks in Organized Baseball." *Nine* 13 (February 2005): 103–109.

Armistead, Myra B. Young. "Revisiting Hotels and Other Lodgings: American Tourist Spaces through the Lens of Black Pleasure-Travelers, 1880–1950." *The Journal of Decorative and Propaganda Arts* 25 (2005): 136–159.

Arnesen, Eric. "'Like Banquo's Ghost, It Will Not Down': The Race Question and the American Railroad Brotherhoods, 1880–1920." *American Historical Review* (December 1994): 1601–1633.

Ashe, Arthur, with Kip Branch, Oceania Chalk, and Francis Harris. *A Hard Road to Glory: A History of the African-American Athlete*. 3 vols. New York: Warner, 1988.

Asinof, Eliot. *Eight Men Out: The Black Sox and the 1919 World Series*. New York: Holt, Rinehart and Winston, 1963.

Astor, Gerald. *... And a Credit to His Race: The Hard Life and Times of Joseph Louis Barrow, a.k.a. Joe Louis*. New York: Saturday Review, 1974.

Atwan, Robert, Donald McQuade, and John W. Wright. *Edsels, Luckies and Frigidaires: Advertising the American Way*. New York: Dell, 1979.

Ayers, Edward L. *The Promise of the New South: Life After Reconstruction*. New York: Oxford University Press, 1992.

Bak, Richard. *Turkey Stearnes and the Detroit Stars: The Negro Leagues in Detroit, 1919–1933*. Detroit: Wayne State University Press, 1994.

Baker, Aaron. "From Second String to Solo Star: Classic Hollywood and the Black Athlete." *Classic Hollywood, Classic Whiteness*. Daniel Bernardi, ed. Minneapolis: University of Minnesota Press, 2001.

Baker, William J. *Jesse Owens: An American Life*. New York: The Free Press, 1986.

Baldassaro, Lawrence. "Dashing Dagos and

Walloping Wops: Media Portrayal of Italian American Major Leaguers before World War II." *Nine* 14 (October 2005): 98–106.

Banker, Stephen. *Black Diamonds: An Oral History of Negro Baseball.* Washington: Tapes for Readers, 1978, 1992. Cassette Tapes.

Bankes, James. *The Pittsburgh Crawfords.* Jefferson, NC: McFarland, 2001.

Bartley, Abel. "Selected reactions of the African American and White press to the Italian invasion of Ethiopia." *The Griot* 19:1 (Spring 2000) 13–23.

Bates, Beth Tompkins. *Pullman Porters and the Rise of Protest Politics in Black America, 1925–1945.* Chapel Hill: University of North Carolina Press, 2001.

Bederman, Gail. *Manliness and Civilization: A Cultural History of Gender and Race in the United States, 1880–1917.* Chicago: University of Chicago Press, 1995.

Beeching, Barbara J. "Paul Robeson and the Black Press: the 1950 Passport Controversy." *The Journal of African American History* 87 (Summer 2002): 339–354.

Belton, Don, ed. *Speak My Name: Black Men on Masculinity and the American Dream.* Boston: Beacon, 1995.

Berger, Asa. *The Comic-Stripped American.* Baltimore: Penguin, 1974.

Best, Wallace D. *Passionately Human, No Less Divine: Religion and Culture in Black Chicago, 1915–1952.* Princeton, NJ: Princeton University Press, 2005.

Betts, John R. *America's Sporting Heritage, 1850–1950.* Reading, Mass: Addison-Wesley, 1974.

_____. "Sporting Journalism in Nineteenth Century America." *American Quarterly* 5 (Spring 1953): 39–56.

_____. "The Technological Revolution and the Rise of Sport, 1850–1900." *The Mississippi Valley Historical Review* 40 (Sep 1953): 231–256.

Bjarkman, Peter C. *Baseball with a Latin Beat: A History of the Latin American Game.* Jefferson, NC: McFarland, 1994.

Blackmon, Douglas A. *Slavery by Another Name: The Re-Enslavement of Black Americans from the Civil War to World War II.* New York: Anchor, 2009.

Blum, John Morton. *V Was for Victory: Politics and American Culture During World War II.* New York: Harcourt Brace Jovanovich, 1976.

Boskin, Joseph. *Sambo: The Rise and Demise of an American Jester.* New York: Oxford University Press, 1986.

Boyd, Robert L. "Residential Segregation by Race and the Black Merchants of Northern Cities during the Early Twentieth Century." *Sociological Forum* 13 (December 1998): 595–609.

Bracey, John H., Jr., August Meier, and Elliott Rudwick. *Black Nationalism in America.* Indianapolis and New York: Bobbs-Merrill, 1970).

Brashler, William. *The Bingo Long Traveling All-Stars and Motor Kings.* New York: Signet, 1973.

_____. *Josh Gibson: A Life in the Negro Leagues.* New York: Harper and Row, 1978.

Brock, Lisa, and Digna Castañeda Fuertes, eds. *Between Race and Empire: African-Americans and Cubans before the Cuban Revolution.* Philadelphia: Temple University Press, 1998.

Broderick, Francis L., and August Meier. *Negro Protest Thought in the Twentieth Century.* Indianapolis and New York: Bobbs-Merrill, 1965.

Browder, Laura. *Slippery Characters: Ethnic Impersonators and American Identities.* Chapel Hill: University of North Carolina Press, 2000.

Bruce, Janet. *Kansas City Monarchs: Champions of Black Baseball.* Lawrence: University of Kansas Press, 1985.

Burgos Adrian, Jr. *Cuban Star: How One Negro-League Owner Changed the Face of Baseball.* New York: Hill and Wang, 2011.

_____. *Playing America's Game: Baseball, Latinos, and the Color Line.* Berkeley: University of California Press, 2007.

_____. "Playing Ball in a Black and White Field of Dreams": Afro-Caribbean Ballplayers in the Negro League 1910–1950."

Journal of Negro History 82 (Winter 1997): 67–104.

Burstyn, Varda. *The Rites of Men: Manhood, Politics, and the Culture of Sport.* Toronto: University of Toronto, 1999.

Cahn, Susan. *Coming On Strong: Gender and Sexuality in Twentieth-Century Women's Sports.* Cambridge: Harvard University Press, 1994.

Caponi, Gena Dagel. *Signifyin(g), Sanctifyin', and Slam Dunking: A Reader in African American Expressive Culture.* Amherst: University of Massachusetts, 1999.

Caponi-Tabery, Gena. *Jump for Joy: Jazz, Basketball, and Black Culture in 1930s America.* Amherst: University of Massachusetts Press, 2008.

Captain, Gwendolyn. "Enter Ladies and Gentlemen of Color: Gender, Sport, and the Ideal of African American Manhood and Womanhood During the Late Nineteenth and Early Twentieth Century." *Journal of Sport History* 18 (Spring 1991): 81–102.

Cavallo, Dominick. *Muscles and Morals: Organized Playground and Urban Reform, 1880–1920.* Philadelphia: University of Pennsylvania Press, 1981.

Chadwick, Bruce. *When the Game Was Black and White: The Illustrated History of the Negro Leagues.* New York: Abbeville, 1992.

Chalk, Oceania. *Pioneers in Black Sport: The Early Days of the Black Professional Athlete in Baseball, Basketball, Boxing, and Football.* New York: Dodd, Mead, 1975.

Clemetson, Lynette. "The racial politics of speaking well." *New York Times,* 4 February 2007.

Cohen, Lizabeth. *Making a New Deal: Industrial Workers in Chicago, 1919–1939.* New York: Cambridge University Press, 1990.

_____. *A Consumers' Republic: The Politics of Mass Consumption in Postwar America.* New York: Alfred A. Knopf, 2003.

Conningham, F.A. *Currier & Ives.* Cleveland, World Publishing, 1950.

Cottrell, Robert C. *Blackball, the Black Sox, and the Babe: Baseball's Crucial 1920 Season.* Jefferson, NC: McFarland, 2002.

Couvares, Francis G. *The Remaking of Pittsburgh: Class and Culture in an Industrializing City, 1877–1919.* Albany: State University of New York Press, 1984.

Craft, David. *The Negro Leagues: 40 Years of Black Professional Baseball in Words and Pictures.* New York: Crescent, 1993.

Cramer, Richard Ben. *Joe DiMaggio: The Hero's Life.* New York: Simon & Schuster, 2000.

Creamer, Robert W. *Babe: The Legend Comes to Life.* New York: Fireside, 1974, 1992.

Cripps, Thomas. *Slow Fade to Black: The Negro in American Film 1900–1942.* New York: Oxford University Press, 1977.

Cronon, E. David, ed. *Marcus Garvey.* Englewood Cliffs, NJ: Prentice-Hall, 1973.

Cumbler, John T. *Working-Class Community in Industrial America: Work, Leisure, and Struggle in Two Industrial Cities, 1880–1930.* Westport, CT: Greenwood, 1979.

Dagavarian, Debra. *Say It Ain't So: American Values as Revealed in Children's Baseball Stories 1880–1950.* New York: Peter Lang, 1988.

Davis, Angela Y. *Blues Legacies and Black Feminism.* New York: Random House, 1998; reprint, New York: Vintage, 1999.

Dennis, Rutledge M. "Social Darwinism, Scientific Racism, and the Metaphysics of Race." *Journal of Negro Education* 64 (1995): 243–252.

Dorinson, Joseph, and William Pencak, eds. *Paul Robeson: Essays on His Life and Legacy.* Jefferson, NC: McFarland, 2002.

Drake, St. Clair, and Horace R. Cayton. *Black Metropolis: A Study of Negro Life in a Northern City.* Chicago: University of Chicago, 1945, 1993.

Driggs, Frank, and Chuck Haddix. *Kansas City Jazz: From Ragtime to Bebop—A History.* New York: Oxford University Press, 2005.

Duberman, Martin B. *Paul Robeson,* New York: New Press, 1995.

DuBois, W.E.B. *The Souls of Black Folk.* New York: Viking Penguin, 1903, 1989.

Dudziak, Mary L. *Cold War Civil Rights:*

Race and the Image of American Democracy. Princeton: Princeton University Press, 2000.

_____. "Josephine Baker, Racial Protest, and the Cold War." *Journal of American History* 81 (1994): 543–570.

Dyreson, Mark. "Marketing National Identity: The Olympic Games of 1932 and American Culture." *Olympika: The International Journal of Olympic Studies* (1995): 23- 48.

_____. "Nature by Design: Modern American Ideas About Sport, Energy, Evolution, and Republics, 1865–1920." *Journal of Sport History* 26 (1999): 447–470.

Early, Gerald. *The Culture of Bruising: Essays on Prizefighting, Literature, and Modern American Culture*. Hopewell, New Jersey: Ecco, 1994.

Edwards, Harry. *The Revolt of the Black Athlete*. New York: Free Press, 1970.

Eisen, George, and David K. Wiggins, eds. *Ethnicity and Sport in North American History and Culture*. Westport, CT: Greenwood, 1994.

Ellis, Mark. "'Closing Ranks' and 'Seeking Honors': W. E.B. Du Bois in World War I." *Journal of American History* 79 (June 1992): 96–124.

_____. "W.E.B. Du Bois and the Formation of Black Political Thought in World War I: A Commentary on 'The Damnable Dilemma.'" *Journal of American History* 81 (March 1995): 1584–1590.

Ellison, Ralph. *Going to the Territory*. New York: Vintage International, 1986.

_____. *Invisible Man*. New York: Vintage International, 1947, 1995.

_____. *Shadow and Act*. New York: Quality Paperback Book Club, 1964, 1994.

Enstad, Nan. *Ladies of Labor, Girls of Adventure: Working Women, Popular Culture, and Labor Politics at the Turn of the Twentieth Century*. New York: Columbia University Press, 1999.

Epstein, Abraham. *The Negro Migrant in Pittsburgh*, reprint edition. New York: Arno Press and The New York Times, 1918, 1969.

Erdman, Andrew L. *Blue Vaudeville: Sex, Morals, and the Mass Marketing of Amusement, 1895–1915*. Jefferson, NC: McFarland, 2004.

Evans, Art. "Joe Louis as Key Functionary: White Reactions Toward a Black Champion." *Journal of Black Studies* 16 (September, 1985): 95–111.

Ewen, Stuart, and Elizabeth Ewen. *Channels of Desire: Mass Images in the Shaping of American Consciousness*. New York: McGraw Hill, 1982.

Fabre, Michel. "International Beacons of African-American memory: Alexandre Dumas pere, Henry O. Tanner, and Josephine Baker as Examples of Recognition." *History and Memory in African American Culture*. Genevieve Fabre and Robert O'Meally, eds. New York: Oxford University Press, 1994.

Farr, Finis. *Black Champion: The Life and Times of Jack Johnson*. New York: Scribner, 1964.

Ferguson, Roderick A. "African American Masculinity and the Study of Social Formations." *American Quarterly* 58 (March 2006): 213–219.

Fetter, Henry D. "The Party Line and the Color Line: The American Communist Party, the Daily Worker, and Jackie Robinson" *Journal of Sport History* 28 (Fall 2001): 375–402.

Fields, Wilmer. *My Life in the Negro Leagues*. Westport, CT: Meckler, 1992.

Fine, Gary Alan, and Patricia A. Turner. *Whispers on the Color Line: Rumor and Race in America*. Berkeley: University of California Press, 2001.

Fitts, Robert K. "Baseball Cards and Race Relations." *Journal of American Culture* 17 (Fall 1994): 75–85.

Fordin, Hugh. *Getting to Know Him: A Biography of Oscar Hammerstein II*. New York: Da Capo, 1995.

Foster, Mark S. "In the Face of 'Jim Crow': Prosperous Blacks and Vacations, Travel and Outdoor Leisure, 1890–1945." *Journal of Negro History* 84 (Spring 1999): 130–149.

Frazier, E. Franklin. *The Negro Church in America.* New York: Schocken, 1963, 1974.

Fredrickson, George M. *The Black Image in the White Mind: The Debate on Afro-American Character and Destiny 1817–1914.* New York: Harper and Row, 1971.

Fuller, Todd. "60 Feet 6 inches and Other Distances from Home: A Creative Biography about Mose YellowHorse, Baseball, Cartoons, and the Pawnee." PhD dissertation, Oklahoma State University, May 1999.

Gaston, John C. "The Destruction of the Young Black Male: The Impact of Popular Culture and Organized Sports." *Journal of Black Studies* 16 (June 1986): 369–384.

Gates, Henry Louis, Jr. *The Signifying Monkey: A Theory of African American Literary Criticism.* New York: Oxford University Press, 1988.

Gems, Gerald R. *Windy City Wars: Labor, Leisure, and Sport in the Making of Chicago.* Landham, MD: Scarecrow, 1997.

Gerlach, Larry R. "Baseball's Other 'Great Experiment': Eddie Klep and the Integration of the Negro League." *Journal of Sport History* 25 (Fall 1998): 453–481.

Gilbert, Tom. *Baseball and the Color Line.* New York: Franklin Watts, 1995.

Gill, Glenda E. *White Grease Paint on Black Performers: A Study of the Federal Theatre, 1935–1939.* New York: Peter Lang, 1988.

Gilmore, Al-Tony. *Bad Nigger! The National Impact of Jack Johnson.* Port Washington, NY: 1975.

_____. "Jack Johnson: A Magnificent Black Anachronism of the Early Twentieth Century." *The American Sporting Experience: A Historical Anthology of Sport in America.* Steven A. Riess, ed. Champaign, IL: Leisure Press, 1984.

_____. "Jack Johnson and White Women: The National Impact." *Journal of Negro History* (January 1973): 18–38.

Goldstein, Warren. *Playing for Keeps: A History of Early Baseball.* Ithaca: Cornell University Press, 1991.

Goodman, Cary. *Choosing Sides: Playground and Street Life on the Lower East Side.* New York: Schocken, 1979.

Gorn, Elliot J. *The Manly Art: Bare-Knuckle Prize Fighting in America.* Ithaca: Cornell University Press, 1986.

Gottlieb, Peter. *Making Their Own Way: Southern Blacks' Migration to Pittsburgh, 1916–1930.* Urbana: University of Illinois Press, 1987.

Green, Ben. *Spinning the Globe: The Rise, Fall, and Return to Greatness of the Harlem Globetrotters.* New York: HarperCollins, 2005.

Gregorich, Barbara. *Women at Play: The Story of Women in Baseball.* New York: Harcourt, Brace, 1993.

Gregory, Robert. *Diz: The Story of Dizzy Dean and Baseball During the Great Depression.* New York: Penguin, 1992.

Grossman, James R. *Land of Hope: Chicago, Black Southerners, and the Great Migration.* Chicago: University of Chicago Press, 1989.

Guridy, Frank Andre. *Forging Diaspora: Afro-Cubans and African Americans in a World of Empire and Jim Crow.* Chapel Hill: University of North Carolina Press, 2010.

Guttmann, Allen. *From Ritual to Record: The Nature of Modern Sports.* New York: Columbia University Press, 1978.

_____. *Games and Empires: Modern Sports and Cultural Imperialism.* New York: Columbia University Press, 1994.

_____. *Sports Spectators.* New York: Columbia University Press, 1987.

_____. *A Whole New Ball Game: An Interpretation of American Sports.* Chapel Hill: University of North Carolina Press, 1988.

_____. *Women's Sports: A History.* New York: Columbia University Press, 1991.

Hale, Grace Elizabeth. *Making Whiteness: The Culture of Segregation in the South.* New York: Pantheon, 1998.

Hall, Alvin L. *Cooperstown Symposium on Baseball and the American Culture, 1989.* Westport, CT: Mecklermedia, 1989.

_____. *Cooperstown Symposium on Baseball and the American Culture, 1990.* Westport, CT: Mecklermedia, 1991.

Hall, Patricia Kelly, and Steven Ruggles. "'Restless in the Midst of Their Prosperity': New Evidence on the Internal Migration of Americans, 1850–2000." *Journal of American History* 90 (December 2004): 829–846.

Hardy, Stephen. *How Boston Played.* Boston: Northeastern University Press, 1982.

Harris, Michael D. *Colored Pictures: Race and Visual Representation.* Chapel Hill: University of North Carolina Press, 2006.

Harris-Lacewell, Melissa Victoria. *Barbershops, Bibles, and BET: Everyday Talk and Black Political Thought.* Princeton: Princeton University Press, 2004.

Haywood, Harry. *Black Bolshevik: Autobiography of an Afro-American Communist.* Chicago: Liberator Press, 1978.

Heaphy, Leslie A. *The Negro Leagues, 1869–1960.* Jefferson, NC: McFarland, 2003.

_____, ed. *Satchel Paige and Company: Essays on the Kansas City Monarchs, Their Greatest Star and the Negro Leagues.* Jefferson, NC: McFarland, 2007.

Henderson, Edwin B. *The Negro in Sports.* Washington, D.C.: The Associated Publishing Company, 1949.

Henry, Charles P. "The Political Role of the 'Bad Nigger.'" *The Journal of Black Studies* 11 (June 1981): 461–482.

Higginbotham, Evelyn Brooks. "African-American Women's History and the Metalanguage of Race." *Signs* 17 (1992): 261–274.

Hoberman, John M. *Darwin's Athlete: How Sports Has Damaged Black America and Preserved the Myth of Race.* Boston: Houghton Mifflin, 1997.

Hoch, Paul. *Rip Off the Big Game: The Exploitation of Sports by the Power Elite.* Garden City, NY: Anchor, 1972.

_____. *White Hero, Black Beast: Racism, Sexism, and the Mask of Masculinity.* London: Pluto, 1979.

Hoffbeck, Steven R., ed. *Swinging for the Fences: Black Baseball in Minnesota.* St. Paul: Minnesota Historical Society, 2005.

Hogan, Lawrence D. *Shades of Glory: The Negro Leagues and the Story of African-American Baseball.* Washington, D.C.: National Geographic, 2006.

Holway, John, *Blackball Stars: Negro League Pioneers.* Westport, CT: Meckler, 1988.

_____. *The Complete Book of Baseball's Negro Leagues: The Other Half of Baseball History.* Fern Park, FL: Hastings House, 2001.

_____. *Voices from the Great Black Baseball Leagues.* New York: DaCapo, reprint edition, 1992.

hooks, bell. *Black Looks: Race and Representation.* Boston: South End, 1992.

_____. "Micheaux: Celebrating Blackness" *Black American Literature Forum* 25 (Summer 1991): 351–360.

Hoose, Phillip M. *Necessities: Racial Barriers in American Sports.* New York: Random House, 1989.

Howard, Arlene, and Ralph Wimbish. *Elston and Me: The Story of the First Black Yankee.* Columbia: University of Missouri Press, 2001.

Howell, Colin. *Northern Sandlots—A Social History of Maritime Baseball.* Toronto: University of Toronto Press, 1995.

Huizinga, Johan. *Homo Ludens: A Study of the Play Element in Culture.* Boston: Beacon, 1955.

Humber, William. *Diamonds of the North: A Concise History of Baseball in Canada.* Toronto: Oxford University Press, 1995.

Hutchinson, Earl Ofari. *The Assassination of the Black Male Image.* New York: Simon and Schuster, 1996.

Irvin, Monte, with James A. Riley. *Monte Irvin: Nice Guys Finish First.* New York: Carroll and Graf, 1996.

Jackson, Bruce. *Get Your Ass in the Water and Swim Like Me.* Cambridge: Harvard University Press, 1974.

Jaher, Frederic Cople. "White America Views Jack Johnson, Joe Louis, and Muhammad Ali," in Donald Spivey, ed. *Sport in America: New Historical Perspectives.* Westport, CT: Greenwood, 1985.

Jarmon, Laura C. *Wishbone: Reference and Interpretation in Black Folk Narrative.* Knoxville: University of Tennessee Press, 2003.

Johnson, Charles S. *Growing Up in the Black*

Belt: Negro Youth in the Rural South. Washington, D.C.: American Council on Education, 1941.

Johnson, Jack. *Jack Johnson is a Dandy, An Autobiography.* New York: Chelsea House, 1969.

Jordan, William. "'The Damnable Dilemma': African American Accommodation and Protest During World War I." *Journal of American History* 81 (March 1995): 1562–1583.

Kadzielski, Mark A. "As a Flower Needs Sunshine: The Origins of Organized Children's Recreation in Philadelphia, 1886–1911." *Journal of Sport History* 4 (Summer 1977): 169–188.

Kasson, John F. *Amusing the Million: Coney Island at the Turn of the Century.* New York: Hill and Wang, 1978.

Katovich, Michael A. "Humor in Baseball: Functions and Dysfunctions." *Journal of American Culture* 16 (Summer 1993): 7–15.

Kaye, Andrew M. *The Pussycat of Prizefighting: Tiger Flowers and the Politics of Black Celebrity.* Athens: University of Georgia Press, 2004.

Kelley, Brent. *Voices from the Negro Leagues: Conversations with 52 Baseball Standouts of the Period 1924–1960.* Jefferson, NC: McFarland, 1998.

_____. *The Negro Leagues Revisited: Conversations with 66 More Baseball Heroes.* Jefferson, NC: McFarland, 2000.

Kelley, Robin D.G. *Hammer and Hoe: Alabama Communists During the Great Depression.* Chapel Hill: University of North Carolina Press, 1990.

_____. *Race Rebels: Culture, Politics, and the Black Working Class.* New York: Free Press, 1994.

_____. "'We Are Not What We Seem': Rethinking Black Working-Class Opposition in the Jim Crow South." *Journal of American History* (June 1993): 75–113.

Kennedy, David M. *Over Here: The First World War and American Society.* New York: Oxford University Press, 1980.

Kern-Foxworth, Marilyn. *Aunt Jemima,*

Uncle Ben, and Rastus: Blacks in Advertising, Yesterday, Today, and Tomorrow. Westport, CT: Greenwood, 1994.

Kimball, Richard Ian. "Beyond the Great Experiment: Integrated Baseball Comes to Indianapolis." *Journal of Sport History* 26 (Spring 1999): 142–162.

King, Gilbert. *Devil in the Grove: Thurgood Marshall, the Groveland Boys, and the Dawn of a New America.* New York: Harper Perennial, 2013.

Kirby, John. *Black Americans in the Roosevelt Era.* Knoxville: University of Tennessee Press, 1980.

Kirsch, Geroge B. *Baseball in Blue and Gray: The National Pastime During the Civil War.* Princeton: Princeton University Press, 2003.

Klein, Alan M., *Sugarball: The American Game, The Dominican Dream.* Knoxville: University of Tennessee Press, 1983.

_____. *Baseball on the Border: A Tale of Two Laredos.* Princeton: Princeton University Press, 1997.

Klinetobe, Charles, and Steve Bullock. "Complicated Shadows: Ty Cobb and the Public Imagination." *Nine: A Journal of Baseball History and Culture* 18 (Fall 2009), 22–23.

Knight, Arthur. "Star Dances: African-American Constructions of Stardom, 1925–1960." *Classic Hollywood, Classic Whiteness.* Daniel Bernardi, ed. Minneapolis: University of Minnesota Press, 2001.

Krasner, David. "Parody and Double Consciousness in the Language of Early Black Musical Theatre." *African American Review* 29 (Summer 1995): 317–323.

Kuklick, Bruce. *To Every Thing a Season: Shibe Park and Urban Philadelphia.* Princeton: Princeton University Press, 1991.

Lanctot, Neil. *Fair Dealing and Clean Playing: The Hilldale Club and the Development of Black Professional Baseball.* Jefferson, NC: McFarland, 1994.

_____. *Negro League Baseball: The Rise and Ruin of a Black Institution.* Philadelphia: University of Pennsylvania Press, 2004.

Lansbury, Jennifer H. "'The Tuskegee Flash'

and 'the Slender Harlem Stroker': Black Women Athletes at the Margins." *Journal of Sport History* 28 (Summer 2001): 233–252.

Leab, Daniel J. *From Sambo to Superspade: The Black Experience in Motion Pictures.* Boston: Houghton Mifflin, 1976.

Lemons, J. Stanley. "Black Stereotypes as Reflected in Popular Culture, 1880–1920." *American Quarterly* 21 (Spring 1977): 102–116.

Leonard, Buck, with James A. Riley. *Buck Leonard: The Black Lou Gehrig: The Hall of Famer's Story in His Own Words.* New York: Carroll and Graf, 1995.

Levine, Lawrence W. *Black Culture and Black Consciousness: Afro-American Folk Thought from Slavery to Freedom.* New York: Oxford University Press, 1977.

_____. *Highbrow/Lowbrow: The Emergence of Cultural Hierarchy in America.* Cambridge: Harvard University Press, 1988.

Lewis, David Levering. *W.E.B. Du Bois: The Fight for Equality and the American Century, 1919–1963.* New York: Henry Holt, 2000.

_____. *When Harlem Was in Vogue.* New York: Vintage, 1982.

Lewis, Earl. *In Their Own Interests: Race, Class, and Power in Twentieth Century Norfolk.* Berkeley: University of California Press, 1991.

Lewis, Ronald L. "From Peasant to Proletarian: The Migration of Southern Blacks to the Central Appalachian Coalfields." *Journal of Southern History* 55 (February 1989): 77–102

Lipsitz, George. *Rainbow at Midnight: Labor and Culture in the 1940s.* Urbana: University of Illinois Press, 1994.

_____. *Time Passages: Collective Memory and American Popular Culture.* Minneapolis: University of Minnesota Press, 1990.

Litwack, Leon F. *Trouble in Mind: Black Southerners in the Age of Jim Crow.* New York: Alfred A. Knopf, 1998.

Locke, Alain. "The Negro and the American Stage." *Theatre Arts Monthly* 10.2 (Feb. 1926): 112–120.

Lomax, Michael E. "The African American Experience in Professional Football." *Journal of Social History* 33 (1999), 163–178.

_____. "Black Baseball, Black Community, Black Entrepreneurs: The History of the Negro National and Eastern Colored Leagues, 1880–1930." PhD dissertation, Ohio State University, 1996.

_____. *Black Baseball Entrepreneurs, 1860–1901: Operating by Any Means Necessary.* Syracuse: Syracuse University Press, 2003.

_____. "Black Entrepreneurship in the National Pastime: The Rise of Semiprofessional Baseball in Black Chicago, 1890–1915." *Journal of Sport History* 25 (Spring 1998): 43–64.

Louis, Joe, with Edna and Art Rust, Jr. *Joe Louis: My Life.* New York: Harcourt Brace Jovanovich, 1978.

Lucas, John A., and Ronald A. Smith. *Saga of American Sport.* Philadelphia: Lea and Febiger, 1978.

Luke, Bob. *The Baltimore Elite Giants: Sport and Society in the Age of Negro League Baseball.* Baltimore: Johns Hopkins University Press, 2009.

Manley, Effa, and Leon Herbert Hartwick. *Negro Baseball ... Before Integration.* Chicago: Adams, 1976.

Marchand, Roland. *Advertising the American Dream: Making Way for Modernity, 1920–1940.* Berkeley: University of California Press, 1985.

Martin, Tony. *Race First: The Ideological and Organizational of Marcus Garvey and the Universal Negro Improvement Association.* Westport, CT: Greenwood, 1976.

McGimpsey, David. *Imagining Baseball: America's Pastime and Popular Culture.* Bloomington: University of Indiana Press, 2000.

McGowan, Philip. *American Carnival: Seeing and Reading American Culture.* Westport, CT: Greenwood, 2001.

McKay, Jim, Michael A. Messner, and Don Sabo., eds. *Masculinities, Gender Rela-*

tions, and Sport. Thousand Oaks, CA: Sage, 2000.

McNary, Kyle P. *Ted "Double Duty" Radcliffe: 36 Years of Pitching and Catching in Baseball's Negro Leagues.* Minneapolis: McNary, 1994.

McNeill, William F. *Cool Papas and Double Duties: The All-Time Greats of the Negro Leagues.* Jefferson, NC: McFarland, 2001.

McRae, Donald. *Heroes Without a Country: America's Betrayal of Joe Louis and Jesse Owens.* New York: HarperCollins, 2002.

Mead, Chris. *Champion Joe Louis: Black Hero in White America.* New York: Scribner's, 1995.

Meltzer, Milton, ed. *In Their Own Words: A History of the American Negro 1916–1966.* New York: Thomas Y. Crowell, 1967.

Messner, Michael. *Power at Play: Sports and the Problem of Masculinity.* Boston: Beacon Press, 1992.

_____, and Donald A. Sabo. *Sex, Violence and Power in Sports: Rethinking Masculinity.* New York: Crossing Press, 1994.

Miller, Marvin. *A Whole New Ball Game: The Inside Story of Baseball's New Deal.* New York: Fireside, 1991.

Miller, Patrick B. "The Anatomy of Scientific Racism: Racialist Responses to Black Athletic Achievement." *Journal of Sport History* 25 (1998): 119–151.

_____. "To 'Bring the Race Along Rapidly': Sport, Student Culture, and Educational Mission at Historically Black Colleges during the Interwar Years." *History of Education Quarterly* 35 (Summer 1995): 111–133.

Moffi, Larry, and Jonathan Kronstadt. *Crossing the Line: Black Major Leaguers, 1947–1959.* Jefferson, NC: McFarland, 1994.

Moore, Joseph Thomas, *Pride Against Prejudice: The Biography of Larry Doby.* New York: Greenwood, 1988.

Moran, Jeffrey P. "Reading Race into the Scopes Trial: African American Elites, Science, and Fundamentalism." *Journal of American History* 89 (December 2003): 891–911.

Mormino, Gary Ross. "The Playing Fields of St. Louis: Italian Immigrants and Sports,

1925–1941." *Journal of Sport History* 9 (Summer 1982): 5–19.

Mrozek, Donald J. *Sport and the American Mentality: The Rise to Respectability.* Knoxville: University of Tennessee Press, 1983.

Mullan, Michael L. "Ethnicity and Sport: The Wapato Nippons and Pre–World War II Japanese American Baseball." *Journal of Sport History* 26 (Spring 1999): 82–114.

Nasaw, David. *Going Out: The Rise and Fall of Public Amusements.* New York: Basic Books, 1993.

_____. *Children of the City: At Work and At Play.* Garden City, NY: Anchor, 1985.

Nash, Gerald D. *The Great Depression and World War II: Organizing America, 1933–1945.* New York: St. Martin's, 1979.

Nathan, Dainiel A. "Bearing Witness to Blackball: Buck O'Neil, the Negro Leagues, and the Politics of the Past." *Journal of American Studies* 35 (2001), 453–469.

Nowatzki, Robert. "Foul Lines and the Color Line: Baseball and Race at the Turn of the Twentieth Century." *Nine* 11 (2003): 82–88.

Okrent, Daniel, and Harris Lewine, eds. *The Ultimate Baseball Book.* Boston: Houghton Mifflin, reprint 1991.

O'Neil, Buck, with Steve Wulf and David Conrads. *I Was Right on Time: My Journey from the Negro Leagues to the Majors.* New York: Fireside, 1997.

Oriard, Michael. *King Football: Sport & Spectacle in the Golden Age of Radio & Newsreels, Movies & Magazines, the Weekly & the Daily Press.* Chapel Hill: University of North Carolina Press, 2003.

Overmyer, James. *Queen of the Negro Leagues: Effa Manley and the Newark Eagles.* Metuchen, NJ: Scarecrow, 1993.

Ownby, Ted. *Subduing Satan: Religion, Recreation, and Manhood in the Rural South.* Chapel Hill: University of North Carolina Press, 1990.

Paige, LeRoy (Satchel), as told to David Lipman. *Maybe I'll Pitch Forever: A Great Baseball Player Tells the Hilarious Story*

Behind the Legend. Lincoln: University of Nebraska, 1962, 1993.

Paxson, Frederick L. "The Rise of Sport." *Mississippi Valley Historical Review* 4 (September 1917): 144–168.

Pearson, Nathan W., Jr. *Goin' to Kansas City.* Urbana: University of Illinois Press, 1987.

Pegg, Bruce. *Brown Eyed Handsome Man: The Life and Hard Times of Chuck Berry.* New York: Routledge, 2002.

Peiss, Kathy. *Cheap Amusements: Working Women and Leisure in Turn-of-the-Century New York.* Philadelphia: Temple University Press, reprint edition, 1987.

_____. *Hope in a Jar: The Making of America's Beauty Culture.* New York: Henry Holt, 1999.

Perez, Louis A. *On Becoming Cuban: Identity, Nationality, and Culture.* Chapel Hill: University of North Carolina, 1999.

Pesavento, Wilma J. "Sport and Recreation in the Pullman Experiment, 1880–1900." *Journal of Sport History* 9 (Summer 1982): 38–62.

Peterson, Joyce Shaw. "Black Automobile Workers in Detroit, 1910–1930." *The Journal of Negro History* 64 (Summer, 1979): 177–190.

Peterson, Robert. *Only the Ball Was White: A History of Legendary Black Players and All-Black Professional Teams.* New York: McGraw Hill, 1984.

Phillips, Kimberley L. *AlabamaNorth: African-American Migrants, Community, and Working-class Activism in Cleveland, 1915–45.* Urbana: University of Illinois Press, 1999.

_____. *War! What is it Good For? Black Freedom Struggles & the U.S. Military from World War II to Iraq.* Chapel Hill: University of North Carolina, 2012.

Pietrusza, David. *Lights On! The Wild Century-Long Saga of Night Baseball.* Lanham, MD: Scarecrow, 1997.

Pilz, Jeffrey J. "The Beginnings of Organized Play for Black America: E.T. Attwell and The PRAA." *The Journal of Negro History* 70 (1985): 59–72.

Pollock, Alan. J. *Barnstorming to Heaven:* *Syd Pollock and His Great Black Teams.* James A. Riley, ed. Tuscaloosa: University of Alabama Press, 2006.

Pope, S.W., ed. *The New American Sport History: Recent Approaches and Perspectives.* Urbana: University of Illinois Press, 1997.

Pruitt, Bernadette. "'For the Advancement of the Race': The Great Migration to Houston, Texas, 1914–1941." *Journal of Urban History* 31 (May 2005): 435–478.

Pruter, Robert. "Youth Baseball in Chicago, 1868–1890: Not Always Sandlot Ball." *Journal of Sports History* 26 (Spring 1999): 1–28.

Putney, Clifford. *Muscular Christianity: Manhood and Sports in Protestant America, 1880–1920.* Cambridge: Harvard University Press, 2003.

Quillin, Frank U. *The Color Line in Ohio: A History of Race Prejudice in a Typical Northern State.* Ann Arbor: George Wahr, 1913.

Rader, Benjamin. *American Sports: From the Age of Folk Games to the Age of Spectators.* Upper Saddle River, NJ: Prentice Hall, 1996.

_____. *Baseball: A History of America's Game,* 2d ed. Urbana: University of Illinois Press, 2002.

_____. "The Quest for Subcommunities and the Rise of American Sport." *American Quarterly* 29 (Autumn, 1977): 355–369.

Rampersad, Arnold. *Jackie Robinson: A Biography.* New York: Alfred A. Knopf, 1997.

_____, ed., *The Collected Poems of Langston Hughes.* New York: Random House, 1995.

Ramsey, Calvin Alexander. *Ruth and The Green Book.* Carolrhoda, 2010.

Reich, Steven A. "Soldiers of Democracy: Black Texans and the Fight for Citizenship, 1917–1921." *Journal of American History* 82 (March 1996): 1478–1504.

Reisler, Jim. *Babe Ruth: Launching the Legend.* New York: McGraw Hill, 2004.

_____. *Black Writers/Black Baseball: An Anthology of Articles from Black Sportswriters who covered the Negro Leagues.* Jefferson, NC: McFarland, 1994.

Remnick, David. *King of the World: Muhammad Ali and the Rise of an American Hero. New York: Random House, 1998.

Rendle, Ellen. *Judy Johnson: Delaware's Invisible Hero*. Wilmington, DE: Cedar Tree, 1994.

Ribowsky, Mark. *A Complete History of the Negro Leagues, 1884–1955*. New York: Birch Lane, 1995.

_____. *Don't Look Back: Satchel Paige in the Shadows of Baseball*. New York: Simon and Schuster, 1994.

_____. *The Power and The Darkness: The life of Josh Gibson in the shadows of the game*. New York: Simon and Schuster, 1996.

Riess, Steven A. *The American Sporting Experience: A Historical Anthology of Sport in America*. Champaign, IL: Leisure, 1984.

_____. *City Games*. Urbana: University of Illinois Press, 1989.

_____. "The New Sport History." *Reviews in American History* 18 (September 1990): 311–325.

_____. "Professional Baseball and Social Mobility." *Journal of Interdisciplinary History* 11 (Autumn, 1980): 235–250.

_____. "Sport and the American Dream: A Review Essay." *Journal of Social History* 14 (December 1980): 295–303.

_____. *Touching Base: Professional Baseball and American Culture in the Progressive Era*. Westport, CT: Greenwood, 1980.

Riley, James A. *The Negro Leagues*. Philadelphia: Chelsea House, 1997.

Roberts, Gene, and Hank Klibanoff. *The Race Beat: The Press, the Civil Rights Struggle, and the Awakening of a Nation*. New York: Vintage, 2007.

Roberts, John W. *From Trickster to Badman: The Black Folk Hero in Slavery and Freedom*. Philadelphia: University of Pennsylvania Press, 1989.

Roberts, Randy. *Joe Louis: Hard Times Man*. New Haven: Yale University Press, 2010.

Robinson, Frazier "Slow," and Paul Bauer. *Catching Dreams: My Life in the Negro Baseball Leagues*. Syracuse: Syracuse University Press, 1999.

Rogosin, Donn. *Invisible Men: Life in Baseball's Negro Leagues*. New York: Kodansha International, 1983, 1995.

Roorda, Eric Paul. *The Dictator Next Door: The Good Neighbor Policy and the Trujillo Regime in the Dominican Republic, 1930–1945*. Durham, NC: Duke University Press, 1998.

Roosevelt, Theodore. *The Selected Letters of Theodore Roosevelt*, H.W. Brands, ed. New York: Cooper Square, 2001.

Rosenzweig, Roy. *Eight Hours for What We Will: Workers and Leisure in an Industrial City 1870–1920*. Cambridge: Cambridge University Press, 1983.

Ross, Marlon B. *Manning the Race: Reforming Black Men in the Jim Crow Era*. New York: New York University Press, 2004.

Ruck, Rob. *Raceball: How the Major Leagues Colonized the Black and Latin Game*. Boston: Beacon, 2011.

_____. *Sandlot Seasons: Sport in Black Pittsburgh*. Urbana: University of Illinois Press, 1987.

_____. *The Tropic of Baseball: Baseball in the Dominican Republic*. Lincoln: University of Nebraska Press, 19999.

Rusinack, Kelly Elaine. "Baseball on the Radical Agenda: The Daily and Sunday Worker on the Desegregation of Major League Baseball, 1933 to 1947." Master's thesis, Clemson University, 1995.

Rust, Arthur, Jr. *Get That Nigger Off the Field: An Oral History of Black Ballplayers from the Negro Leagues to the Present*. New York: Delacourt, 1976.

Ryczek, William J. *When Johnny Came Sliding Home: The Post-Civil War Baseball Boom, 1865–1870*. Jefferson, NC: McFarland, 1998.

Sack, Marcy S. "'To Show Who Was in Charge': Police Repression of New York City's Black Population at the Turn of the Twentieth Century." *Journal of Urban History* 31 (September 2005): 799–819.

Salyer, Lucy E. "Baptism by Fire: Race, Military Service, and U.S. Citizen Policy, 1918–1935." *Journal of American History* 90 (December 2004): 847–876.

Sammons, Jeffrey T. "'Race' and Sport: A

Critical Historical Explanation." *Journal of Sport History* 21 (Fall 1994): 203–278.

Schaap, Jeremy. *Triumph: The Untold Story of Jesse Owens and Hitler's Olympics.* New York: Houghton Mifflin, 2007.

Schleppi, John R. "It Pays: John H. Patterson and Industrial Recreation at the National Cash Register Company." *Journal of Sport History* 6 (Winter 1979): 20–28.

Schultz, Jaime. "'A wager concerning a diplomatic pig': A Crooked Reading of the Floyd of Rosedale Narrative." *Journal of Sport History* 32 (Spring 2005): 1–21.

Scott, Emmett J., and Stowe, Lyman Beecher. "Booker T. Washington: Builder of a Civilization." *Booker T. Washington and His Critics: Black Leadership in Crisis.* Hugh Hawkins, ed. Lexington, MA: D.C. Heath, 1962, 1974.

Scott, James C. *Domination and the Arts of Resistance: Hidden Transcripts.* New Haven: Yale University Press, 1990.

Seiler, Cotton. "'So that we as a race might have something authentic to travel by': African American automoblity and Cold-War liberalism." *American Quarterly* 58 (December 2005), 1091–1117.

Seymour, Harold. *Baseball: The Early Years.* New York: Oxford University Press, 1960.

_____. *Baseball: The Golden Age.* New York: Oxford University Press, 1971.

_____. *Baseball: The People's Game.* New York: Oxford University Press, 1990.

Shaw, Stephanie J. "Using the WPA Ex-Slave Narratives to Study the Impact of the Great Depression." *Journal of Southern History* 69 (August 2003): 623–658.

Sidran, Ben. *Black Talk: How the Music of Black America Created a Radical Alternative to the Values of Western Literary Tradition.* New York: Holt, 1971.

Simons, William M. *The Cooperstown Symposium on Baseball and American Culture, 2002.* Jefferson, NC: McFarland, 2003.

Singer, Barry. *Black and Blue: The Life and Lyrics of Andy Razaf.* New York: Schirmer, 1992.

Skipper, James K., Jr. *Baseball Nicknames: A Dictionary of Origins and Meanings.* Jefferson, NC: McFarland, 1992.

Smith, J. David. *The Eugenic Assault on America: Scenes in Red, White, and Black.* Fairfax, VA: George Mason University Press, 1992.

Smith, Leverett. *The American Dream and the National Game.* Bowling Green, OH: Bowling Green State University Popular Press, 1970.

Smith, Steven D. "The African American Soldier at Fort Huachuca, 1892–1946." Report Prepared for U.S. Army Fort Huachuca, Arizona and the Center of Expertise for Preservation of Historic Structures& Buildings, U.S. Army Corps of Engineer, Seattle District, February 2001, http://artsandsciences.sc.edu/sciaa/PDF docs/military-research/AfricanAmerican Soldier-FortHuachuca.pdf accessed 17 August 2013.

Smitherman, Geneva. *Talkin and Testifyin: The Language of Black America.* Detroit: Wayne State University Press, 1986.

Sobol, Ken. *Babe Ruth and the American Dream.* New York: Random House, 1974.

Spalding, Albert. *America's National Game.* New York: American Sports, 1911.

Spalding, Henry D., ed. *Encyclopedia of Black Folklore and Humor.* Middle Village, NY: Jonathan David, 1972.

Spaulding, Norman W. "History of Black Oriented Radio in Chicago 1929–1963. PhD Dissertation, University of Illinois at Urbana-Champaign, 1981.

Spear, Allan H. *Black Chicago: The Making of a Negro Ghetto 1890–1920.* Chicago: University of Chicago Press, 1967.

Spivey, Donald. "The Black Athlete in Big-Time Intercollegiate Sports, 1941–1968." *Phylon* 44 (1982): 116–125.

_____. "End Jim Crow in sports: The protest at New York University, 1940–1941." *Journal of Sport History* 15 (Winter 1988): 282–303.

_____. "*If Only You Were White*": *The Life and Times of Leroy "Satchel" Paige.* Columbia: University of Missouri Press, 2012.

Spring, Joel H. "Mass Culture: School

Sports." *History of Education Quarterly* 14 (Winter 1974): 483–500.

Springwood, Charles Fruehling. *Cooperstown to Dyersville: A Geography of Baseball Nostalgia.* Boulder, CO: Westview, 1996.

Stein, Judith. *The World of Marcus Garvey: Race and Class in Modern Society.* Baton Rouge: Louisiana State University Press, 1986.

Sternsher, Bernard, ed. *Hitting Home: The Great Depression in Town and Country.* Chicago: Quadrangle, 1970.

Strother, T. Ella. "The Race Advocacy Function of the Black Press." *Black American Literature Forum* 12 (Autumn 1978): 92–99.

Sugar, Bert Randolph. *Boxing's Greatest Fighters.* Guilford, CT: Lyons, 2006.

Sullivan, Dean A. ed. *Middle Innings: A Documentary History of Baseball, 1900–1948.* Lincoln: University of Nebraska Press, 2001.

Sumner, Jim L. *Separating the Men from the Boys: The First Half Century of the Carolina League.* Winston-Salem, NC: John F. Blair, 1994.

Threston, Christopher. *The Integration of Baseball in Philadelphia.* Jefferson, NC: McFarland, 2003.

Tolan, Sandy. *Me and Hank: A Boy and His Hero Twenty-Five Years Later.* Free Press: 2000.

Treder, Steve. "The Persistent Color Line: Specific Instances of Racial Preference in Major League Player Evaluation Decisions After 1947." *Nine* 10 (Fall 2001): 1–30.

_____. "A Legacy of What-If's: Horace Stoneham and the Integration of the Giants." *Nine* 10 (Spring 2002): 71–101.

Trouppe, Quincy. *20 Years Too Soon: Prelude to Major League Integrated Baseball.* St. Louis: Missouri Historical Society, 1977, 1995.

Tucker, Sherrie. *Swing Shift: "All-Girl" Bands of the 1940s.* Durham: Duke University Press, 2000.

Turner, Patricia A. *I Heard It Through the Grapevine: Rumor in African American Culture.* Berkeley: University of California Press, 1993.

Tygiel, Jules. *Baseball's Great Experiment: Jackie Robinson and His Legacy.* New York: Vintage, 1984.

_____. *Extra Bases: Reflections on Jackie Robinson, Race, & Baseball History.* Lincoln: University of Nebraska Press, 2002.

_____. *Past Time: Baseball as History.* New York: Oxford University Press, 2000.

Van der Linden, Marcel. "Labour History: An International Movement." *Labour History* November 2005 <http://www.historycooperative.org/journals/lab/89/linden2.html> (20 Dec. 2005)

Vertinsky, Patricia. "Gender Relations, Women's History and Sport History." *Journal of Sport History* 21 (Fall 1994): 1–25.

_____, and Gwendolyn Captain. "More Myth Than History: American Culture and Representations of the Black Female Athletic Ability." *Journal of Sport History* 25 (1998): 532–561.

Vignola, Patricia. "The Enemies at the Gate: An Economic Debate about the Denouement of Negro League Baseball." *Nine* 13 (February 2005): 71–81.

_____. "The Patriotic Pinch Hitter: The AAGBL and How American Woman Earned a Permanent Spot on the Roster." *Nine* 12 (February 2004): 102–113.

Voigt, David Q. *American Baseball: From Gentleman's Sport to the Commissioner System.* Vol. 1. Norman: University of Oklahoma Press, 1966.

_____. *American Baseball: From the Commissioner System to Continental Expansion.* Vol. 2. Philadelphia: University of Pennsylvania Press, 1982.

Von Eschen, Penny M. *Race Against Empire: Black Americans and Anticolonialism, 1937–1958.* Ithaca: Cornell University Press, 1997.

_____. *Satchmo Blows Up the World: Jazz Ambassadors Play the Cold War.* Cambridge: Harvard University Press, 2004.

Votano, Paul. *Late and Close: A History of*

Relief Pitching. Jefferson, NC: McFarland, 2002.

Walker, Donald E., and B. Lee Cooper. *Baseball and American Culture: A Thematic Bibliography of Over 4,500 Works*. Jefferson, NC: McFarland, 1995.

Ward, Geoffrey C. *Unforgivable Blackness: The Rise and Fall of Jack Johnson*. New York: Alfred A. Knopf, 2004.

Weems, Robert E., Jr. *Black Business in a Black Metropolis: The Chicago Metropolitan Assurance Company, 1925–1985*. Bloomington: Indiana University Press, 1996.

Welky, David B. "Viking Girls, Mermaids, and Little Brown Men: U.S. Journalism and the 1932 Olympics." *Journal of Sport History* 24 (Spring 1997), 24–49.

Westcott, Rich. *Philadelphia's Old Ball Parks*. Philadelphia: Temple University Press, 1996.

"Where have you gone Jackie Robinson?: In College the Baseball Diamonds Are Almost All White." *The Journal of Blacks in Higher Education* (Summer 2001): 50–52.

White, Deborah Gray. *Too Heavy a Load: Black Women in Defense of Themselves 1894–1994*. New York: W.W. Norton, 1999.

White, G. Edward. *Creating the National Pastime: Baseball Transforms Itself 1903–1953*. Princeton: Princeton University Press, 1996.

White, Graham, and Shane White. *Stylin': Black Expressive Culture from Its Beginnings to the Zoot Suit*. Ithaca: Cornell University Press, 1998.

White, Richard. "Civil Rights Agitation: Emancipation in Central New York in the 1880s." *Journal of Negro History* 78 (Winter 1993): 16–24.

White, Sol. *Sol White's History of Colored Base Ball, with Other Documents on the Early Black game, 1886–1936*. Lincoln: University of Nebraska Press, 1907, revised edition, 1995.

Whitehead, Charles E. *A Man and His Diamonds: A Story of Andrew "Rube" Foster and His Famous American Giants*. New York: Vantage, 1980.

Wiese, Andrew. "The Other Suburbanites: African American suburbanization in the North before 1950." *The Journal of American History* 85 (March 1999): 1495–1524.

Wiggins, David K. *Glory Bound: Black Athletes in a White World*. Syracuse: Syracuse University Press, 1997.

_____. "Great Speed but Little Stamina: The Historical Debate Over Black Athletic Superiority." *Journal of Sport History* 16 (Summer 1989): 158–185.

_____, and Patrick B. Miller. *The Unlevel Playing Field: A Documentary History of the African American Experience in Sport*. Urbana: University of Illinois Press, 2003.

_____. "Wendell Smith: The Pittsburgh Courier-Journal and the Campaign to include Blacks in Organized Baseball, 1933–1945." *Journal of Sport History* 10 (Summer 1983): 5–29.

Wiggins, William H. Jr. "Jack Johnson as Bad Nigger: The Folklore of His Life." *Black Scholar* (January 1971): 4–19.

William, Harlan S. "Jim Crow at the Bat: Apartheid in Baseball, 1846–1900." www.negro-league.columbus.oh.us/jimcrow2.htm. October 25, 2003.

Willis, Joe D., and Richard G. Wettan. "Social Stratification in New York City Athletic Clubs, 1865–1915." *Journal of Sport History* 3 (Spring 1976): 45–63.

Wolters, Raymond. *Negroes and the Great Depression: The Problem of Economic Recovery*. Westport CT: Greenwood, 1970.

Wood, Peter H. *Black Majority: Negroes in Colonial South Carolina from 1670 through the Stono Rebellion*. New York: Norton, 1996.

Zang, David W. *Fleet Walker's Divided Heart: Baseball's First Black Major Leaguer*. Lincoln: University of Nebraska Press, 1995.

Zingg, Paul. "Diamond in the Rough: Baseball and the Study of American Sports History." *The History Teacher* 19 (May 1986): 385–403.

_____, ed. *The Sporting Image: Readings in American Sport History*. Lanham, MD: University Press of America, 1988.

Index